PRAISE FOR

INTO THE CANNIBAL'S POT

"The Western press promptly forgot all about South Africa after Nelson Mandela assumed the presidency. The commissars of allowable opinion pretend atrocities have not been taking place, and smear anyone who mentions them. Ilana Mercer will have none of the lies and omissions of the commissars and the cowards. For the sake of white and black South Africans alike, her compelling account deserves a wide and sympathetic audience."

– **THOMAS E. WOODS**, Ph.D., historian, author of the New York Times best-sellers, *Nullification*, *Meltdown*, *The Politically Incorrect Guide to American History*, and the critically acclaimed, *The Church Confronts Modernity*

"Ilana Mercer's well-documented, encompassing study is at once heartbreaking, infuriating, illuminating and instructive. Ethnic cleansing is underway in the once great nation of South Africa, but Americans hear nothing of it; they are deliberately shielded by the same parties that served to bring it about, the liberal elites in Western governments and the press who believe that white South Africans 'have it coming.' It is white guilt and the so-called right of black reprisal extrapolated to ghastly extremes; political correctness on steroids, and all in the name of craven progressive ideology. If the West is ever to occupy anything resembling moral high ground – not to mention avoiding this fate itself – it will have to come to terms with its part in South Africa's demise, and the misery, degradation and naked horror of those who now suffer."

– **ERIK RUSH**, columnist and author of *Negrophilia: From Slave Block to Pedestal–America's Racial Obsession*. Erik was the first to break the story of President (then Senator) Barack Obama's ties to the militant, Afrocentric, Chicago preacher Reverend Jeremiah Wright.

"The truth shall set you free," a memorable Biblical phrase tells us. It does not say the truth shall make us comfortable or happy. *Into The Cannibal's Pot* fits this mold: it is an interesting, important, well-written and well-documented book that informs the reader but is likely to upset, perhaps even anger, some or many of them.

– **THOMAS SZASZ**, the author of *The Myth of Mental Illness*, *Psychiatry: The Science of Lies*, and many other books

"Egalitarianism leads to democracy; democracy leads to socialism; socialism leads to economic destruction; and democratic socialism in multicultural societies leads to death and democide. This, in shocking detail, is what Ilana Mercer illustrates superbly in her case study of post-apartheid South Africa. America's political and intellectual 'elites' will ignore this book, because it is politically 'incorrect.' We can only do so at our own peril."

– **HANS-HERMANN HOPPE**, Austrian school economist, libertarian political philosopher, emeritus professor of economics, University of Nevada, distinguished fellow, the Ludwig von Mises Institute, author of *Democracy: The God That Failed*, and *The Economics and Ethics of Private Property*

"If you want to witness the end result of what in America is called 'diversity,' you must read *Into the Cannibal's Pot*. 'Diversity' is a euphemism for racial retribution administered mostly by guilty white liberals in universities, corporations, and government. It is a thoroughly collectivist notion that condones punishing the current generation of white males for the sins of the past. It's most extreme form is practiced in post-Apartheid South Africa, and its effects are meticulously documented by Ilana Mercer (who also writes marvelously): rampant black-on-white crime, racist labor laws that have created 'The world's most extreme affirmative action program'; the confiscation of private property; economic socialism; state-sponsored terrorism; and, most sickeningly, the idolization of the corrupt and murderous Zimbabwean dictator, Robert Mugabe. The Western media ignore all of this because of their ideological love affair with the communistic African National Congress and, frankly, their support for many of these same policies."

– **THOMAS J. DILORENZO**, professor of economics, Loyola College, Maryland, author of the best-selling *The Real Lincoln*, *Lincoln Unmasked*, and most recently, *Hamilton's Curse*

ALSO BY ILANA MERCER

Broad Sides: One Woman's Clash with a Corrupt Culture

INTO THE CANNIBAL'S POT

Lessons For America From Post-Apartheid South Africa

Ilana Mercer

The daughter of a leading anti-apartheid activist blows the lid off the new South Africa

STAIRWAY PRESS

A CURVA PELIGROSA BOOK
STAIRWAY PRESS
SEATTLE

Visit Ilana online: www.ilanamercer.com

Library of Congress Cataloguing-in-Publication data

Mercer, Ilana

Into the Cannibal's Pot: Lessons For America From Post-Apartheid South Africa/by Ilana Mercer, 1st ed.

Includes bibliographical references and index.

ISBN 978-0-9827734-3-7

1. United States –Diplomatic history- Foreign and general relations.
2. Social Sciences – Social pathology - criminology.
3. Law – Natural law – property.

Library of Congress Control Number: 2011930725

Cover Design by Guy Corp, www.grafixCORP.com

www.stairwaypress.com
1500A East College Way #554
Mount Vernon, WA 98273

Dedicated to my Afrikaner brothers betrayed, and to my African sisters, Nomasomi Khala and Annie Dlahmini, whose lives touched mine

Publisher's Note

This is a book about ideas and ideology. When losing an intellectual argument, there are despicable people who point an accusing finger and shout racism. In our dark times where mob rule and collectivist ideas resonate with so many, this appalling strategy can be very effective.

To those who support colorblind civil discourse, rule of law, equality of opportunity, freedom, the golden rule (do unto others as you wish them to do unto you), liberty, freedom of expression and religion and private property rights...regardless of skin color or ethnic background (black, red, white, yellow, brown, green or violet), we extend the hand of friendship.

To those who support all forms of thuggery—including totalitarianism, collectivism, fascism, extremist fundamentalism, unequal treatment under law, income redistribution, nanny state government programs and the soft bigotry of low expectations—your skin color and ethnicity are irrelevant...and your ideas belong in the dustbin of history.

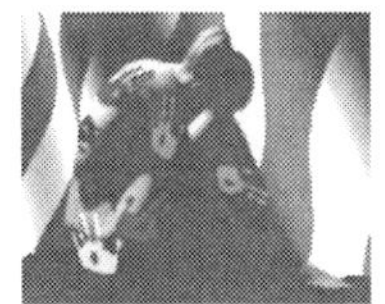

PREFACE

IT IS NO surprise that a manifesto against majoritarianism would not find favor with the mission of most American publishers. Opposition to mass society was once an accepted (indeed, unremarkable) theme in the richly layered works of iconic conservatives such as Edmund Burke, Russell Kirk, and James Burnham. Today, by contrast, such opposition is considered as damning as it is impolitic.

And don't even think of writing a less-than hagiographical account of Nelson Mandela. *Time* magazine's Richard Stengel has serialized his tributes to Saint Mandela. (Stengel has completed two. Perhaps a third is planned?) But an opposing voice to the media paean for the democratic South Africa and its deity, written by a dissenting South African exile—this cannot be countenanced.

"What menaces democratic society in this age is not a simple collapse of order," forewarned Alexis de Tocqueville, "but a tyranny of mediocrity, a standardization of mind and spirit and condition." In the context of post-apartheid South Africa, this sameness of mind and spirit manifests in a convergence of opinion—even in the neatly bifurcated America.

Thus, while almost every other postcolonial insurgency in Africa has been scrutinized, rival views of post-apartheid South Africa are unwelcome. Despite the country's body count since "freedom," the foundations of what was a joint Anglo-American undertaking are not to be faulted or questioned.

The loss of 300,000 innocents murdered since democracy dawned is therefore regularly diminished. People slide into extenuation: "We have our problems, but we now have, I'm proud to say, a working, wonderful democracy in South Africa." These words were uttered by the roaming Justice Richard Goldstone, who—unlike this writer's father—attached himself to the anti-apartheid cause only once it became fashionable, safe and professionally expedient.

In itself, the tale of the publication of *Into the Cannibal's Pot: Lessons For America From Post-Apartheid South Africa* bears telling. For while this polemic respects no political totems or taboos, it is faithful to facts. These facts cried out to be chronicled. They should not have had a struggle to find their way into print.

Yet struggle they did.

"Ilana, if you'd only give me something like Corinne Hofmann's *Back from Africa*, publishers would pounce," promised one literary agent. Hofmann's salacious account of her time as the sexual plaything of a virile African tribal chief was described by *The Times Literary Supplement* as "a dated tale of exotic desire and disillusionment."

As the PC pecking order stands, *Into the Cannibal's Pot* might also have been pounced upon had its author been more like economist Dambisa Moyo of the trendy *Dead Aid*. That popular book consists of derivative deductions which had been reached decades ago by Peter Thomas Bauer, the doyen of development economics. (To give Ms. Moyo her dues, *Dead Aid* is dedicated to the late Lord Bauer.)

The following is an assessment from a well-known academic publisher whose stock does not exactly fly off the shelves:

> I've long been aware of Mercer's writing. Though I rarely agree with her, she's quite a presence on the right side of the blogosphere. This is an extremely well-written and provocative work. I was riveted as I read it.

> ...The problem here is that the market for a book with such a clear political bias is that much smaller. So I just don't think we could take it on.

"There is no settling the point of precedency between a louse and a flea," said Dr. Johnson. This is my position with respect to political parties stateside and in South Africa. How can a book that discounts the venerated vote and disavows all political parties have a political bias? *Into the Cannibal's Pot* is manifestly *against* politics! A partiality for *small government* and *big society*—in other words, for civilization—is not a "political bias." No, the prejudice was that of the petitioned publisher; his was a prejudice against an unorthodox perspective that comports with the classical liberal philosophy, and with reality.

Another publisher made the following excuse:

> We recently had the chance to review your manuscript. Like everything you do, it is well-written and worthy of publication. However, we do not believe we can successfully market it.

This particular editor added that the imprint would be concentrating instead on the timeless topic of the Olympic Games in China. Obviously that is a far more inspiring subject than this writer's "unhealthy" preoccupation with the methodical ethnic cleansing of the Afrikaner farmer.

Other respondents lavished praise on a "closely argued stylish effort" (for which, of course, they did not care to make an effort).

To go by the Left's postmodern strictures, truth is not immutable but subject to a process of discovery. As a practical matter, then, how is a synthesis of the South-African situation to emerge if the antithesis is disallowed?

Let us not discount the publishing world's ongoing drive for the bottom line and the lowest common denominator. (The publisher who refused to bear Christian Witness, citing the prospects of poor profits, is an example.) This uncompromising dedication does not lend itself to contrarian material, not even when the facts are pressing (and almost too horrible for words). After all, a complicit publishing establishment can shirk responsibility and seek comfort in the fact that the marketplace for books no longer adjudicates the product's worth. Actually, nowadays this marketplace does no more than offer an aggregate snapshot of the millions of subjective preferences consumers demand and publishers deliver. Mackenzie Phillips' squalid story of incest and insanity outsells Ludwig von Mises' pearls of wisdom. For some this cultural foot-and-mouth will be faith-inspiring, for others deeply distressing.

ABBREVIATIONS USED

Association of Community Organizations for Reform Now (ACORN)
African National Congress (ANC)
Black Economic Empowerment (BEE)
Central Business District (CBD)
Congress of South African Trade Unions (COSATU)
Dutch Reformed Church (NGK)
Firearm Control Act (FCA)
Human Sciences Research Council (HSRC)
Inkatha Freedom Party (IFP)
South Africa Institute for Race Relations (SAIRR)
Movement for Democratic Change (MDC)
National Party (NP)
Palestine Solidarity Committee (PSC)
People Against Gangsterism and Drugs (PAGAD)
Progressive Federal Party (PFP)
South Africa (SA)
South African Medical Research Council (MRC)
South African Police Service (SAPS)
Supreme Court of the United States (SCOTUS)
University of South Africa (UNISA)
White Anglo-Saxon Protestant (WASP)
Transvaal Agricultural Union (TAU)

CONTENTS

INTRODUCTION

Rambo Nation

When South Africa was governed by a racist white minority, it was scorned by the West and treated as Saddam Hussein was, with boycotts and sanctions. Now that a racist, black-majority government controls the country; that it is as violent as Iraq, Liberia, or the Congo and rapidly becoming another Islamist-friendly, failed African state, it is the toast of the West.

Indeed, world leaders and the liberal lickspittle media seldom speak of the embarrassment that is the democratic South Africa—the crumbling infrastructure of this once First World country, and the out-of-control crime—down to an ongoing mini-genocide. Rocker Bono certainly isn't moved to tears over the seemingly systematic extermination of the Afrikaner farmers of South Africa. The cultural *cognoscenti* in the US are equally silent about the New South Africa's unparalleled, radical, race-based wealth-distribution policies.

As *Into The Cannibal's Pot* demonstrates, South Africa's democratically elected African leaders are as committed as their political predecessors, apartheid-era Afrikaners, to restructuring society around race. With one distinction: more people are murdered in one week under African rule than died under the detention of the Afrikaner government over the course of roughly four decades.* Consequently, the much-maligned Western stronghold established in South Africa under Boer—and before that British—rule is rapidly reverting to type. Gone is the European strongman who suppressed the seething African kraal. What has arisen instead is best captured by Joseph Conrad's Kurtz: "The horror, the horror." Dubbed the "Rainbow Nation," for its multiculturalism, South Africa is now, more than before, a "Rambo Nation."

Americans, who take for granted their domestic tranquility, can't afford to finesse the fate of the dying Christian civilization at the tip of Africa. *Into The Cannibal's Pot* compels them to stare into "The Heart of Darkness" that is the New South Africa, and by so doing, offers a cautionary tale: in their unqualified paeans to the will of the majority everywhere, Americans must understand that traditionally Western legal institutions, however flawed, are preferable to institutions riven by tribal feuds, fetishes, and factional loyalties.

Universal suffrage is not to be conflated with freedom.

As the democratic South Africa (and Iraq) amply demonstrates, political rights don't secure the natural rights to life, liberty, property, and the pursuit of happiness; ink-stained fingers don't inoculate against blood stains. Extant societal structures that safeguard life and property can always be improved upon. But once these bulwarks against mob rule and mayhem disintegrate, they are seldom restored. A civilized society, ultimately, is one in which the individual can go about the business of life unmolested. If he can't do that simple thing, of what value is the vote?

Post-apartheid South Africa serves as a reminder that such societies, however imperfect, are fragile. They can, *and will*, crumble in culturally inhospitable climes; the new South Africa

---

* See Chapter 1, Crime, the Beloved Country

reminds us that, for better or for worse, societies are built slowly from the soil up, not from the sky down. And by people, not by political decree. Sadly, the facts as this writer tells them indicate that, while the Old South Africa could only have improved; the New South Africa can but decline.

So why is this book so very crucial at this juncture? Simply this: Although grisly horror stories have percolated into the popular press, the emetic facts about the New South Africa have never before been told. They must be! *Into the Cannibal's Pot* fills this knowledge gap. This book, moreover, is crucial in curbing the naïve enthusiasm among American elites, and those they've gulled, for radical, imposed, top-down transformations of relatively stable, if imperfect, societies, including their own. As the example of South Africa demonstrates, a highly developed Western society can be dismantled with relative ease. In South Africa, this deconstruction has come about in the wake of an almost overnight shift in the majority/minority power structure.

In the U.S., a slower, more incremental transformation is under way. It began with a state-orchestrated, historically unparalleled, mass importation of inassimilable ethnic groups into a country whose creed is that it has no creed any longer. American institutions no longer assimilate immigrants.

Rather, they acculturate them to militant identity politics aimed at doing away with merit. Dissolving the American people and electing another, to paraphrase Bertolt Brecht, will likely erode American institutions further, and may well replicate on American soil the terrifying conflicts that mar the Third World. Ever the source of deafening demagoguery about the virtues of democracy, American leaders might wish to consider that, "Severely divided societies are short on community," and "community is a prerequisite for majority rule."[1]

Still, American leaders refused to rest until South Africa became a democracy. And before that Zimbabwe. And after that Iraq. (They were not alone. I trace that chain of culpability in

Chapter Seven, "The Anglo-American-Australian Axis of Evil.") The consequences in each case have been catastrophic. While all people want safety and sustenance for themselves, not everyone is prepared to allow those whom they dislike to peacefully pursue the same. This maxim applies both to Mesopotamia and to Azania (the term once used for South Africa by the governing African National Congress). The time is historically ripe to challenge some of the central tenets of liberal democratic ideology through the prism of another democratic disaster: post-Apartheid South Africa.

If the sanctity of life is the highest value in a civilized society, then the New South Africa has little to recommend it. Societies are only as good as the individuals of whom they are comprised; individuals only as good as their actions. Democratic South Africa is now preponderantly overrun by elements, both within and without government, which make a safe and thriving civil society impossible to sustain. The salient feature of mass politics in the New South Africa is a government unable to control itself and unwilling to control a sinecured criminal class. As a consequence, sundered is the individual's right to live unmolested.

Our unhappy trek through the wreck of the New South Africa begins with the facts, nothing but the facts. The realities of crime-riddled democratic South Africa are relayed in Chapter One: "Crime, the Beloved Country." The title parodies Alan Paton's poignant tale titled *Cry, the Beloved Country*. The story of the life of Zulu pastor Stephen Kumalo was to apartheid South Africa what Harriet Beecher Stowe's *Uncle Tom's Cabin* was to antebellum America.

Victims of crime in South Africa garner some sympathy, but it is sympathy on a sliding scale. Thus, worldwide, the press extended liberal pieties to liberal Nobel Prize-winning author Nadine Gordimer. She had survived an attack in her Johannesburg home. The Prince of Wales bewailed the murder of another prominent liberal, Anglo-Zulu War historian David Rattray. He was killed by six armed Zulus. When the nephew of South Africa's finest novelist (no; it's not J. M. Coetzee), the liberal André Brink, was shot and killed in front of his wife and daughter, *The Economist* took note:

> 'First he thought it was a mouse, then a rat—and then the rat shot him in the face.' That is how André Brink, one of South Africa's most famous novelists, described the recent killing of his nephew Adri, at home at 3am in the morning.[2]

Former First Lady Marike de Klerk, brutally stabbed in her Cape Town apartment, received a fair amount of international attention too. Not so the Afrikaner farmers who are being culled like springbok in a hunting safari. This brings us to the mini-genocide underway in the democratic South Africa, chronicled in Chapter Two, "The Kulaks of South Africa Vs. The Xhosa Nostra."

The ruling African National Congress (ANC) is largely composed of the Xhosa Bantu tribe. The Xhosa are also well-represented among the Africans armed with automatic weapons, who roam the countryside killing Afrikaner farmers. These rural folk—who, by law, must battle their ubiquitous assailants with only a shotgun, a handgun and a legally limited number of rounds at their disposal[3]—are convinced that the assaults are state-sanctioned, the ANC's idea of an early eviction notice; "land reform," if you will. The evidence suggests that they may have a point, hence the title pitting the "Kulaks" against the "Xhosa Nostra."

But before we recount how upward of 3,000 members of this once 40,000-strong community—almost ten percent—have hitherto been exterminated, we explain who the Boers are and provide a brief, action-packed, history of Boer, Briton and Bantu. Americans will want to hear this! Decades of emasculation—legal and cultural—have created a hunger among American men, especially, for heroic, historic narrative. The story of the South African settlers, circa 1652, is every bit as epic as that of the American settlers. Despite their comparable foibles and frailties, the last haven't been blackened by historians as much as the first.

It is commonly argued, in defiance of emerging facts to the contrary,[4] that crime is an equal opportunity offender in South Africa: whites, blacks and browns are all in it together. What is incontrovertible, however, is that, where economic opportunities are concerned, the minority that dare not speak its name is on the wane. White males, strictly speaking, are not supposed to comprise more than ten percent of the payroll in a South African company. As during apartheid, a class of people is being dispossessed because of their pallor.

Chapter Three, "Dispossession is Nine-Tenths of the Law," explores this legal attack on property known as Black Economic Empowerment (BEE). BEE is yet another unique feature of the South African democracy, whereby racist labor laws have made for what Robert Guest, Africa editor of *The Economist,* has charitably termed "The world's most extreme affirmative action program."[5] The upshot of such a coercive transfer of private wealth from those who create it to those who consume it is that societal institutions—state and civil—are being hollowed out like husks. South Africa's gutted institutions serve as a harbinger of things to come in the U.S., where affirmative action is still dismissed as a "minor irritant,"[6] but ought not to be.

South Africa *is a microcosm of what America could become, unless it returns to the principles that made it great.* If American institutions continue to subordinate their *raison d'être* to politically dictated egalitarianism, reclaiming them from the deforming clutches of affirmative action will become harder and harder. Sadly, it is probably already too late for South Africa, where the majority opposes a meritocracy. Americans, however, must once again embrace merit and individualism. Be it in the U.S. or in South Africa, preferential treatment, enforced by legal fiat and rooted in the characteristics of a group (race) rather than the value of the individual, flouts justice in every respect.

The West has grown accustomed to Thabo Mbeki, South Africa's refined former president. Having spent most of his adult life abroad in exile, Mbeki has the mannerisms of an English gent, not a man of the people. But the baton has been passed from the pukka proper Mbeki to the populist polygamist Jacob Zuma, whose favorite jingle is called "Bring Me My Machine Gun." (It only has two lines; the second beseeches, rather politely, "Please bring me my machine gun."[7]) In a country in which crimes are seldom prosecuted, the newly-installed President Zuma has the dubious distinction of having stood trial on 783 charges of corruption, racketeering, tax evasion, and rape.[8]

Against Mbeki's reserved style, there is Zuma's unbuttoned conduct, dancing half naked in tribal dress. In one of his Noble-Savage moments, after forcing sex on an HIV-positive acquaintance, Zuma promised, disarmingly, that he took a shower as a prophylactic against AIDS. It has been suggested that Zuma has done for South Africa's international image what Borat Sagdiyev has done for Kazakhstan.[9] With one distinction: Borat is a fictitious character, the product of Sacha Baron Cohen's comedic genius; Zuma is "for real."

Since Zuma's ascension, wealth transfer in South Africa is expected to accelerate considerably and to resemble ever more closely the unabashed confiscation and dispossession brought about by Robert Mugabe in Zimbabwe. "Mandela, Mbeki, And Mugabe Sitting In A Baobab Tree K-I-S-S-I-N-G," or Chapter Four, analyzes the significance of the unqualified support Zuma's predecessors, Mandela and Mbeki, have lent the Zimbabwean dictator Robert Mugabe over the decades. "If you want to see the future of South Africa, it might not be a bad idea to look at the present in Zimbabwe."[10]

The Old South Africa had been governed by Puritans. But as Christianity receded in influence after the 1994 transition, the void left has been filled by Islam. The unintended consequences of bringing the Old South Africa to its political knees, to the detriment of American interests, are covered in Chapter Six, "Why Do WASP Societies Wither?"

America, a humane society, ought to take pity on the persecuted descendants of another Protestant patriarchy. However, even if American immigration policy welcomed white South Africans, which it doesn't, Afrikaners would find it hard to leave. The Boers (and British) built the place. Like Heidi away from the Alps, Afrikaners tend to wilt when separated from their homeland. Not for nothing have the Afrikaners been dubbed "The White Tribe of Africa."[11] They are as African as black South Africans. What is to be done, then, in light of the fact that Afrikaner farmers, in particular, are being killed off at alarmingly high rates? While it remains for the secessionists to "give territorial content"[12] to their aspirations, secession is one of the escape routes suggested in the conclusion, "Saving South Africans S.O.S."

Into the Cannibal's Pot is topped and tailed with hard evidence that allows conclusions vis-à-vis the aggregate characteristics of South African society. Although not necessarily politically correct, such conclusions are perfectly proper. With this in mind, a word about the titular tease. Cannibalism, attests Leonard Thompson, author of *The Oxford History of South Africa,* was widespread during the upheaval associated with rise of the Zulu Kingdom in the 1820s.[13] These days, in northeastern Congo, two prominent militias, the Lendu and the Hema, delight in demonstrating to UN observers their culinary creativity with human hearts and livers.[14] While cannibalism—motivated by aggression, ancestral reverence, or survival—has seldom been anathema in Africa, *Into the Cannibal's Pot* is meant as a metaphor, and is inspired by Ayn Rand's wise counsel against prostrating civilization to savagery:

> In America, religion is relatively nonmystical. Religious teachers here are predominantly good, healthy materialists. They follow common sense. ... The majority of religious people in this country do not accept on faith the idea of jumping *into a cannibal's pot* and giving away their last shirt to the backward people of the world. Many religious leaders preach this today, because of their own leftist politics; it's not inherent in being religious.[15] [Emphasis added]

Daniel Etounga-Manguelle, a Cameroonian thinker, and a former adviser to the World Bank, contends that "What Africans are doing to one another defies credulity. Genocide, bloody civil wars, and rampant violent crime suggest African societies at all social levels are to some extent cannibalistic."[16] Why? In part, because of the inveterate values held by so many Africans. These, and other causes—and excuses—are examined in Chapter Five, "The Root-Causes Racket."

Based on the evidence presented in this book, both Ms. Rand and Mr. Etounga-Manguella would have agreed that South Africans had been tossed into the metaphorical cannibal's pot. Washington and Westminster insisted that the country pass into the hands of a voracious majority. Unwise South African leaders acquiesced. Federalism was discounted. Minority rights for the Afrikaner, Anglo and Zulu were dismissed. Ironically, America's founding fathers had attempted to forestall raw democracy by devising a republic. Yet under the wing of the American eagle a dispensation was negotiated in this writer's former homeland, the consequence of which is the raw, ripe rule of the mob and its dominant, anointed party.

Since *Into the Cannibal's Pot* stands for peaceful, progressive, and sustainable change, it will resonate with those who saw the folly of imposing majority rule on Iraq. Democratizing Mesopotamia has resulted in horrifying material destruction and lasting moral damage. Democratizing Azania has, similarly, made it abundantly clear that the franchise is not to be equated with freedom and that political rights do not safeguards natural rights. The cause and the consequence of the almost over-night, top-down transformation of South Africa is a society where might makes right.

In the interstices of this polemic, the reader will find my story and the story of those I love and had to leave behind. Above all, this tome is a labor of love to my homelands, old and new.

CHAPTER 1

Crime, the Beloved Country

It is bad to be oppressed by a minority, but it is worse to be oppressed by a majority...from the absolute will of an entire people there is no appeal, no redemption, no refuge but treason.

—Lord Acton*

If a young South African were to ask me whether to stay or leave, my advice would be to go.

—Breyten Breytenbach†

THE WILLIAMS FAMILY is emigrating—leaving South Africa for good. The family will be departing for the UK without their twelve-year-old daughter. Emily Williams was killed at seven in the morning on her way to school, a victim of an armed robbery underway at the home of a classmate who was being fetched by Emily and her mother. Many of the family's friends are following Roger Williams' lead. An executive director and chief financial officer at AECI, a South African chemicals group, Mr. Williams believes "everybody should have the right to go about their

---

* *The History of Freedom In Antiquity*, 1877

† The Afrikaner poet who was incarcerated for anti-apartheid activism.

business and go to school without worrying that you're going to become a victim of crime."[1]

René Burger is the little sister of Schalk Burger, a young rising star in South African rugby. Twenty-year-old René, a medical student, was headed for classes at the Tygerberg hospital in Cape Town when she was abducted from the well-patrolled hospital grounds by three men. They drove her to a remote location and gang-raped her at knife-point.

Young Noah Cohen emerged from soccer practice in time to watch his father die. Sheldon Cohen had been sitting in his car outside a Johannesburg sports stadium waiting for Noah when he was shot by "three young men."[2]

An elderly Jew is murdered on his way to synagogue in Johannesburg on Saturday morning, shot for refusing to hand over the "valuables" in his tallit bag, the pouch in which an observant Jew carries his prayer shawl.[3]

A family friend writes: "Crime is out of control down here—you hear of truly horrific stuff all the time. Johannesburg is particularly bad. I recently sold my house and moved into a security village where all the houses are accessible only through one entrance. There are guards who phone you if someone you know wants to get in to see you. Insane!"

This is a snapshot of life in suburban South Africa circa 2008, fourteen years since freedom. Ordinarily, case studies do not a rule make, but you'd be hard pressed to find a family in democratic South Africa whose members have not been brutalized. The travails of this writer's extended family are fairly typical. They tell of the lives of good people ruined by rubbish: A sister's partner suffering permanent neurological damage after being brutally assaulted by five Africans; a brother burglarized and beaten in his suburban fortress at two in the morning by an African gang (his wife and infant son were miraculously spared); a father whose neighbor was shot point-blank in front of his little girls as he exited his car to open the garage gates; a spouse, two of whose colleagues were murdered (one shot by African taxi drivers in broad daylight, left to bleed to death on the pavement near his girlfriend's place), and whose cousin and uncle were hijacked, aunt raped and beaten within an inch of her life. Sean Mercer, Ph.D., found out recently that a fondly remembered professor at his alma mater had been beaten to death with an umbrella by an angry African student.[4] A Cambridge graduate, Brian D. Hahn was a prodigious applied mathematician at the University of Cape Town.[5] He is no longer, but his webpage is still online. Hahn, it states, was born in November 1946 in Cape Town, born again in August of 1966, and died in February of 2005. His colleagues tell of a humble man who practiced his profession and faith faithfully. Rest in Peace.

"The circle narrows," mourns Afrikaner poet and former anti-apartheid activist, Breyten Breytenbach in an essay for *Harper's Magazine*:

> The grandmother of a close friend—she's as old as [Mandela]—pleads with her robbers not to be sexually violated, she even claims to be infected with a communicable disease; the nephew of a fellow writer is shot in the face, killed in his own house by a night intruder whom he mistook for a rat; the son of my eldest brother is stabbed in a parking lot outside a restaurant, the blade pierces a lung, the police never turn up, he is saved because his companion calls her boyfriend all the way in Australia by cell phone and he could summon a nurse he happens to know in Johannesburg. (The woman is on a first visit to the country; she leaves the next day and swears never to return.)[6]

This writer and her immediate family, presciently, left South Africa in 1995, shortly after the white minority ceded power to a black majority. A year prior, we had voted in South Africa's first democratic election. In 1990, I'd been on the Grand Parade in Cape Town, among a crowd of thousands, to witness Nelson Mandela's release after twenty-seven years in prison (it was a riot, literally). In previous decades my father, Rabbi Ben Isaacson, had been a well-known anti-apartheid activist. With him I attended the inauguration of Archbishop Desmond Tutu, and met and took afternoon tea with the Nobel Peace Prize Laureate. Nevertheless, the writing was on the wall.

When we departed, South Africa was still a country with a space program (on which my husband Sean Mercer worked), gleaming skyscrapers, and department stores that rivaled Macy's. The Central Business District in Johannesburg bustled. Crime was controlled, or at least confined. When mobs stoned cars *en route* to the D. F. Malan Airport in Cape Town (geographical names across the country have since been changed to expunge Afrikaner history), a tough and competent police force sprung into action. An equally impressive Western system of Roman-Dutch law, and a relatively independent judiciary, dished out just deserts in response to the ubiquitous "muti-murders" (African ritual killing, including human sacrifice in Venda[7]), and to "necklacing" (the more contemporary African custom of placing a diesel-doused tire around a putative offender's neck and igniting it). Or to the rape of babies. To borrow from Gen. Sir Charles Napier: Before 1994, when African men raped infants because they considered the "practice" a traditional salve for AIDS, South African policemen followed through with their custom: they tied a rope around the rapist's neck and hung him. "Afrikaner rule," the noted liberal historian Hermann Giliomee has observed, "was characterized by an obsession with imposing restrictions through proper legislation and with due process in executing these laws … The government did not attempt to cover up deaths in detention, despite a torrent of unfavorable publicity. Although political opponents were at the mercy of their interrogators in prison, both the policeman and the prisoner knew that neither was outside the law."[8]

It goes without saying that a condemnation of the New South Africa is not an affirmation of the Old. More crucially, realism is not racism. The undeniable reality is that, a decade since this abrupt transfer of power, the rule of the *demos* has turned a once-prosperous, if politically problematic, place into a lawless ramshackle. The BBC World's John Simpson recently—and reluctantly—disclosed that South Africa jostles with Iraq and Colombia[9] for the title of most violent country in the world. So violent is the "free" South Africa that, for a period, the freewheeling ANC government imposed an official blackout on national crime statistics. It now releases them once yearly.

"JACKROLLING"

The surfeit of crime statistics, say those who chronicle crime, can be misleading because "crime definitions vary from one country to the next." This is an argument that the African National Congress' grotesquely mistitled Safety and Security Minister Charles Nqakula often seizes upon, to conceal the blood-soaked facts of violent crime in his country. Following its chief's example, the South African Police Service (SAPS) has developed an agile facility with misleading statistical comparisons. To diminish crime under its jurisdiction, the SAPS is fond of drawing skewed comparisons between low-crime spots in South Africa and high-crime spots in otherwise low-crime countries.

Juxtaposing the incidence of murder in low-crime Pretoria and high-crime Washington, D.C (29.1 per 100,000 inhabitants[10]) is an example of the practice. The same sources like to point to the incidence of rape in Canada: evidently one of the highest *per capita* in the world, having surpassed both the U.S. and Zimbabwe.[11] But the only way First World Canada—with its 1.77

murders per 100,000 population[12]—can lay claim to this dubious distinction is by legally redefining rape. The cause of this is the baleful influence of feminist Catharine Mackinnon on American and Canadian jurisprudence. The consequence of it is that a woman can seek and find in the law a legal remedy to the regret or rage experienced following an impromptu romp between the sheets.

The redefining of rape in American and Canadian law is the product of the collaboration between advocacy groups and feminist stakeholders, and has been exposed by John Fekete in *Moral Panic: Biopolitics Rising*. Undergirding this sub-science are statistically promiscuous surveys such as Statistics Canada's 1993 "Violence Against Women" survey, and its American equivalent. As Professor Fekete has demonstrated, this voodoo consists of single-sex surveys with no input from men; is fraught with problems of unrepresentative sampling, lack of corroboration, a reliance on anecdotes, and a use of over-inclusive survey questions. Suffice it to say that, *contra* North America, in South Africa, where a rape occurs every twenty-six seconds,[13] the crime of rape is unlikely to mean mere sexual harassment or sexual disappointment. Very many South African young men consider rape a form of recreation, their rapacity even finding expression in the vocabulary: gang rape is jocularly referred to as "jackrolling."[14] Ironically, the provincial chauvinism of the cloistered gender feminists of the West has helped trivialize the plight of their African sisters.

Ultimately, murder in all its horrible finality cannot be statistically finessed. This is why, in proportion to population size, it is the best gauge of the precariousness or safety of life in a given society. The U.S. Bureau of Justice concurs: "Homicide is a fairly reliable barometer of all violent crime."[15]

Let us, then, survey homicide statistics for South Africa. They are easy to understand, if hard to digest.

ADAPT AND DIE[‡]

Between April 2004 and March 2005, 18,793 people were murdered in South Africa (population 43 million). In comparison, the "high-crime" United States (population 299,398,000[16]) suffered 16,740 murders. Put differently, South Africa has sixty homicides per 100,000 people; the US approximately six.[17] The European Union (population 728 million) has approximately 1.59 homicides per 100,000 per year.[18] On average, in South Africa, sixty-five people are murdered every day, three times that number are raped; and 300 are violently attacked and robbed daily.[19]

These official figures, say other researches, are more serendipity than science.

According to Robert McCafferty of the United Christian Action, Interpol had pegged South Africa's murder rate at "114.8 murders per 100,000 inhabitants,"[20] roughly double those released by the South African Police Service (SAPS). In 1995 and 1996, Interpol counted 54,298 annual homicides to the SAPS's 26,883. While slightly more optimistic, the South African Medical Research Council (MRC) corroborated the trend Interpol uncovered. It reported approximately a third more murders in South Africa than the official police statistics reveal,"[21] tallying an average of eighty-nine daily deaths, or 32,000 a year. A discrepancy of over 10,000 murders is, shall we say, more than a margin of error.

McCafferty, whose data is a distillation of information from criminology journals, the SAPS, Crime Information Analysis Centre (CIAC), Institute for Security Studies (ISS), Interpol websites, and "the major newspapers on crime statistics and related issues," concluded that "what sets South Africa's crime

‡ Dan Roodt, "Adapt and die—South Africa's New Motto," *Praag*, November 2004.

apart from basically every other country on earth is the incredibly high levels of violent crime"—murder, attempted murder, serious and common assaults, rape, and all categories of robbery: that is, robbery with aggravating circumstances, armed robbery, and car hijacking.

During his term of office, former president Thabo Mbeki wielded the "racist" *ad hominem* deftly. Mbeki ignored the BBC's otherwise incontinent exhilaration about everything else South African, choosing instead to frame as racism the network's newfound realism *vis-à-vis* crime.[22] Mbeki countered a BBC crime exposé by asserting that "nobody can show that the overwhelming majority of the 40-50 million South Africans think that crime is out of control. Nobody can, because it's not true."[23] It so happens that South Africans are fed up ("*gatvol*" in Afrikaans) with crime, as is evident from the petitions, protests and vigils staged across the brutalized country. Asked about their feelings of safety compared to 1994, a majority (seventy percent) of South Africans surveyed by the Human Sciences Research Council (HSRC) in 2001 answered that South Africa was "not safer than it was before 1994."[24] Even if Mbeki had been able to get most South Africans to concede that crime was insignificant, that would not settle the matter. Unfortunately for Mr. Mbeki, truth is not adjudicated by majority vote.

"APARTHEID NOSTALGIA"

To most Western observers, the new dispensation in this writer's old home engenders unconditional praise the world over. For them, not knowing whether you'll survive the day is but a spot of bother. Conservative columnists are as prone as anyone else to be nonchalant about the present situation. One of them described South Africa as "the greatest triumph of chatter over machine-gun clatter. It's not perfect, and crime is at an all-time high in South

African cities, but at least the massacres are a thing of the past and life goes on much better than before." If by "massacres" our correspondent meant Sharpeville, where in 1960, panic-stricken policemen of the apartheid regime shot dead sixty-nine black demonstrators, why, in democratic South Africa that's *the daily* carnage quota.

Few realize that during the *decades* of the apartheid regime a few hundred Africans in total perished as a direct and indirect consequence of police brutality. A horrible injustice, indubitably, but nothing approximating the death toll in "free" South Africa, where hundreds of Africans, white and black, perish *weekly*. Nor did apartheid's casualties come close to the ANC's during "the armed struggle." Freedom's forebears "necklaced" 400 non-combatants, and murdered hundreds more—Zulu opposition, state informers and witnesses, rural headmen, urban councilors, "and others perceived to be collaborators of the system or enemies of the ANC."[25] "Between 1976 and 1994," writes Giliomee, "state agents deliberately killed between two hundred and three hundred people active in the struggle against the state."[26] It takes the free agents of democratic Azania only *five days* to deliberately kill as many of their fellow citizens.

Still fewer realize that during the decades of the repressive—and reprehensible—apartheid regime, which ended officially in 1994, crime rates in South Africa were overall much lower; in whites-only areas they were not dissimilar to those in other Western countries. McCafferty, whose brief it was to compare "the number of murders in the 'Old South Africa' (under apartheid) ... to the 'New South Africa' (post 1994),"[27] counted 309,583 murders over the forty-four years spanning 1950 to 1993. In the first eight years of the "new democratic dispensation," 193,649 people were murdered. In other words, under apartheid, on *average, 7,036 people were murdered each year,* a small number compared to the carnage under the ANCniks: *24,206 annually*. The latter is the South Africa Police Service's low-ball estimation, which both Interpol and the South African Medical Research Council have disputed.

The ANC government now claims that matters have improved and that it is winning the war on violent crime. The Democratic Alliance disputes this. The tiny, tokenistic, opposition to the "all-powerful black majority party" puts the ostensible drop in crime down to the fact that fifty-one percent of victims no longer bothers to report crime, given that corruption is rife, arrests rare, and prosecutions and convictions still rarer.[28] Recent findings suggest that the SAPS's optimistic, homicide statistics are not to be believed. As reported by *The Economist*, the Center for the Study of Violence and Reconciliation has confirmed the existence of a "pervasive pattern of (police) manipulation of statistic." By an amazing coincidence, the reported decline in violent crime and the government's 2004 announcement of its intention to cut such crime have dovetailed.

Doctored or diminished, the SAPS's statistics spanning 2006 to 2007 reveal that 19,202[29] South African lives were lost (population 43,786,115[30]) compared to the United States' 16,574[31] (population 303,824,646[32]). A yearly average of 19,202 murders (under democracy) still constitutes almost three times as many as 7,036 annual murders (under apartheid). Clearly, the era of apartheid remains a Golden Age with respect to the sanctity of life, for blacks and whites alike.

CRIME DESEGREGATED

McCafferty's numbers notwithstanding, such an unsettling claim is usually met with this brittle argument: Murders are not more numerous under majority rule, but merely more evenly spread. Let us celebrate, for democracy has desegregated crime! In his searing 1986 critique of apartheid, *Move Your Shadow: South Africa, Black And White*, Joseph Lelyveld (a former *New York Times* editor) surmised: "Apartheid [ensured] that the victims of most black violence [were] black and the victims of most white violence white."[33] At the time, Lelyveld avoided further damaging deductions, such as that apartheid separated the high-crime from the low-crime communities. The Group Areas Act of 1950, the basic statute that had guaranteed absolute residential segregation under apartheid,[34] served to confine crime to the black townships. Ditto influx control laws: "Africans who had not established a claim to be in urban areas were given only seventy-two hours in towns and cities to find work and were compelled to register at a government labor bureau for this purpose."[35] Let us not beat about the bush; violent crime in the New South Africa is predominantly black on black and black on white. Since the demise of apartheid, it has both increased and spread from slum to suburb. However, even assuming that violent crime has not increased but is only more "equitably" distributed, why is that good or even tolerable? Does parity in the probability of being victimized constitute progress? Does the fact that whites are now as likely as—data[36] suggest more likely than—blacks to be slain herald a more just dispensation? An answer in the affirmative evinces a quest for vengeance, not fairness.

While it is true that "there is nothing new about hideous, sadistic, violent crime in SA,"[37] the Afrikaner National Party, for all its faults, kept the lid on the cauldron of depravity now bubbling over. At the time, Lelyveld, and left-liberals like him, inveighed against the heavily armed "plainclothes white security cops who cruise[d] around the major black townships in big Fords and Datsuns."[38] But, among the many demonstrators forever punching the air, most distinguished between "ordinary (good) police and riot (bad) police." Or so wrote the late Fredrik van Zyl Slabbert, leader of the former anti-apartheid opposition, the Progressive Federal Party (PFP). In *The Last White Parliament*, Slabbert attests that "Without exception, [blacks wanted] ordinary police to remain in the townships and help with [much needed] crime prevention."[39]

Dubbed the father of apartheid, Dr. Hendrik Verwoerd was certainly "[k]eenly interested in urban security." To that end, "township streets were purposely wide so police could control movement easily."[40] Indubitably, law and order in the townships of Old South Africa was less a function of the Boer's brotherly love for the Bantu than of his orderly habits. But it was subject to investigation by a relatively independent judiciary; reports tabled often finding against the police. For example, Justice Kannemeyer's report (which was debated in parliament) of the response to the riots that erupted in 1985 was, to quote the headline in the Johannesburg-based *Star*, at the time, a "'devastating indictment' of police."[41] The only "devastating indictment" of Jacob Zuma's police force issued these days emanates from *outside* the government and well beyond its vengeful reach. (Try as I did, I was unable to get white policemen and women—old hands working deep in the guts of the reconstructed SAPS—to talk about the "workplace": they were afraid.) The ANC's response to a police force shot through with corruption has been the dissolution of the crack, anti-corruption unit known as the "Scorpions."[42]

The Afrikaner's quaint and quintessentially Western practices are etched vividly in journalist Keith Richburg's *Out of America: A Black Man Confronts Africa*. Just before Afrikaners "surrendered without defeat,"[43] Richburg, Africa bureau chief for *The Washington Post* from 1991 to 1994, journeyed to South Africa from the killing fields to the north, on assignment. In the course of his duties, he filed a report from the scene of a tribally motivated killing near Johannesburg. Zulu and Xhosa were embroiled in pre-elections strife. Twelve people had been gunned down. A small massacre by African standards—at least, so thought Richburg, who has described Africa as a continent where everywhere black bodies are stacked up like firewood. Imagine his astonishment when "the police, mostly officious-looking white officers with ruddy complexions—came and did what you might expect police to do in any Midwestern American city where a crime has occurred. They cordoned off the area with police tape. They marked the spots on the ground where the victims had fallen."[44] Topping this *CSI*-worthy protocol was a statement to the press "promising a 'full investigation.'" This civilized routine Richburg characterized as utterly misplaced on a continent where nobody counts the bodies; and where chasing down and charging a man with murder is like "handing out speeding tickets at the Indy 500."[45]

The Old South Africa was the odd man out in Africa. Maligned by Joseph Lelyveld, the Afrikaner's presence in high-crime localities was why a semblance of law and order was maintained and common criminals pursued and prosecuted to the benefit of all.

Little wonder then that "pollsters note a small but growing number of blacks experiencing 'apartheid nostalgia.' 'It's not that they want to return to apartheid, but in retrospect it was a time when things worked better,'" says Robert Mattes, co-director of the Afrobarometer poll.[46] That's an understatement. Certainly back then soccer moms and dads were never shaken down during a match—a common occurrence these days. Back then *The Christian Science Monitor*'s South African correspondent did not compose his dispatches from behind "ten-foot walls, electric fencing, burglar bars," and within reach of "at least one panic button wired directly to an armed-response team."[47] Back then shopkeepers were not compelled to cower behind iron bars, as they do now. Gun battles were unheard of on the streets of South Africa's major metropolises, some of which have come to resemble Mogadishu, pavements strewn with garbage, skyscrapers overrun by squatters, and landmarks vandalized beyond recognition. To wit, the Impala Stampede, a "giant bronze statue that used to adorn the entrance to Anglo American's offices, was torn down and destroyed by the rampaging gangs."[48]

In the New South Africa, rising prices at the pump corresponded to a rising body count, as petrol attendants are targeted for crude.[49] An attendant trend did not accompany the steep gas prices during the 1987 oil embargo against South Africa. This writer would safely fill the tank and travel to Hillbrow to lunch with her late grandfather. Hillbrow was then a hip, cosmopolitan, Johannesburg suburb. Today it is South Africa's Harlem, before gentrification. Equally uneventful for this writer was the walk to work from the Eloff street bus terminal in Johannesburg's city center, where the magnificent five-star Carlton Hotel was open for business. It closed in 1997; the safety of the guests could no longer be guaranteed. The green glass Garden Court Hotel and the Great Synagogue have suffered the same fate.[50] Fearing for its safety, the Johannesburg Stock Exchange, once "the tenth largest in the world,"[51] joined the exodus from the Johannesburg Central Business District (CBD) to the suburb of Sandton.

Defiantly and heroically, a consortium called "Business Against Crime" (BAC) has undertaken to beat back the dirt and decay that had blanketed Johannesburg's CBD. These intrepid entrepreneurs aim to restore the "mothballed" monuments, reopen boarded-up buildings, and replace brothels and shebeens with legitimate businesses. These are not guys with guns: The BAC's frontal assault on crime relies on a system of closed-circuit TV cameras! *The Economist* has proclaimed this "public-private partnership" a success. At the same time, the magazine has conceded that conviction rates in South Africa still hover at a "dismal" eight percent and have only just begun to inch upward.[52]

Optimism aside, it is hard to see how the prospects of being caught on camera would deter a hardcore criminal for long since he has a ninety percent chance of getting away with murder. Considering that the country now has one of the world's highest murder rates and lowest conviction rates, a South Africa thug can safely pursue his vocation without fearing the consequences, confirms criminologist Neels Moolman."[53] Since freedom, the SAPS, a reconstructed, racially "representative" force, has relaxed the pursuit of criminals. Besides, the democratic South Africa's criminal class is unlikely to flee before the regiments of an ill-trained, illiterate and corrupt outfit. If anything, evidence abounds of cooperation between criminals and cops, starting at the top. Jackie Selebi, the SAPS's national police commissioner is a bent and brutal man who's been linked to the mob[54] (and was eventually dismissed by President Zuma).

SUFFER THE LITTLE CHILDREN

The swirl of statistics tends to conceal the casualties of crime. One such casualty is Baby Tshepang. "Tshepang" means "have hope." If Tshepang has hope it is against all odds, for she was raped and sodomized, in 2001, when nine months old. The culprit was a twenty-three-year-old man—Tshepang's sixteen-year-old mother's former lover. Rape of infants in South Africa has reached "epidemic proportions," writes Linda M. Richler in the *Child Abuse Review*, and "occurs with unacceptably high frequency."[55] Roughly ten percent of all rapes in the country—52,425 a year[56]—are committed against children under three years of age. In the span of the two months following Baby Tshepang's rape, another five children under twelve months of age were raped. In two of the cases, media reports suggested the child's caregivers might have accepted money for making the child available to the perpetrator.[57]

Sexperts and sociologists have a habit of sanitizing savagery with odd-ball pseudoscientific assertions: "To penetrate the vagina of a small child," writes Richler ponderously, "the perpetrator must first create a common channel between the vagina and anal canal by forced insertion of an implement."[58] In the gaping wound that was Baby Tshepang before she was sewn back together, Richler has detected a technique where there was only brute, libidinal force. She offers no forensic evidence for her claim. Richler's less iffy inference has it that this nauseating crime wave may well be rooted in the "virgin cleansing myth"—the idea that sex with a virgin cures HIV/AIDS and offers protection against acquiring the virus. (Seen in the context of the late Minister of Health Manto Tshabalala-Msiming's espousal of beetroot, garlic and lemon as antidotes for AIDS,[59] this makes perfect sense.) Oddly enough, when epidemiologists speak of mapping the spread of the epidemic in a country in which *one in five adults* is infected,[60] they are somehow parted from their critical faculties, rarely mentioning epidemic sexual violence as a vector of transmission.

Thankfully, for the victims, political correctness doesn't plague the private, entrepreneurial sector. "The connection between violent crime and AIDS in South Africa was underscored by 'rape insurance' policies launched in November 1999," write Dave Kopel and Drs. Paul Gallant and Joanne Eisen of the Independence Institute. LifeSense, a medical benefits organization underwritten by Lloyds of London, has been offering a "Rape Care" package to rape victims which "provides a top-up policy should the rape survivor become HIV-positive as a result of rape. Dr. Angus Rowe, a spokesperson from LifeSense, stated that 'in an environment where rape is so pervasive we need to extend protections to rape survivors in the families.' Rape Care policy holders will have access to counseling and medical treatment, 'an anti-retroviral starter pack, the home delivery of the full 28-day anti-retroviral treatment, and HIV testing for one year.'"[61] Had the private sector not similarly—and speedily—moved to palliate the South African people's desperate need for protection against criminals, who knows how many more would be ravished or killed? There are now 400,000 "guardian angels" in private security toiling to make up for the state's failure to protect its citizens.[62]

One doesn't have to be an HIV/AIDS counselor to conclude that endemic sexual violence increases the spread of the disease. It so happens that this writer was such a counselor at the Cape Town chapter of ATIC, the AIDS Training, Information and Counseling Centre. The African women I counseled there were educated and well turned out, yet they giggled like girls when prophylactics were mentioned. African patriarchs disdain protection, they told me, coyly cupping their mouths and laughing—at me. They were, however, deadly serious. For these women, insisting on your, "like, reproductive freedoms"—uttered in staccato, tart tones, indigenous to North America—meant risking the wrath of quick-fisted husbands. At the time, the counseling model used at ATIC was developed for gay American men. Based on my experience with these urban, urbane women, I recommended—and was commended for—changing the laughable, gay-centric guidelines. If sophisticated African women were afraid to suggest sheaths to their men, all the more so their rural, uneducated sisters.

One tenet of the gay-centric counseling model applies to Africa in spades: the reality of rutting, rampant sex. When the puritanical apartheid government "finally stirred into action, launching AIDS education and prevention programs, it met considerable resistance,"[63] attests historian Martin Meredith. Anti-apartheid activists accused the government of wanting to prevent Africans from having promiscuous sex so as to retard population growth and "check the advance of African liberation." AIDS, they joked, stood for "Afrikaner Invention to Deprive us of Sex."[64] Although Mbeki persisted in the belief that AIDS is a conspiracy—Big Pharma having replaced the Afrikaner as culprit—there isn't a corner in post-apartheid South Africa that has not been missionized by AIDS educators. Still, infection rates remain, for the most, unaffected. Rocker Bono, the warbling modern father of foreign aid, has praised Africans for being a "rare and spirited people." Sadly, if the spirit didn't move them in so many wild ways, rates of infection in Southern Africa might not have reached twenty to 33.7 percent of the adult population. Africans are having unprotected sex irrespective of the mortal dangers of AIDS, a phenomenon which Austrian economists might explain with reference to time preference rates. In this case, time preference rates signify the degree to which different people will discount the future in favor of immediate gratification. Time orientation, agrees Lawrence E. Harrison, an associate at the Harvard Academy for International and Area Studies, is a central value in progressive as opposed to static cultures.[65] Educational efforts aside, the number of people infected in Southern Africa bespeaks a high time preference: the habit of consistently risking the future for fleeting fun. Put it this way: The Catholic Church's consecration of condoms will likely have the same overall effect on African AIDS infection rates as its condemnation of sex outside marriage.

Let us not forget these child victims. Certainly Breyten Breytenbach does not. Breytenbach, the exiled Afrikaner poet "who served seven years in South African prisons for his anti-apartheid activities,"[66] invokes for our remembrance South Africa's children at large, and Meisi Majola's two-year-old boy in particular. The tot was snatched from his home and his genitals mutilated. "To be used as *muti*...a potency potion." Little Courtney Ellerbeck's broken body mirrors the unremitting violence inflicted on the most innocent members of South African society. The child hobbles about cheerfully with the aid of calipers with lockable knee joints, metal hips, and a walker. She is the country's youngest crime victim. Courtney was born a paraplegic after being shot in utero by a hijacker.[67]

YOUR HOME: THE ANC'S CASTLE

Because the ANC disregards the importance of private property and public order and the remedial value of punitive justice, innocent victims of crime often defend themselves in their own homes on pain of imprisonment. The Amendments to the Criminal Procedure Act demand that, in the course of adjudicating cases of "private defense," the right to life (the aggressor's) and the right to property (the non-aggressor's) be properly balanced. "Before you can act in self-defense," remonstrates Anton du Plessis of the Institute for Security Studies, "the attack against you should have commenced, or at least be imminent. For example, if the thief pulls out a firearm and aims in your direction, [only] then you would be justified in using lethal force to protect your life."[68] In a country where, as columnist Barry Ronge noted, husbands and children are routinely forced to watch while mothers are raped, victims must now "calibrate the extent of the menace" before defending loved ones. Why, even for giving chase, victims may now be prosecuted as aggressors.

Between a rock and a hard place, to use that cliché of in-betweenness, is where Jaco Swart found himself when confronted at two o'clock in the morning with two intruders in his homestead. The twenty-six-year-old Swart hails from Delareyville, a small farming community in South Africa's northwest. This town is named for General Koos de la Rey, hero of the Boer War. Young Swart is a hero too. But for choosing to defend home and hearth in the New South Africa, he was arrested and charged with murder and attempted murder. Swart had dispatched the one assailant and injured the other with a licensed firearm. Not only can self-defense be an offense in the new constitutional democracy, but it may be considered racist when practiced by whites. COSATU, the Congress of South African Trade Unions, under whose auspices, presumably, home invaders fall, accused Swart of racism.[69]

The sixteen-year-old son of Len Parkin of Pretoria was awoken at three in the morning by two armed men, and instructed to lead them to where his parents slept. The boy complied. The criminals shot his father. Despite his injuries, Len Parkin seized his handgun and managed to hasten the descent into hell of the one assailant. An opprobrious police inspector, one Paul Ramaloko, said: "Because Parkin is in hospital, he hasn't been arrested. The public prosecutor will now decide whether the victim was using his firearm in self-defense or not."[70]

An elderly couple—he seventy-seven, she seventy-three—may spend the rest of their days in jail for attempted murder. The plucky pair had overpowered an intruder who had grabbed their pistol and was poised to pounce.[71] Not far from where these heroes reside live my in-laws. I used to rest easier knowing that if a thug entered their Western Cape home, my elderly mother in-law could easily dispatch him with her six-round .32 Special. It was comforting to know that in the unlikely event of her requiring further firepower, my father-in-law could weigh in with his .38 Special. But with the advent of the Firearm Control Act of 2000 (FCA)—whose constitutionality is currently being challenged—the Safety and Security Minister unveiled "an arsenal" of stricter gun-control laws, decreeing that "gun-toting cowboys"[72] such as my elderly mother and father in-law would no longer be tolerated, and "non-threatening" home invaders would no longer face on-the-spot justice. Should my in-laws awaken to find a malefactor beating down the door, they shall have to hold their fire and attempt to ascertain his manifestly acquisitive—and almost certainly murderous—motives.

Lucky are the outlaws in the New South Africa. Less lucky are the in-laws. Their licenses, "granted under the old Arms and Ammunition Act," were supposed to be valid for life and mandatory renewal unconstitutional."[73] Now, they, and each of South Africa's three million legal gun owners, have been required, under the FCA, to re-apply for permits. If she wishes to keep her handgun, my mother-in-law will have to trundle to the only licensed gun seller in the region and, for a fat fee, acquire registration forms and a booklet, which she must study and prepare to be examined on. Once she passes the exam, she will head to the police station, where again, she will be fleeced and forced to fill in more forms that'll be sent to the capital. There, an ANC official will decide whether she truly needs a handgun for "self-defense." This process can take years. Kopel, Gallant and Eisen predicted that Mbeki's FCA would outlaw ninety percent of lawfully owned firearms currently in civilian hands.[74] Preliminary reports appear to substantiate their estimate with respect to new applicants as well.[75]

In a country where almost everyone knows someone who has been raped, robbed, hijacked, murdered, or all of the above, the reasons the revamped SAPS gives for denying an application are: a "lack of motivation," "your husband can protect you," "the police will protect you," "you are too young."[76] Talk about an "eff-off" attitude! The applicant must also prepare for a house call from their protectors for the purpose of inspecting the safety deposit box. Since my seventy nine-year-old infirm mother-in-law has forfeited the pleasure of this procedure—my father-in-law will soldier on—she must surrender her handgun to the police. In this way it can be sold by the notoriously corrupt officers of the law to other industrious trade union workers. For giving up her gun, she will get no official receipt or acknowledgment. If the thing is used in a crime, she's liable. Ditto if she tampers with the mechanism to render it unusable.

As would increasingly be the case, there are those who dismiss as "right-wing scaremongering" any claim that the right to self-defense is seriously circumscribed in a country that needs it more than any other. A case in point is Professor Anthony Minnaar of the Department of Security Risk Management at the University of South Africa (UNISA), my alma mater. Placing "the perpetrator" in irons following a "shooting" in said "perpetrator's" home, and irrespective of the circumstances, is standard—and proper—police practice,[§] maintains Minnaar. In case you wonder, "the perpetrator" in Minnaar's nomenclature is the proper term for a victorious victim of an assault. Besides, admonishes Minnaar, charges are, for the most, dropped. Or if the charges are imposed, they are commuted to a lesser charge such as culpable homicide with a self-defense plea. Beleaguered South Africans, however, need fewer Minnaars and more laws that exempt them from any criminal or civil liability if they are forced to use deadly force in self-defense.

Worlds away from South Africa, Americans have also been subjected to a state-orchestrated volcanic change in their society, the consequence of the unchecked flow of millions of Third World illegal immigrants into the country. As Heather Mac Donald, scholar at the Manhattan Institute, has documented in detail, the sturdy American castle is being catapulted by criminal aliens, although not yet sufficiently so as to make Americans fret over the erosion of the Castle Doctrine. However, as a number of landmark cases would suggest, "Make My Day Laws"[77]—a favored American sobriquet for Castle Laws inspired by the Clint Eastwood *Dirty Harry* character—will become more important commensurate with rapidly changing demographics and the attendant spike in crime.[78]

A man's home is not mere property—it is his castle. In defending his home, an individual is defending a safe haven for his most cherished belongings: his person and his beloved. Someone eager to violate another's inner sanctum will be more than willing to violate the occupant. This applies in spades to South Africa, where life is snuffed out for a cell phone or for the simple pleasure of it, and where home invasions are on the yearly rise, and frequently culminate in torture, rape and murder.[79] Confronted with a home invader, there's precious little a homeowner can do

[§] Email correspondence, September 25, 2009

to divine the intentions of the intruder. This is the distinctively American subtext of the Castle Doctrine, which is unevenly applied across the U.S., despite the fact that the Second Amendment to the American Constitution affirms a natural right to self-defense (recently reaffirmed by the Supreme Court of the United States in *Heller vs. The District of Columbia*).

Not that you'd know it, but South Africans have a right to live free of all forms of violence, "public" or "private" in origin.[80] Section 12 of their progressive Constitution protects the "Freedom and Security of the Person." Clearly "progressive" doesn't necessarily spell progress: Nowhere does this wordy but worthless document state whether South Africans may actually defend this most precious right. A *right that can't be defended is a right in name only*—implicit in the right to life is the right to self-defense. The South African Constitution is descriptive, not prescriptive—full of pitch-perfect verbal obesities that provide little by way of legal recourse for the likes of Messrs Parkin, Swart and all the other good guys with guns.

WHO'S KILLING WHOM

"A typical white woman" is how Barack Obama flippantly dismissed the woman who had raised him with a great deal of devotion: his white maternal grandmother. Richly revealing was the way Obama tarred the late Madelyn Dunham with the taint of racism because she "once confessed her fear of black men who passed her by on the street." Obama's grandma had still not acquitted herself for expressing a visceral fear rooted in the brutal reality of crime in the U.S. Eric Holder, the first African-American to hold the position of Attorney-General, seconded the commander-in-chief's reservations about "typical" Americans. Mr. Holder has called America a nation of cowards and commanded Americans to have an honest conversation about race.

White Americans can be forgiven for cowering. The civil rights division of Holder's Justice Department recently ordered the dismissal of one of the worst cases of voter intimidation to come before it, because, according to a Justice Department attorney, those menaced with batons, instructed to brace for The Black Man's rule—and promised that their babies would be butchered—were "honkies" and "white whores." These were the epithets the defendants, members of the New Black Panthers, used. They were decked up in "black berets, combat boots, battle dress pants, and rank insignia,"[81] and had flanked the entrance to the polling location commanding brothers to kill "crackers" and their kids.

I suspect that rather than a two-way exchange about race, what Mr. Holder really craves is more of the same: a one-way "conversation," where brothers like him, joined by the journalistic herd, talk *at* the errant American people—a people that harbors no racial animus and has elected a black man because they believed he was the right man.

Be that as it may, there are certain facts that will never make it into this highly colored exchange.

According to the 2005 Bureau of Justice's Statistics (BJS) of "Homicide trends in the U.S," blacks were seven times more likely to offend than whites.[82] In that year, 8.8 percent of all murders were of whites by blacks; 3.2 percent of all murders were of blacks by whites.[83] Blacks murder at a rate of 26.5 per 100,000 people; whites—whose criminality the state statistician often inflates by conflating them with Hispanics—committed 3.5 murders per 100,000.[84] As to "Homicide Offenders by Race": Despite blacks comprising a mere 12.3 percent of the population in the US, to whites' 75.1 percent,[85] in 2005, there were 10,285 black murderers to 8,350 white murderers.[86] From the BJS's "Prisoners on death row by race" chart,[87] it can be extrapolated that a black is 4.6 times more likely than a white to be on death row.[88] Similarly, blacks are more likely to murder whites than the reverse. This likelihood is a trend which the BJS downplays by emphasizing the "intraracial" nature of most murders. Black-on-white murder is, moreover, increasing steadily. Not so white-on-black murder.

Still, if you publicize these unexceptional, government-crunched numbers, you run the risk of being treated as though you yourself had committed the crimes that you were reporting. Amicable race relations in the U.S. have come to depend on attaching disproportionate racial significance to the act of dangling a noose—an impolite and impolitic form of expression, admittedly, but hardly more than that. A black man beating a white man to a pulp is deemed racially neutral. Thus the affront *du jour* to the feelings of blacks is debated *ad nauseam*; felonies committed by blacks against whites are debated not at all. Accordingly, there isn't an American who hasn't heard of errant broadcaster Don Imus and his "nappy-headed hos" ugly utterance.[89] There's hardly an American who *has* heard of the habitual, endemic gang rape of white men by black and Hispanic prisoners in the country's prisons.

Although black-on-white crime is more common than the reverse, the category of hate crime applies *de facto* to white-on-black crime. "Whitey" is invariably—and by default—viewed as the chief repository of racial malice. The establishment media, especially, have made a mockery out of real racial hatred. To listen to them, you'd think that being maligned is more hateful than being maimed or murdered. American jurists and journalists, politicians and pundits were oblivious, for the most, to the deep and dark reality buried in the hearts of the individuals who butchered twenty-one-year-old Channon Christian and twenty-three-year-old Hugh Christopher Newsom in Knoxville, Tennessee, in 2007. Five blacks—four men and a woman—anally raped Hugh, then shot him to death, wrapped his body in bedding, soaked it in gasoline and set it alight. He was the lucky one. Channon, his fair and fragile-looking friend, was repeatedly gang raped by the four men—vaginally, anally and orally. Before she died, her murderers poured a household cleaner down her throat, in an effort to cleanse away DNA. She was left to die, either from the bleeding caused "by the tearing," or from asphyxiation. Knoxville officials would not say. She was then stuffed in a garbage can like trash.[90] White trash.

Young, white, and poor: The savage crime against Channon and Hugh was not a statistical outlier. The Bureau of Justice Statistics issued a report, in 2005, the product of a combined effort of the National Crime Victimization Survey (NCV) and the FBI's Uniform Crime Reporting Program (UCR).[91] Accordingly, an annual average of 191,000 hate crimes was documented since 2000. The NCV data is drawn from a 77,600-strong nationally representative sample. The UCR data is collected by 17,300 law enforcement agencies. Youngsters like Channon and Hugh were more likely than any other age group to be well represented among the reported victims.[92] As defined by the report, "an ordinary crime becomes a hate crime when offenders choose a victim because of some characteristic—for example, race, ethnicity, or religion—and provide evidence that hate prompted them to commit the crime."[93]

Hate crimes are extraordinary in unexpected ways. In addition to being among the most serious crimes, NCV data show that approximately eighty-four percent of these assaults are violent—"a sexual assault, robbery or simple aggravated assault."[94] Blacks are less likely than both whites and Hispanics to be targeted for reasons of racial hatred. A significantly higher percentage of victims of violent racial hatred say their attackers were black.[95] Nine out of ten of them identify their race as the reason blacks targeted them. "For victims reporting white offenders, [only] about three in ten victims cited race as a motive."[96] Moreover, and this is crucial, "The number of black hate crime victims was so small, that is statistically insignificant, that it precluded analysis of the race of persons who victimized them."[97]

So much for the libel of a racist America; Americans are not remotely racist. If anything, they are remarkably naïve about human differences—cultural or racial. Alas, as one wag said, "Any idea, plan, or purpose may be placed in the mind through repetition of thought." Relentless propaganda, enforced by the tyranny of political correctness, helps explain why most Americans believe racism saturates their society. As they see it, in electing Barack Obama, they've begun to atone for their original sin.

Sexual Subjugation

The crime of rape is most certainly anything but "intraracial." Every year, approximately 37,460 white women are raped by blacks. As the BJS's 2005 "Criminal Victimization Statistical Tables" reveal, blacks, at 12.3 percent of the population, were responsible for thirty-six percent of the 111,490 incidents in which whites were raped. And blacks committed 100 percent of the 36,620 incidents in which blacks were raped. The legendary miscegenation of the much-maligned white male: could that be a myth too? *Not one* black woman or man—0.0 percent—was ravished by a Caucasian.[98] Human Rights Watch confirms that these unidirectional victimization patterns endure behind bars. "White inmates are disproportionately targeted for abuse." (Rape Human Rights Watch euphemizes as "sexual abuse.") The report titled "No Escape: Male Rape in U.S. Prisons" states: "Inter-racial sexual abuse is common only to the extent that it involves white *non-Hispanic* prisoners being abused by African Americans or Hispanics."[99] "A form of revenge for white dominance of blacks in outside society" is one of the causal factors cited by Human Rights Watch for the sexual subjugation of white by black inmates.[100] In 2008, the United Nations voted to classify rape as a "war tactic," "a systemic means of spreading terror and encouraging displacement."[101] Does the designation extend to jailhouses in America, or does it apply only to hellholes in the Democratic Republic of Congo?

South African authorities, universities, and think tanks no longer provide information about victimization patterns by race of victim and offender. And while the South African Institute of Race Relations (SAIRR) claims to possess such data, it would not share it with this writer unless she forked out a subscriber fee of US $1712 or US $3933. Questionnaires which are used to collect data—many of these questionnaires having been compiled by the UN—do not make provisions for obtaining such demographics.

Only Filling Their Crime Quota

Some South African advocates for criminals claim that blacks are merely filling their crime quota proportionate to their numbers in the population. In 2004, at 76.6 percent of the population, blacks committed 76.4 percent of "intimate femicides" (defined as "the killing of a female person by an intimate partner"). And they committed 68.3 percent of "non-intimate femicides": "the killing of a woman by someone other than an intimate partner." (That snippet came courtesy of a not-yet-binned Medical Research Council report.[102]) Tardy whites are proving woefully inadequate to the task of filling their pro-rata crime quotas: At less than nine percent of the population, the corresponding numbers for white South Africans are 3.9 and 2.6 percent respectively. Whites underperform again with respect to incarceration rates. According to the South African Department of Correctional Services, 113,773 criminals had been sentenced as of June 2008, of whom only 2190 were white.[103] Whites make up only 1.9 percent of the number of sentenced criminals. Weighing in with 90,013[104] sentenced individuals—approximately 79.1 percent of the total number of criminals sentenced—blacks more than fill their per-population crime allotment.

The minority that dare not speak its name is on the wane. Of the approximately forty-eight million South Africans, whites number only 4.3 million[105]; blacks more than thirty-eight million. By the estimate of the SAIRR, the white population had shrunk from 5,215,000 in 1995 to 4,374,000 in 2005. Almost a fifth.[106] "Since 1996," reports *The New York Times*, "the black population has risen to a projected 38.5 million from 31.8 million."[107] (Submerged in this sentence is the fact that the same population has been increasing since Europeans settled South Africa.) While the number of whites is shrinking as a percentage of the total population, their proportion among the scalded, shot, sliced and garroted is growing. Constituting less than nine percent of the population, whites nevertheless made up ten percent of the 33,513 "non-natural deaths," recorded in 2007 by The National Injury Mortality Surveillance System, a project of the MRC and UNISA. At around eighty percent of the population, black "Africans constituted seventy-six percent of all cases."[108] Are whites beings purposefully sought out by the swelling black criminal class that has turned crime into a sinecure? Is it any wonder that the most pressing problem in the lives of whites is violent crime, causing an exodus of those who're able to leave?

As the old adage goes, "figures don't lie but liars can figure."

White Hot Hatred

The SAIRR categorically denies that there is a racial component to crime in South Africa. Its thinking, presumably, is that the handiwork of the demons who do the deeds described doesn't conclusively prove white hot hatred. Such motivation can only be properly ascertained by the administration of, say, standardized questionnaires to a representative sample of killers, with all the methodological pitfalls such tests entail. On the rare occasions that the Institute's scholars have deigned to pair race and crime, it has been in the context of "the killing of four blacks by a white youth in Skierlik, near Swartruggens," in the country's northwest.[109] Or, the "murder of a black man in 2001 by four white teenagers from the wealthy suburb of Waterkloof, in Pretoria.[110] These statistical anomalies notwithstanding, a study conducted by the market research company Markinor for the ISS reveals: "Only thirty-two percent of all blacks questioned knew someone who was a victim of crime," compared to sixty-six percent of Indian adults and fifty six percent of white adults.[111] By logical extension, "there were also marked differences in feelings of safety between the race groups. Indians followed by white South Africans were least likely to feel safe."[112] Conversely, thirty-two percent of black South Africans were likely to know someone who made a living from crime while less than seventeen percent of Indians and just seven percent of whites said this was the case.[113] As of June 2008, the South African Department of Correctional Services reported that 90,013 blacks had been sentenced. Conviction rates stand at a dismal eight percent.[114] The black criminal class is thus 1.13 million strong, at least one million of whom are still at large.[115] The SAIRR would have evinced a modicum of intellectual honesty had it argued that wealth was a confounding variable in crime: Because Indian and white South Africans tend to be wealthier than blacks, the theory runs, they are likelier than blacks to be targeted.

To counter evidence for the hue of hatred here at home, America's own self-styled anti-racism activists will typically claim that whites make up most of the population and are therefore natural targets for crimes. The probability of a black encountering a white is simply many times the reverse,[116] their argument goes. However, interracial encounter rates do not account for the sheer hatred manifested in the appalling attacks on white South Africans. Similarly, they fail to explain away what was done to the white

American couple from Knoxville. Or to the four whites from Wichita, Kansas, who were slain by blacks in 2000.[117] Probabilities belie the stalking and savaging, in 2008, of a Columbia University student at the hands of Robert Williams; he black, she white. Her nineteen-hour ordeal ended with Williams setting the twenty-three-year-old student on fire. It began with Williams raping the girl orally, vaginally, and anally, pouring bleach in her eyes, boiling water on her body, slicing her face and slitting her eyelids with a carving knife.[118]

The American student and Daleen Pieterse, a prototypal South African victim of racial hatred, have parallel fates. And Williams and the Pieterse assailants share a *modus operandi*. Indeed, wealth disparities fail to explain away the sadism invested in the onslaught against white South Africans like Daleen. From the liberal *Cape Argus*: "Pieterse's husband was tortured with a hot kettle, stabbed and finally strangled with shoelaces. She and her ten-year-old son were viciously assaulted with molten plastic; her calf muscle was lacerated, clothes cut off and a knife forced between her legs. Her three-year-old daughter was threatened with abduction and rape."[119] The Pieterses of the North-Western Cape are but one South African family among thousands; run-of-the-mill victims of black crime.

Still harder to finesse are the telltales of racial hatred seared into the mangled white bodies of over three thousand dead Afrikaner farmers. More about that in Chapter Two.

In all, no color should be given to the claim that race is not a factor in the incidence of crime in the US and in South Africa. The vulgar individualist will contend that such broad statements about aggregate group characteristics are collectivist, ergo false. He would be wrong. Generalizations, provided they are substantiated by hard evidence, not hunches, are not incorrect. Science relies on the ability to generalize to the larger population observations drawn from a representative sample. People make prudent decisions in their daily lives based on probabilities and generalities. That one chooses not to live in a particular crime-riddled county or country in no way implies that one considers all individual residents there to be criminals, only that a sensible determination has been made, based on statistically significant data, as to where scarce and precious resources—one's life and property—are best invested.

AN EXISTENTIAL CRISIS

Whites have been told to accept their lot. Or "[to] continue to whinge until blue in the face," as Charles Nqakula counseled those who carp about crime.[120] Securing subjects in their lives and property has not been a priority for the ANC. South African historian Rodney Warwick believes that the state's stout indifference does not exist in a void. Ditto the steady, anti-white venom the ANC cobra-head keeps spitting. "The *de facto* situation is that whites are under criminal siege explicitly because of their 'race,'" he writes in the *Cape Argus*. "The black criminal collective consciousness understands whites are now 'historical fair game.'"[121] Warwick sees the physical vulnerability of white South Africans as flowing from a confluence of historical antecedents that have placed them in a uniquely precarious position. "The white minority," he writes, "surrendered [its] political dominance for non-racial constitutional safeguards."[122] By foreswearing control over the state apparatus, whites ceded mastery over their destiny, vesting their existential survival in a political dispensation: a liberal democracy. In a needlessly optimistic assumption, whites imagined blacks too would be bound by the same political abstractions, and would relinquish race in favor of a constitutional design as an organizing principle in the society they now controlled. Having surrendered without defeat,[123] for a tepid peace, Europeans are, moreover, particularly and uniquely vulnerable within this political dispensation because of their history on the continent. Remedial historical revisionism notwithstanding, South Africa—with its space program and skyscrapers—was not exactly the product of the people currently dismantling it. Instead, it was the creation of British and Dutch colonists and their descendants. For what they've achieved and acquired—and for the sins of apartheid—they are the objects of envy and racial enmity.

A chronicler of Africa, the observations of African-American journalist Keith Richburg agree with Warwick's. Richburg believes that on the Dark Continent, tribal allegiance trumps political persuasion and envy carries the day. He cites the fate of the Tutsi—an alien, Nilotic African people, who formed a minority in Rwanda and Burundi—among the Hutu who are a Bantu people. The Hutu have always resented the tall, imposing Tutsis, who had dominated them on-and-off since the fifteenth century, and whose facial features the lovely supermodel Iman instantiates. When Hutus picked up machetes to slash to bits nearly a million of their Tutsi neighbors in the 1994 Rwandan genocide, they were, on a deeper level, contends Richburg, "slashing at their own perceived ugliness, as if destroying this thing of beauty, this thing they could never really attain, removing it from the earth forever."[124] Are shades of this impulse alive in the savagery inflicted on the European "settlers" of South Africa (and Zimbabwe and the Congo before them)? Who can say for sure? This much I do know: Empowering majorities in Africa has helped, not hindered, the propensity of hostile masses to exact revenge on helpless minorities.

CHAPTER 2

The Kulaks of South Africa vs. the Xhosa Nostra

...the disappearance of nations would have impoverished us no less than if all men had become alike, with one personality and one face. Nations are the wealth of mankind, its collective personalities; the very least of them wears its own special colors and bears within itself a special facet of divine intention.

—Alexander Solzhenitsyn*

My people will not listen unless they are killed.

—Cetshwayo, Zulu King, 1878

THE FARMERS OF South Africa are being killed off at genocidal rates," I said to broadcaster John Safran during a 2007 interview on the Australian Broadcasting Corporation. Was I being hyperbolic? For the answer, an incredulous Mr. Safran quizzed Dr. Gregory H. Stanton, who heads "Genocide Watch." Stanton confirmed what scant few among Western media care to chronicle. "The rates at which the farmers are being eliminated, the torture and dehumanization involved—all point to systematic extermination."[1] Since the dawn of democracy, close to ten

* From his Nobel Prize speech (1970)

percent of farming South Africa has been slaughtered in ways that would do Shaka Zulu proud.

The reader will be accustomed by now to gauging murder rates per units of 100,000 people. In low-crime Europe, that rate stands at two murders per 100,000 people a year. In American inner-city ghettoes it rises to about forty and above (according to the FBI Uniform Crime Reports, in New Orleans it's fifty six per 100,000). By Chris van Zyl's assessment—van Zyl is safety and security manager for the Transvaal Agricultural Union—Boers are being exterminated at the annual rate of 313 per 100,000 inhabitants,[2] 3,000 since the election of Mandela in 1994[3]; two a week,[4] seven in March of 2010[5], "four times as high as is for the rest of the [South African] population," says Dr. Stanton. This makes farming in South Africa the most dangerous occupation in the world. (Miners, by comparison, suffer 27.8 fatalities per 100,000 workers[6].)

But no one who matters is counting. And some are even denying it, the South African Institute of Race Relations (SAIRR), for instance. Back in 2004, *The Economist* had already counted 1,500 rural whites dead "in land-related violence."[7] By 2010, the deniers at the SAIRR were finally willing to concede that "not all murders in the country are a function of simple criminal banditry."[8] They still put the figure "conservatively" at only 1,000, even as most news outlets are reporting upwards of 3,000 farmers murdered. The 3,000 figure consists of "some 1,000 white farmers, along with 2000 of their family members."[9] Perhaps the SAIRR has forgotten to factor in the families. The uncomfortable fact that South Africa's farmers are conservative, Christian, and Caucasian might help explain why the likes of CNN's Anderson Vanderbilt Cooper have yet to show up in fashionable fatigues to report from this unfashionable front.

As *Carte Blanche*, a South African current affairs television program, has documented, the victims of this onslaught are almost invariably elderly, law-abiding, God-fearing Afrikaners, murdered in cold blood in ways that beggar belief. The heathens will typically attack on Sundays. On returning from church, the farmer is ambushed. Those too feeble to attend Sunday service are frequently tortured and killed when the rest are worshiping. In one crime scene filmed by *Carte Blanche*, Bibles belonging to the slain had been splayed across their mangled bodies. In another, an "old man's hand rests on the arm of his wife of many years."[10] She raped; he, in all likelihood, made to watch. Finally, with their throats slit, they died side by side.

The Lord Saved Her

There's an ethereal quality about Beatrice Freitas, who has survived two farm attacks. Her equanimity belies the brutality she has endured. Beatrice and her husband immigrated to South Africa from Madeira forty years ago. They built a thriving nursery near the Mozambican border. It supplied the entire region with beautiful plants. Some people build; others destroy. Beatrice tells her story as she drifts through the stately cycads surrounding the deserted homestead.

When the four men attacked her, Beatrice says, her mind "disappeared." She and her permanently disabled husband, José, were tied up while the home was ransacked. When the brutes were through, they wanted to know where she kept the iron. They then took her to the laundry room, where two of them raped her, coated her in oil, and applied the iron. They alternated the iron with kicks from their boots. When they were through, twenty five per cent of Beatrice's body was covered in third-degree burns. They suffocated her with a towel, and left her for dead, but she survived. She says the Lord saved her. No one was ever arrested—not then, and not after the couple was attacked three years later. This time José died "in a hail of bullets." Arrests and convictions are rare. *Carte Blanche* tells of

Dan Lansberg, shot dead in broad daylight. Members of his courageous farming community caught the culprits, but they "escaped" from the local police cells.

Sky News[11] sent its correspondent to the northern province of South Africa, where viewers are introduced to Herman Dejager. Before retiring every night, Herman prepares to fight to the death to protect what's his. He checks his bulletproof vest, loads the shotgun, and drapes ammunition rounds on the nightstand. You see, Herman's father died in his arms, shot in the face by intruders.

Kaalie Botha's parents were not so lucky: "You can't kill an animal like they killed my mom and father. You can't believe it." The Achilles tendons of Kaalie's seventy-one-year-old father had been severed, so he couldn't flee. He was then hacked in the back until he died, and his body was dumped in the bush. His wife, Joey, had her head bashed in by a brick, wielded with such force that the skull "cracked like an egg."

Murdered farmers are often displayed like trophies. According to Dr. Stanton, who was "responsible for drafting the UN resolutions that created the International Criminal Tribunal for Rwanda," there are eight stages of genocide. Dehumanization is the third. Stanton is convinced that these "hate crimes" amount to genocide under the convention.[12] "Genocide is always organized, usually by the state," he has written at Genocide Watch's website. The farmers believe, seconds Sky News, that "these attacks are a government-sanctioned attempt to purge South Africa of white land owners, as has already happened in Zimbabwe."[13]

"Rather than simply reflecting SA's overall high crime rate, murders against farmers," contends van Zyl, "… are part of an orchestrated strategy to drive white farmers from their land."[14] This verdict accords with the truth that for these murders, robbery is seldom the motive. Rarely is any valuable item removed from these grisly crime scenes. For the edification of "racism"-spotters in the West, the *assailants*, confirms Stanton, are as ethnically distinct as their *victims*.

Reluctantly, the South African Human Rights Commission agrees. Its commission's report fails to break down their figures by color; but it does admit that "the majority of attacks in general … are against white people" and that "there was a considerably higher risk of a white victim of farm attacks being killed or injured than a black victim."[15]

Conspiracy is difficult to prove; depraved indifference less so. That the ANC plans to dismantle the Commando System is damning—the Commandos are a private Afrikaner militia that has existed since the 1770s, and is the sole reliable defense at the farmers' disposal. Contrary to the pro-forma denials issued by the ANC's fulsome officials, the *Daily Mail* newspaper confirmed, in February 2006, that the government is still set on forcibly seizing the land of thousands of farmers, should they refuse to settle. By the year 2014, a third of Boer property will have been given to blacks.

True to the dictum that the victim must always be denounced, lodestars for the left like the SA Human Rights Commission, the ANC, "development organizations,"[16] and the malfunctioning mass media the world over blame the farmers for mistreating their farmhands, who, understandably, retaliate. Much to its disgrace, America's Ford Foundation goes as far as to fund "local land NGOs in their efforts to encourage people to claim productive farmland, in many cases without legal basis."[17] However, the Helen Suzman Foundation—whose mission it is to continue the life's work of the famed progressive parliamentarian for which it is named—found that ninety three percent of farm workers indicate their relationship with their employers is good."[18]

In one respect, and in one alone, the excuse-making industry is right: the crimes are indeed personal in nature. As mentioned, theft is seldom the motive. The trouble with excuse-makers is that the extent of such violence is far worse under democracy than it was under apartheid. Back then, farmhands were presumably treated more inhumanely than they are now. But also, back then, those who perpetrated capital crimes were very likely to get caught, and the threat of the scaffold loomed over them. Sixty-nine-year old fourth generation Natal farmer and stockman Nigel Ralfe was but a lad when an elderly farming husband and wife, the Lowes, were murdered by three men who worked near the victims' Natal-lowlands farm. Once the culprits were eventually captured and tried—not before they had sliced a guard's throat with a bread knife—their families were ferried to Pretoria for free to see their sons swing on the gallows. Years elapsed before another such crime was committed in that area. The occasion of Mr. Ralfe's reminiscing? In March of 2010, his own wife Lynette was shot to death by laborers. Given that South Africa now has a political system which, as Mr. Ralfe puts it, is "run by jailbirds,"[19] he does not expect his Lynette to get justice.

Could it be that killers kill not because of "racism" or "oppression," but because they can? Perish the thought.

"Kill the Fucking Whites" On Facebook

In the new South Africa, there is a renewed appreciation for the old slogan, "Kill the Boer, kill the farmer," chanted at political rallies and funerals during "The Struggle" (against apartheid). ANC youth leader Peter Mokaba is credited with originating the catch phrase. Mokaba went on to become a legislature and a deputy minister in the Mandela cabinet. By the time he expired in 2002 at the age of only forty-three (rumor has it of AIDS), Mokaba had revived the riff, using it liberally, in defiance of laws against incitement to commit murder. Given the mesmerizing, often murderous, power of the chant—any chant—in African life, many blame Mokaba for the current homicidal onslaught against the country's white farmers.

Mokaba's legacy lives on. Late in February of 2010, a senior member of the Pan Africanist Congress of Azania (PAC)—a competing socialist, racialist political party whose motto is "Africa for the Africans"—set-up a page on the social networking site Facebook. For all to see were comments such as the following, written by one Ahmed El Saud:

> Kill the fucking whites now!!! If you afraid for [sic] them, lets [sic] do it for you. In return, you can pay us after the job has been done...text us... We are not afraid for [sic] the whites like your own people...its disgrace [sic]...he ask you and you dont [sic] want to...we will do it Mandela! [sic].[20]

Other messages matched the savagery of El Saud's sentences, if not their syntax. One boasted of "an army of 3000 people ready to kill white people within a day if it were called upon to do so."[21] Western Cape PAC chairman Anwar Adams, the responsible functionary, refused to remove the page. Needless to say, his sinecure has not been affected.

The ANC took a pixilated page out of the PAC's Facebook. Days later, the following eloquent post appeared on a Facebook page under the name of ANC Youth League president Julius Malema:

> You fucking white pigs. Malema is our leader. He will kill [President Jacob] Zuma within the next six weeks. "Look ahead, my fellow black people. We will then take our land, and every trespasser, namely white whores, *we will rape them and rape them till the last breath is out. "White kids will be burned, especially those in Pretoria and Vrystaat.* Men will be tortured while I take a video

> clip and spread it on YouTube," read one post. It continued: "Its [sic] true what Malema said, silently we shall kill them... Police will stand together...our leader will lead us to take our land over. Mandela will smile again. "White naaiers, we coming for you! Households will be broken into and families will be slaughtered.[22] [Emphasis added]

Was the murderer of seventeen-year-old Anika Smit, also in March of 2010, a Facebook friend of Malema? When Johan Smit bid his bonny daughter goodbye, before leaving the home they shared in north Pretoria, he did not imagine he'd never again see her alive. Once he had returned from work, he found the naked and mutilated corpse of his only child. Her throat had been slashed sixteen times and her hands hacked off.[23] She had been raped.

Eugène Terre'Blanche, leader of the Afrikaner Resistance Movement (AWB) that seeks the establishment of a homeland for the Afrikaners,[24] was alone on his homestead, over the Easter 2010 period, when two farmhands bludgeoned the sixty-nine-year-old separatist to a pulp with pangas[†] and pipes. To leave the old man without a shred of dignity—*Crimen injuria* in South African law—they pulled down his pants, exposing his privates. Based on hearsay, the pack animals of the Western media insisted that the motive for the murder was a "labor dispute."

In Malema's defense, the ANC claimed he was not responsible for the Facebook page. The youth leader might be hard to track down in cyberspace, but Malema performed in person at the University of Johannesburg, stomping about with a group of students and singing, in Zulu, "Shoot the Boers, they are rapists."[25] ANC Secretary-General Gwede Mantashe spin-doctored Malema's live performance by choosing to dismiss the

---

[†] A kind of machete

power of "Kill the Boer." He maintained, implausibly enough, that the killer phrase does no more than pay homage to the Party's illustrious history and is "not meant as an incitement to violence against whites."[26]

No one who remembers the role of Radio Rwanda (first) and *Radio-Télévision Libre des Milles Collines* (RTLM), next, in galvanizing the Hutu to exterminate the Tutsi "inyenzi" ("cockroaches") in 1994, can shrug off what is under way in South Africa. Many South African blacks have a pathological preoccupation with variants of "Kill the Boer; kill the farmer" (which is why it is naïve to imagine that banning an incitement to murder will do anything to excise a dark reality embedded so deep in the human heart). In its hypnotic hold on the popular imagination, the mantra resembles the "Kill them before they kill you" slogan that helped excite Hutus to massacre 800,000 of their Tutsi fellow countrymen. In Rwanda, it was the old media that transmitted older hatreds; in Mandela's South Africa the new media are doing the same.

Is Facebook the face of incitement to genocide in South Africa?

Peter Mokaba's funeral was attended by Jacob Zuma (not yet President) and his two predecessors, Thabo Mbeki and Nelson Mandela.[27] At the sight of the coffined Mokaba, the crowd roared, "Kill the Boer, kill the farmer!" Witnesses will not say whether "Madiba" (to use Mandela's African honorific) partook, but to dispel any doubts about the esteem in which Mokaba is still held despite his savage slogan, the ANC named a soccer stadium, built for the soccer World Cup, after this son of the New South Africa.

THE WHITE TRIBE OF AFRICA

So "who are the Afrikaners, or Boers, as they are often called?", mused Afrikaner activist Dan Roodt. "A hundred years ago, Sir Arthur Conan Doyle, the popular British writer of the Sherlock Holmes mysteries, asked [and answered] much the same question in his book":

> Take a community of Dutchmen of the type of those who defended themselves for fifty years against all the power of Spain at a time when Spain was the greatest power in the world. Intermix with them a strain of those inflexible French Huguenots who gave up home and fortune and left their country forever at the time of the revocation of the Edict of Nantes. The product must obviously be one of the most rugged, virile, unconquerable races ever seen upon earth. Take this formidable people and train them for seven generations in constant warfare against savage men and ferocious beasts, in circumstances under which no weakling could survive, place them so that they acquire exceptional skill with weapons and in horsemanship, give them a country which is eminently suited to the tactics of the huntsman, the marksman, and the rider. Then, finally, put a finer temper upon their military qualities by a dour fatalistic Old Testament religion and an ardent and consuming patriotism. Combine all these qualities and all these impulses in one individual, and you have the modern Boer—the most formidable antagonist who ever crossed the path of Imperial Britain.[28]

In a recent translation of Tacitus' *Annals,* a question was raised as to whether "there were any 'nations' in antiquity other than the

Jews."[29] Upon reflection, one suspects that the same question can be posed about the Afrikaners in the modern era. In April of 2009, President Zuma infuriated the "multicultural noise machine" the world over by stating: "Of all the white groups that are in South Africa, it is only the Afrikaners that are truly South Africans in the true sense of the word. Up to this day, they [the Afrikaners] don't carry two passports, they carry one. They are here to stay."[30] As a white South African who traded her passport for another, I have to agree with the president. A social conservative and a proud Zulu, Zuma has exhibited a far greater understanding of—and affinity for—the Afrikaner than did his deracinated predecessors.

"I am an Afrikaner!"

How formidable an antagonist "the modern Boer" was could have been deduced from history well before Conan Doyle wrote. Admittedly, the first European ever to see South Africa was not a Dutchman but a Portuguese: Antonio de Saldanha, back in 1503.[31] Saldanha Bay still bears this sea-captain's name. For all practical purposes, though, South Africa's white history begins a century and a half later, with the first Dutch settlement in the region (and the foundation of what would become Cape Town) occurring in 1652. The Puritans have 350 years of history on the continent of Africa—as long as their American cousins have been in North America.

Despite the climatic problems that Dutch settlers found locally—poor soil, few local industry prospects, extreme distance from major world markets, and nothing like the trading opportunities supplied by other outposts of the Dutch empire, such as the East Indies (today's Indonesia)—a robust spirit of independence and patriotism soon manifested itself. As early as 1707, a youth named Hendrik Bibault, of Stellenbosch, defied the local authorities who had come to arrest him for a misdemeanor by shouting "I am an Afrikaner!" ("*Ik ben een Afrikaander!*")[32]. That exclamation has become epochal in tracing the birth of Afrikaner nationhood. Woe to those Britons who underestimated such pride. The great age of the *voortrekkers*—that is, Afrikaners seeking to leave British-controlled territory to settle what would afterwards become Natal, Transvaal, and the Orange Free State—started in the 1830s. Most notable of all was the 1836-1837 Great Trek, which included among its participants the very young (eleven years old) Paul Kruger, future Boer President. Affectionately known by his supporters as "Oom [Uncle] Paul", Kruger would achieve world fame in the 1890s for the Old Testament-derived fervor which he shared with so many of his compatriots—a fervor analogous to that of American Puritans in the seventeenth century—and for his tenacious championship of Boer rights against anyone who might threaten them.

The Grahamstown Manifesto, issued in February 1837 by Afrikaner leader Piet Retief, became a founding document of the Afrikaner heritage. It set out the grievances which Retief and his people felt at the way Britain had treated them as second-class citizens: particularly in the matter of slavery, which Britain had recently abolished without adequately compensating Afrikaners. Overall, the Boers favored a "loose master-servant relationship." "What they could not accept," explains historian Donald R. Morris, "was the concept that their servants were their legal equals."[33] Matters were further inflamed by the influx of missionaries who "displayed more zeal than common sense," and began laying charges of murder and maltreatment against the Boers. "Most of the accusations evaporated in the cold light of evidence," but "the very fact that a man could be forced to leave his family unprotected while he traveled to a distant court to defend himself against the capricious charges of an irresponsible Hottentot was deeply disturbing"[34] to the Boers.

The following year, Zulu king Dingane slew Retief and one hundred of his followers. Retief "had proceeded openly and carelessly, and made no effort to understand Dingane. The Zulu monarch was in a state of deadly fear, and he had no intention of allowing an armed European folk who had beaten the Matabele—something the Zulus had tried to do but failed—to settle in numbers on his borders."[35] But a terrible revenge came at the December 1838 Battle of Blood River (*Slag van Bloedrivier,* to quote the Afrikaans phrase). There, 3,000 Zulus perished at the hands of Retief's fellow Boer general Andries Pretorius.

For as long as white rule lasted, this victory (attained by a spectacularly outnumbered force, it should be noted: Pretorius commanded only around five hundred men, not a single one of whom was killed) retained a sacred significance in Afrikaner culture. Especially notable was Pretorius's defense strategy: the *laager,* whereby wagons would be placed to form the shape of a circle, with horses and cattle on the inside of the circle, to protect them from marauders. Pretorius did not invent this method himself. After all, there are records of similar formations being made by rebels in Bohemia (the modern Czech Republic) as early as the fifteenth century. But he used the method to devastating effect. In 1949, as an act of homage to Blood River's heroes, the government unveiled a Voortrekker Monument in Pretoria, the city which owes its very name to Pretorius. The dome of this monument's roof is structured so that at noon on the anniversary of the battle, a ray of sunlight falls directly onto the cenotaph.[36]

"Methods of Barbarism"

With the discovery of gold and diamonds in the late nineteenth century, dreams of Anglo-Saxon empire made a British-versus-Afrikaner conflict inevitable. In the 1899-1902 Boer War, a guerrilla-dominated force of no more than 87,000 Afrikaners—who had been perfecting guerrilla strategies for decades—held at bay, for nearly three years, no fewer than 447,000 troops from Canada, Australia, and New Zealand as well as Britain. Through sheer frustration, British commander-in-chief Lord Kitchener established concentration camps in which approximately 26,000 Afrikaners, mostly women and children, perished.

The outrage which these camps inspired burned itself into the Afrikaner soul, and remains vivid there even now.[‡] Surviving photographs from the camps can still give today's beholders—however desensitized they might be by the legacy of two world wars and countless other massacres—a salutary shock. They suggest nothing so much as emaciated Jewish victims of Nazi atrocities. During the early twentieth century nothing like these pictures had ever been imagined in the West before. As a result, the condemnation which the camps provoked in Europe and America was fully matched by British censure of them. Britain's future Prime Minister Sir Henry Campbell-Bannerman called them "methods of barbarism." Boer commander Louis Botha

---

[‡] Which has not stopped Andrew Roberts, veteran apologist for British governmental crimes, from attempting (*A History of the English-Speaking Peoples Since 1900*, London, 2007) to deny the camps' horrors: "The 'war crime' [Roberts wrote] for which the British have been most commonly held responsible during the Boer War was the supposed [sic!] ill-treatment of Afrikaans women and children in camps there. In fact, these 'concentration' camps – the term had no pejorative implication until the Nazi era – were set up for the Boers' protection off the veldt, and were run as efficiently and humanely as possible … A civilian surgeon Dr Alec Kay, writing in 1901, gave a further reason why the death rates were so high: 'The Boers in the camps often depend on home remedies, with deplorable results'" (p. 31). Further details of (and quotations from) Roberts's propaganda can be found in R. J. Stove, "Court Historian," *The American Conservative*, September 22, 2008.

subsequently paid tribute to Campbell-Bannerman's outspokenness: "Three words made peace and union in South Africa: 'methods of barbarism'." It deeply impressed Botha that "the leader of one of the great English parties had had the courage to say this thing, and to brave the obloquy which it brought upon him. So far from encouraging them [the Boers] to a hopeless resistance, it touched their hearts and made them think seriously of the possibility of reconciliation."[37]

By the Treaty of Vereeniging (May 1902) Afrikanerdom finally surrendered. Representatives at the surrender ceremony included three future South African Prime Ministers: Louis Botha, Jan Smuts, and J. B. M. Hertzog. Nevertheless, reconciliation proved superficial. Conan Doyle saluted the Afrikaners as valiant opponents; such generosity of spirit was all too rare among the British elsewhere. Britain's High Commissioner in South Africa, Lord Milner, announced his intention to "knock the bottom out of the great Afrikaner nation."[38] The preferred method took the form not of violence, but of petty slights. South African schools thereafter had to conduct instruction in English, save for three hours a week in Dutch, with severe and humiliating punishment for any schoolchild caught speaking Dutch outside those hours. "I am a donkey—I speak Dutch," was the sort of sign a refractory Dutch-speaking schoolchild would be compelled to wear in public.[39] Admittedly, during World War I both Botha and Smuts favored Britain; but beneath the Anglophile surface an increasing Afrikaner linguistic consciousness simmered, particularly after Afrikaans became an official tongue in 1924.[40] There occurred a new emphasis on Afrikaans in literary and academic contexts. As one leading recent historian puts it: "Afrikaans became one of four languages in the world—Hebrew, Hindi and Indonesian are the others—which, in the course of the twentieth century, were standardized and used in all branches of life and learning."[41]

With World War II's outbreak, Prime Minister Hertzog, openly neutralist, lost office; Smuts (espousing a renewed alliance with Britain) took his place; and many who found both men insufficiently radical formed their own movement, the *Ossewabrandwag* (OB), which—while clandestine—succeeded in pulling Afrikaner opinion toward the political right. Smuts, more popular abroad than at home, fatally underestimated his opponents, telling the *Rand Daily Mail* newspaper in 1948: "I anticipate victory in the election."[42] That year Smuts' United Party lost easily to the rurally-oriented Nationalist Party, led by hard-liner Daniel Malan.[§]

Going For Gold

Under Malan (Prime Minister till his retirement in 1954), apartheid in the true sense began. His government outlawed mixed marriages, banned sexual relations between races, and set up the Group Areas Act to regulate internal migration. J. G. Strijdom, Malan's successor as Prime Minister, continued such policies from 1954 to 1958 (he died in office). So did Strijdom's own successor, the more charismatic and intellectual Hendrik Verwoerd, who had a philosophy doctorate from Stellenbosch University. Once Verwoerd assured an interviewer that he always slept well, however demanding the circumstances, since "one does not have the problem of worrying whether one

---

[§] Smuts's defeat infuriated King George VI, who conferred on him the Order of Merit at Cape Town the following year. Nationalist leaders boycotted the ritual, and "the King burst out characteristically, 'I'd like to shoot them all!' to which the Queen [Elizabeth, later the Queen Mother] replied in her voice of gentle remonstrance, half-smiling, 'But Bertie, you can't shoot everybody'—as though he could at least shoot *some*." (Elizabeth Longford, *The Oxford Book of Royal Anecdotes* [Oxford, 1991], p. 483.)

perhaps could be wrong."[43] Confirming his enviable self-confidence is his portrait—published August 26, 1966—on the cover of *Time* magazine: a publication which, it is fair to suggest, would not dream of even attempting to discuss such a figure disinterestedly these days.

"South Africa," *Time* conceded in its accompanying article, "is in the middle of a massive boom. Attracted by cheap labor, a gold-backed currency and high profits, investors from all over the world have plowed money into the country, and the new industries that they have started have sent production, consumption—and the demand for labor—soaring." Again, from the same article: "Verwoerd often boasts that the blacks of South Africa are better off than anywhere else on the continent. Economically he is right. What with decent paychecks (minimum daily wage for an unskilled laborer is $2.80) and easy credit, many an urban African can afford to buy … wood furniture for his dining room, neat school uniforms for his children, and in some cases even a car for himself. Every year countless thousands of blacks from nearby countries flood into the republic looking for work."[44] Despite or because of these facts, Verwoerd became *personally* detested overseas, as his predecessors had not been: particularly after the 1960 Sharpeville shootings (in which sixty-nine blacks perished), South Africa's withdrawal from the British Commonwealth, its move to republicanism, and the 1964 sentencing of Nelson Mandela to life behind bars for terrorism. (Who would have guessed back in 1964 that Mandela would, in little more than a generation, be regarded as everyone's favorite cuddly role-model?)

Yet Demitrio Tsafendas, a parliamentary messenger who stabbed Verwoerd to death in Cape Town (September 1966), had no political agenda. He blamed his action, instead, on "a huge tapeworm with serrated edges, which tormented his body."[45] This being surely the most surreal alibi any killer had hitherto provided (though California's 1979 "Twinkie Defense" subsequently rivaled it), a bemused court spared Tsafendas the supreme penalty; and he eventually died of natural causes in a mental home.

From Muldergate to Mandela

Upon Verwoerd's murder, former Police Minister J. B. Vorster—whose ultra-rightist background and OB membership had sent him to prison during the war—became head of government.[46] In foreign affairs he modified his predecessor's policy by doing what to Verwoerd would have seemed unthinkable: abandoning support for white Rhodesia. Since 1965 Rhodesia's Prime Minister Ian Smith had defied Western elite opinion by refusing to countenance black majority rule for his country; and for the decade after 1965 he had been able to count on South African support for his policy. Then Vorster altered course, deciding that in order to get black African nations on side, it would be needful to abandon South Africa's support for the Smith government. Some might see—certainly Smith, when writing his memoirs, saw—in the subsequent fate of Vorster's party a lesson on the theme "What goes around, comes around."[**]

In home affairs, nonetheless, Vorster kept his promise "to walk further along the road set by ... Verwoerd."[47] It is now known that under Vorster, South Africa covertly began a nuclear weapons project.[48] What drove Vorster from power was a

** Ian Smith, *Bitter Harvest: Zimbabwe and the Aftermath of Independence* (London, 2001), quotes acidly (p. 194) a South African politician who "had worked with all four National Party prime ministers—Malan, Strijdom, Verwoerd and Vorster—since 1948. With the first three, when they gave an undertaking they kept it, he said; but Vorster would tell you one thing today, and do the opposite tomorrow...too cunning by half!"

domestic scandal which quickly became known as "Muldergate," after Vorster's Information Minister Connie Mulder. Three of the cabinet's most powerful men—Vorster himself, Mulder, and Mulder's deputy Eschel Roodie—were using, it turned out, funds secretly siphoned off from the Defense Department, in order to subsidize ostensibly "independent" English-language pro-government newspapers. Nowadays, when terms such as "spin-doctors," "astroturf" and "sock puppets" have entered common discourse, such media tactics by a beleaguered political party would surprise nobody; but in 1978 even those who most detested white rule in South Africa assumed that it was run by personally incorruptible individuals. All the greater was the public outrage at the discovery that this personal honesty no longer prevailed. (Americans in 2010 scarcely have the right to complain about the methods of "Muldergate," since Iraq's Radio Sawa—controlled by the U.S. government—has always operated on much the same principle, while still being considered perfectly legitimate by neoconservatives. As part of "exporting democracy," conquered Iraqi youngsters were flooded with the sounds of J.Lo's caterwauling and Jay-Z's gutter grunts, piped through American-controlled airwaves.)

Suitably disgraced, Vorster resigned from the Prime Ministry in 1978 to make way for P. W. Botha, yet another wartime OB member (and, incidentally, someone who had opposed the Muldergate chicanery from the start). Although Botha modified apartheid legislation, sometimes softening it, the international campaign against white rule—involving shrill demands for disinvestment—intensified. In 1984 Botha (made President under a new constitution) declared a state of emergency; but the domestic situation grew worse and worse, while the practice—particularly among the Xhosa—of "necklacing" suspected police informers attained international ill repute. (This has already been alluded to in Chapter One of the present book.) According to a 1997 statement by the South African Press Association, the first-ever necklacing was of a girl named Maki Skosana, who in July 1985 was necklaced after being accused baselessly of involvement in the killing of several youths.[49] "With our boxes of matches and our necklaces, we shall liberate this country," proclaimed Mandela's increasingly deranged wife Winnie to *The New York Times* on February 20, 1989.[50] Between September 1984 and December 1993 the death toll from civil strife amounted to 18,997, including approximately 600 white deaths.[51]

A severe stroke forced Botha from power in 1989. Nothing in the background of his successor, President, F. W. de Klerk, indicated the revolutionary policies he would pursue. Among much else, De Klerk scrapped the ban on the ANC and other opposition parties; freed Mandela from incarceration; acceded to Namibia's independence; and junked the nuclear weapons. As is mentioned in Chapter Seven, a 1992 referendum, asking white voters if they favored de Klerk's reforms, resulted in sixty eight percent of respondents saying "yes." And for good reason: de Klerk had made his views clear to constituents: "negotiations would only be about power-sharing."[52] At the time, these respondents generally trusted de Klerk, who had specifically condemned majority rule. "While quite prepared to abolish apartheid and remove obstacles to negotiations, de Klerk did not envisage competitive elections and a system that could reduce the NP to a perpetual opposition party."[53] By the time the average "yes" voter discerned the fact that de Klerk had no intention of maintaining this opposition when push came to shove, it was too late. With Mandela, de Klerk shared the Nobel Peace Prize the following year; and a Transitional Executive Council was set up, to oversee the forthcoming general election. This event, occurring on April 27, 1994, brought Mandela to power with over sixty percent of the vote.

Of course, the election was scarcely the peace-and-love-fest you might have gathered from Jimmy Carter or his fellow Western pundits. Even the election report issued by the Library of Congress, hardly a hotbed of Afrikaner sentiment, admitted that "in ANC-controlled areas, some of that party's activists intimidated IFP, NP, and even liberal Democratic Party (DP) organizers and disrupted their campaign rallies, despite ANC leaders' pleas for tolerance."[54] The harsh truth is that "large-scale intimidation made it nearly impossible for rival parties to campaign in the African townships."[55] (More about the racial aspects of the 1994 poll can be found in Chapter Seven.) Severe class divisions also marked the poll, and would go on to mark subsequent polls in 1999 and 2004.[56] No such considerations have been allowed to impinge upon the typical cosseted Western journalist, for whom dreams about the "Rainbow Nation" continue as a substitute for reality. So much about modern South Africa is reminiscent of the famous line in *The Man Who Shot Liberty Valance:* "When the legend becomes fact, print the legend."

APARTHEID IN BLACK AND WHITE

How paradoxical, then, that a people, "who are widely credited with having fought Africa's first anticolonial struggles, who are native to the land and not colonist in any normal sense, came to establish [what came to be considered] one of the world's most retrogressive colonial systems."[57] But so the Afrikaner leadership did. The honing of apartheid by the Afrikaner National Party started in 1948 after Daniel Malan assumed the Prime Minister's post, although elements of the program were part of the policy first established in 1923 by the British-controlled government. There was certainly nothing Mosaic about the maze of racial laws that formed the edifice of apartheid. The Population Registration Act required that all South Africans be classified by bureaucrats in accordance with race. The Group Areas Act "guaranteed absolute residential segregation." Pass laws regulated the comings-and-goings of blacks (though not them alone), and ensured that black workers left white residential areas by nightfall.

Easily the most egregious aspect of flushing blacks out of white areas was the manner in which entire communities were uprooted and dumped in bleak, remote, officially designated settlement sites—"vast rural slums with urban population densities, but no urban amenities beyond the buses that represented their slender lifelines to the cities."[58] Still, apartheid South Africa sustained far more critical scrutiny for its non-violent (if unjust) resettlement policies than did the U.S. for its equally unjust but actively violent mass resettlement agenda in South Vietnam. Between 1964 and 1969, the American army uprooted 3.5 million South Vietnamese, the process including massacres and the razing of numerous villages.[59]

Nor should we forget previous American military misdeeds. There was, for instance, the 1890 Wounded Knee bloodbath in South Dakota (where a U.S. cavalry regiment wiped out, within an hour, between 150 and 300 Native Americans, women and children included). A decade later occurred the war in the Philippines, where a million Filipinos perished at American hands. The 1990 book *In Our Image*, written by historian Stanley Kurnow, reports that at least 200,000 of the dead Filipinos in that war were civilians. Many of the civilians breathed their last in disease-ridden concentration camps which were known as *reconcentrados*. Conservative writer Michelle Malkin credits herself with shattering the "liberal" libel of equivalence between America's World War II internment camps and Germany's World War II death camps. Other than Holocaust deniers who claim the gas chambers were really Jacuzzis, no one thinks Manzanar or Minidoka matched the horror of Majdanek. The fact is, however, that between 1942 and 1945, the FDR administration dispensed with *habeas corpus* in order to relocate en masse, and confine in camps, some 112,000 Japanese aliens and American-born citizens of Japanese ancestry. That the Japanese internees were not gassed, starved or shot does not justify penning them in camps, often for years, without charging them with any crime, and while freezing their bank accounts. Nothing in Afrikaner rule, even at its least enlightened, can match such episodes in American history.

The offending Nats, as they were known, began to dismantle apartheid almost a decade before the transition to democracy; by 1986, the party had already brought down apartheid's pillars. "Beginning in the early 1980s, the South African government expanded democracy by drawing colored people and Indians into Parliament"[60] By the end of the 1980s, the pernicious influx control laws had been scrapped, public facilities desegregated, and racial sex laws repealed. "Blacks were allowed full freehold rights to property,"[61] and admission to historically white universities.

As the vignette following the next will attest, I was still doing battle with what remained of apartheid in 1995.

A Strategy for Survival

America, being a rib from the British ribcage, was built on liberal individualism; Afrikaner culture was first and foremost grounded in the survival of the *Volk*. This is not to say that Afrikaners were not fiercely individualistic; they were, even more so than early Americans. However, to perceive the fundamental way in which the Afrikaner and American creeds differed early on we must first examine the former's ideas of what a nation and a state were, respectively. For the Boers, the nation encompassed "the land, the culture, the terrain, the people."[62] The state, on the other hand, had no such prestige for the Boers, who regarded it as just "the coercive apparatus of bureaucrats and politicians."[63] Against this apparatus, above all, the Boer rebelled. The nineteenth century found him still resisting majority rule, by which time Americans had thoroughly submitted to it. Although the Boer's outlook remained passionately political, his preference was for a parochial self-rule.[64] It might be said, then, that if in the Americans the vagaries of the frontier bred an atomistic individualism, those same vagaries bred in the Afrikaner a very different attitude, namely, a keen sense of the collective and the need to preserve it. "The worth of the nation is even higher than the worth of the individual,"[65] exclaimed one *Volk* philosopher.

To the existential threat which they faced on the Dark Continent, Afrikaners responded by circling the wagons metaphorically (much as, during the 1830s, they had done literally) and devising the corpus of racial laws known as apartheid. Monomaniacal Westerners have come to think and speak of apartheid as a theory of white supremacy. It was not. The policy of "separate development," as it was euphemized, was not a theory of racial supremacy, but a strategy for survival. "We shall fight for our existence and the world must know it. We are not fighting for money or possessions. We are fighting for the life of our people," thundered Verwoerd.[66] Malan had already used different words for the same sentiment, announcing his devotion to "My God, my people, my country."[67] Strijdom believed unswervingly that if they were to survive as a group, whites would need to retain a position of guardianship,[68] and that ultimately, white hegemony was indispensable for the good of *all*. Those intellectuals who heralded from the University of Stellenbosch phrased the issue thus:

> The granting of political rights to the Bantu, of the kind which would satisfy their political aspirations, was altogether impossible in a mixed community, since such a step would endanger the present position and survival of the European population. If this danger was to be avoided, and at the same time the Europeans

> were not to violate their own conscience and moral standards, a policy of separate development would prove the only alternative.[69]

To that end, a "tortuous social structure" was erected to keep blacks from forming a political majority in South Africa proper. Africans were assigned to homelands in accordance with tribal affiliation, still a central organizing principle across Africa. These "black satrapies"[70] were to function as "national and political homes for the different Bantu communities"[71]; in the "Bantustans," blacks were to exercise political rights.

Hermann Giliomee—whose grand historical synthesis, *The Afrikaners: Biography of a People,* is referenced extensively in this work—agrees that Afrikaner anxieties were overwhelmingly existential, rather than racial. Giliomee is adamant that the apartheid policy did not spring from "racist convictions or antiquated religious doctrines" (even if these convictions were at times present in specific Afrikaners themselves), but from an overriding need for security.

> For leading thinkers in the NP such arguments almost completely missed the point because the security of the Afrikaners as a dominant minority, and not as a race *per se*, was what concerned them. The Cape Town-Stellenbosch axis of the nationalist intelligentsia, which was the most influential lobby in Malan's NP, almost without exception defended apartheid not as an expression of white superiority but on the grounds of its assumed capacity to reduce conflict by curtailing points of interracial contact.[72]

Giliomee contends that "apartheid was not uniquely abhorrent and had much in common with Western colonialism and American segregation."[73] Another of the historian's apparent heresies has it that "attempts to depict the nationalist leaders as proto-fascists showed a poor understanding of both the Nazi and the Afrikaner nationalist movement."[74] Giliomee's deviationism has prompted a critical mauling, courtesy of Patrick J. Furlong—another liberal historian, an expatriate safely ensconced in the U.S. since 1983. Furlong accused Giliomee of coming close to "perilously defending the system that he so long opposed"—even growling at Giliomee for becoming an "outspoken champion of the Afrikaans language and culture" (as if these were intrinsically bad).

In retrospect, it is easy for me to see the merits of Giliomee's argument for "the essential moderation of Afrikaner nationalism."[75] Anybody who lived, as I lived, among Afrikaners during the apartheid era can testify that crime and communism were foremost on their minds. To rationalize the cruel, Kafkaesque laws of apartheid, Afrikaners spoke of the Swart Gevaar (which meant the "Black Threat"), and of the Rooi Gevaar (the "Red Threat"). My Afrikaner neighbor would regularly admonish me for my incipient liberalism: "You want Black rule so badly, look around you at the rest of Africa! Anglos like you simply don't understand what's at stake."

We didn't. But when the going got tough, the Afrikaners, stayed behind; we upped and left, leaving those we loved. One beloved person was Ethel, whose Xhosa name was Nomasomi.

Up Close and Personal

I was on time; Ethel, my longtime housekeeper, was early. That was her habit; her work ethic. She and I had arranged to meet at the equivalent of what is today the Department of Home Affairs in Cape Town. Before departing for Canada (and then the U.S.), I had paid Ethel a lump sum in lieu of a pension. However, I wanted to see about getting government retirement benefits for her. Ethel doesn't know this book is dedicated to her, among others. We corresponded for years. I'd send self-addressed envelopes and bank drafts; she, brief, achingly beautiful letters. Ethel was near illiterate, but the power of her idiom was enough to punch a hole in my heart. She addressed me as "My Dear Eyes."

Dressed to the nines, Jim (Ethel's husband) and the children sat on the bench waiting. To claim welfare benefits one had to be in The System. Although this was 1995, by which time apartheid was all but dismantled, these were early days still. The laws on the books had not caught up with *de facto* law. At this stage, most blacks remained assigned to a specific Bantustan, and as a result, they were officially considered to be aliens in South Africa proper. This would explain why Ethel and her family did not appear on the lists of South African citizens. The lady clerk raised an eyebrow; our little group must have made quite an impressive spectacle. I knew we were in for a tussle when said clerk told me that there was no trace of the family in "The System"—and certainly no birth certificates. If the family wished to claim benefits, they'd have to "go home" to their designated "homeland," Transkei. It was going to be a long day.

"The Cape is their home," I told the clerk. They have been here for a generation. I introduced each child to the clerk by name, and suggested that she bring them all into official existence by issuing them with birth certificates. "Start with the youngest, Peliwe, please." We would not be budging without these items. The clerk left and reappeared with the requested certificates.

Ethel's children were now in The System and eligible for a variety of assistance programs. I persisted: "What about Mr. and Mrs. Khala?" Jim had a debilitating, work-related lung ailment and would need disability benefits. He could hardly walk more than five feet. The clerk was coy: "Mrs. Mercer, the two are not married. They must have had a tribal ceremony." "Well then, let's have us a wedding," I smiled, as it appeared, winningly. For

I won. The woman was beginning to understand what it would take to be rid of me. She departed and returned accompanied by the in-house magistrate. With me as their witness, Jim and Ethel solemnized their twenty-five-year-old union.

LAND, LANGUAGE AND LANDMARKS LOST

To the orgiastic killing spree that threatens the "Teutonic folk who have burrowed so deeply into Africa,"[76] recent years have added the horrors of a Stalinist land grab. The ANC regime is preoccupied with redistributing white-owned land to poor blacks.[77] By 2015 (so the Commission on Restitution of Land Rights has promised), thirty percent of all agricultural land will have been handed over to blacks. It looks as if, in the ANC leaders' eyes, the fewer farmers there are to negotiate with, the better.

Eminent Domain or Domination?

Simon Barber, "the United States representative of the International Marketing Council of South Africa," categorically rejects the common perception that South Africa "looks set to sail the same course as Zimbabwe's Robert Mugabe in pursuing a policy of 'uncompensated expropriation of land held by whites for black resettlement.'"[78] Barber wants there to be no misunderstanding about the "South African government's land restitution and redistribution policies". He'd like Americans to think of the process—which has seen thousands of white citizens turned out of homesteads which their black compatriots covet—as no different to the eminent domain process in the United States.

Sadly, he has a point. Eminent domain abuses in the U.S. are wide-ranging. Although the Fifth Amendment to the U.S. Constitution sanctions taking for public use only and with just compensation, as with all things constitutional, case law has intervened to redefine and broaden the meaning of public use. There exists, however, one big difference between the two countries. It is this: America's eminent-domain depredations notwithstanding, *the U.S. has yet to establish a legal procedure to effect the forcible transfer of property from one private owner to another in the name of social justice.*

More closely resembling the American eminent-domain laws was the apartheid-era Expropriation Act of 1975. The new "improved" Expropriation Bill of 2008 is a different matter entirely. Enforcing this procedure took longer than expected, but the ANC finally tired of the old-style courts-adjudicated legal system (with its long-standing mixture of Roman and Dutch traditions) as it applied to land restitution, replacing it with a blend of tribal and totalitarian laws. These laws duly dispensed with pesky due-process formalities, such as matching a willing buyer with a willing seller and arriving at fair compensation. With the 2008 Bill, the dominant ruling party had empowered itself—and "any organ of state, at any level of government"[79]—to take ownership and possession of property "simply by giving notice to the expropriated owner." "The state would make the 'final' determination of the compensation due, subject only to a limited form of court review." Both movable and immovable property is up for grabs—"livestock and farming implements, residential homes, business premises and equipment, patents, and shares."[80] The 2008 Bill, shelved temporarily before the 2009 elections but not forgotten, has led in short order to talk about nationalization.

However short the shrift the SAIRR gives to the evidence of racial rage imprinted in the ravaged remains of thousands of rural white South Africans, it is, mercifully, willing to disbelieve Zuma and his Land Reform director-general. Despite the evidence to the contrary, they claim they do not intend to nationalize farm land. The facts speak otherwise. In March 2010 a plan was tabled in Parliament for turning "all productive land into a national asset leased to farmers."[81] Such sentiments are hardly new. True to a promise made in its 1955 communistic Freedom Charter, the ANC has already nationalized the "mineral wealth beneath the soil," and the water rights. And now, to supplement the Expropriation Bill, the Party has published a policy paper that suggests two land-use models other than the system of freehold title, and warns of the need to water-down the already weak property-rights provision in the Constitution.

This should pose no great problem. The entrenchment of a property clause in the South African Constitution has angered judicial activists, who conflate the protection of private property with the entrenchment of white privilege. Their fears are overblown. I wager that nationalization might not necessitate a change to the South African Constitution, since the latter allows a good deal of mischief in the name of the greater good, including land expropriation in the "public interest."

The Hobbesean choice which the ANC plans to present to white farmers is between making them mere tenants of the state (by declaring all productive land a national asset under state control) and, on the other hand, "placing a ceiling on how much land individual farmers can own."[82] Which, in practice, limits economies of scale, and with them successful commercial agriculture. "One farmer, one farm" was how Zimbabwe's Zanu-PF described this policy. The government still asserts that it is merely putting in place a "mechanism for taking back failed farms from black farmers." But the SAIRR has exposed such assurances as "a red herring to conceal the State's more plausible intention to wrest control of agricultural production from white commercial farmers."[83]

Channeling the ANC, *The Economist* has mouthed about the alleged need for "making white farmers transfer forty percent of their farms by value to black shareholders."[84] This magazine endearingly describes the ANC as a "friendly monolith." Friendly? The ANC has already nationalized water and mineral rights, has tabled the Expropriation Bill of 2008, and shares with its Western governmental cheer-squad a willingness to "sacrifice performance for racial ideology." So talk of further anti-white economic persecution is only logical.

As a matter of daily practice, white farmers are currently being terrorized and threatened with land claims. As if this were not bad enough, they can now expect nationalization. In case Zimbabwe is a distant memory, the nationalization of South Africa's farms will increase unemployment in the agricultural sector, and with it, rural poverty. That will guarantee mass migration to the cities, with all the attendant problems which this exodus poses. Also, it will undermine South Africa's ability to meet its food needs and deter investment in the country. And these, so help us, are the positive aspects of land parity.

The Law of the Land 'Indigenized'

When former farm laborer Mooiman Elias Mahlangu came before Justice Antonie Gildenhuys' Court, in 1996, to initiate proceedings against farmer Breggie Elizabeth de Jager—claiming her house, land, *bakkie* (pick-up truck) and other possessions of which he had availed himself during his tenure on her land—Justice Gildenhuys searched the plaintiff's affidavit for facts. He looked high and low for evidence to support the claims. In what was a harbinger of things to come, Mr. Omar, the plaintiff's lawyer, asserted that the mere fact of Mahlangu making allegations shifted the burden of proof to the respondent. Justice Gildenhuys, in a crisp, concise decision, reminded Mr. Omar that "substantive law determines where the burden of proof lies," and that "such a burden is not shifted in the course of the litigation." The Judge granted the applicant leave to renew the application when all relevant facts had been placed before the Court.[85]

The same search for facts and fairness is evinced in the claim on Macleantown, a small hamlet approximately forty kilometers northwest of East London, which "was declared a white group area" during 1970. Land owned by blacks was expropriated. The residents were not compensated for the land they lost, and received no title to the land on which they were resettled. The same Court, Justice Gildenhuys,' affirmed that the expelled residents had a right to be compensated and ruled that "the forced removal during 1970 had been clearly established." Once "the involvement of each of the claimants" had been properly shown, alternative state-owned sites were set aside for the purpose of restitution.[86]

In 2005, by which stage apartheid was little more than a memory, individuals calling themselves the Popela community laid claim to farms in the Moketsi area of the Northern Province, on the grounds that they were dispossessed of their land rights by racially discriminatory law. They cited, in particular, the abolition of the labor tenancy system on the farms, and the institution of a wage-earning system. But Gildenhuys did not oblige them. He ruled that this conversion could not be considered racially discriminatory, and did not constitute grounds for a land claim.[87]

These decisions exemplify the South African Land Claims Court at its inception, when rules of procedure and evidence applicable in civil actions and familiar to the West were still followed. Some decisions are for the plaintiff; others against him, as expected. This was the law before it was thoroughly "indigenized."

Cut to 2010. Gildenhuys and his ilk are increasingly marginalized in decision-making. The most fashionable judge today is Fikile Bam. On his résumé, under "National Service," Bam lists "political prisoner on Robben Island during apartheid." Now judge-president of the South African Land Claims Court, Bam is presiding over the transfer of the opulent Eastern Cape Fish River Sun Resort owned by "Sun International" over to the "Mazizini Community." Even he concedes that the community does not presently possess the financial or managerial wherewithal "to maintain the existing developments and improve upon them." For this, "public money" will be allocated. Yet after acknowledging "the many instances where the beneficiaries of restored land have failed dismally to sustain, let alone develop, commercial projects on the land"—Bam cheerily grants the Mazizini Community its wish. The validity of the Pedi Tribe's right to the seafront fishing, hiking and golfing retreat is nowhere debated in Bam's 2010 decision, other than in a vague statement that "the grazing rights which the claimants previously enjoyed were, in themselves, commercial activity." Particularly tragicomic—and certainly instructive in matters of law—is the claimant's assertion, during the proceedings, that the "bellowing of cattle to Africans was like the jingling of the coins in the pocket of a European."[88]

Killing God's Creatures

The putative pleasure which some Africans derive from the "bellowing of cattle" extends increasingly to the sounds of the beasts in the throes of death. Farm attacks on animals have been every bit as cruel as the onslaught on their owners, with one exception: the expiration in agony of animals is more likely to move the animal-loving West to tears.

No sooner does a "tribe" or an individual launch a claim with the Department of Rural Development and Land Reform, than squatters—sometimes in the thousands—move to colonize it, defile its grounds and groundwater by using these as one vast toilet, and terrorize, often kill, its occupants and their animals in the hope of "nudging" them off the land. Dr. Philip du Toit, a farmer (with a doctorate in labor law) and author of *The Great South African Land Scandal*, speaks of recurrent attacks on farm animals that "hark back to the Mau Mau terror campaign which drove whites off Kenyan farms." *Farmer's Weekly* is packed with pitiful accounts of cows poisoned with exotic substances, battered with heavy metal bars, their Achilles tendons severed, writhing in agony for hours before being found by a distraught farmer.

"Encroachment is the right word," a farmer told du Toit. "They put their cattle in, then they cut the fences, then they start stealing your crops, forcing you to leave your land. And then they say: 'Oh well, there's vacant land, let's move on to it.' It's a very subtle way of stealing land."[89] According to Agri SA, an organization representing small and large-scale commercial farmers, "Up to 121,000 livestock, worth about R365 million [about $48.5 million US] was stolen in the 2008-2009 financial year alone." "When there is a farm claim I say 'Look out!' because attacks may follow to scare the farmers," says Piet Kemp, the regional director of the Transvaal Agricultural Union (TAU)."[90]

The ANC's old Soviet-inspired Freedom Charter promised this: "All shall have the right to occupy land wherever they choose." And so they do today. The adapted, indigenized law allows coveted land, owned and occupied by another, to be obtained with relative ease. It signals a free-for-all on the lives of white owners and their livestock. Because of legal claims which they are powerless to fight, squatters whom they cannot fend off, and cattle, crops and families which they can no longer protect, farmers have been pushed to abandon hundreds of thousands of hectares of prime commercial farmland.

"Since the end of apartheid in 1994, when multi-racial elections were held," writes Dan McDougal of the London *Times,* "fifteen million acres of productive farmland have been transferred to black ownership. Much of it is now lying fallow, creating no economic benefit for the nation or its new owners. Last year South Africa became a net importer of food for the first time in its history."[91] "My visit to Mpumalanga came immediately after crossing the frontier from Zimbabwe," attests Aidan Hartley, also of the *Times*, "and what struck me was how similar the landscapes were after redistribution had taken place. Once productive maize fields now grow only weeds. Citrus orchards are dying, their valuable fruit rotting on the branches. Machinery lies about rusting. Irrigation pipes have been looted and farm sheds are derelict and stripped of roofing. Windbreak trees have been hacked down and roads are potholed."[92] Dr. du Toit has traversed the "beloved country" from the Limpopo to the Cape, from Natal to the North West to document the transfer and consequent trashing of the country's commercial farms. Without exception, splendid enterprises that fed the country many times over have been reduced to "subsistence operations with a few mangy cattle and the odd mealie patch."[93] (*Mealie* is Afrikaans for "maize," deriving, apparently, from the Portuguese word *milho.*) In even the best-case scenario, farms belonging to the whites who feed the country and produce surpluses are being handed over to subsistence farmers who can barely feed themselves.

Tot Siens (Farewell) To The Taal (The Language)

"He who controls the past controls the future." So wrote Orwell in *Nineteen Eighty-Four*. The ANC now commands past, present and future. Yet, *The Economist* derisively dismisses Afrikaner discontent over the loss of "status, flag, party, geographical place-names and most of their schools."[94] What will the magazine mock next? Will it consider ethnic cleansing campaigns against farmers to be screamingly funny?

It may be a trifling issue to deracinated sophisticates, but landmarks in the country's founding history are slowly being erased, as demonstrated by the ANC's decision to give an African name to Potchefstroom, a town founded in 1838 by the *Voortrekkers*. Pretoria is now officially called Tshwane. Nelspruit, founded by the Nel Family (they were not Xhosa), and once the seat of the South African Republic's government during the Boer War, has been renamed Mbombela. Polokwane was formerly Pietersburg. Durban's Moore Road (after Sir John Moore, the hero of the Battle of Corunna, fought in 1809 during the Napoleonic Wars) is Che Guevara Road; Kensington Drive, Fidel Castro Drive. Perhaps the ultimate in tastelessly hip nomenclature is Yasser Arafat Highway, down which the motorist can careen on the way to the Durban airport.

The Afrikaans tongue, in particular, has come under the ANC's attack, as the government attempts to compel Afrikaans schools to adopt English. Afrikaans-speaking universities have been labeled "racist" in the New South Africa, and have been forced to merge with "third-rate black institutions so that campuses may be swamped by blacks demanding instruction in English." On the supplanting of the Afrikaans language, Dan Roodt relates: "Not so long ago, an Indian employee at my local branch of the Absa Bank demanded to know if I was a legal resident in South Africa upon hearing me speak a foreign language, Afrikaans."

The ANC's attempt to tame and claim South African history mimics the effort by American elites to deconstruct American history and memory, documented by Samuel P. Huntington in *Who Are We?*. Wishing to purge America of her "sinful European inheritance," bureaucrats, mediacrats, educrats, assorted policy wonks and intellectuals trashed the concept of America as melting pot. In its place, they insisted on ensconcing multiculturalism, inherent in which is a denunciation of America's Western foundation and a glorification of non-Western cultures. This mindset does not permit pedagogues to reject Afrocentric faux-history outright. They dare not—not if the goal of education is to be achieved, and that goal is an increase in self-esteem among young Africans, in particular. Other self-styled victim groups, notably natives and women, have had their suppurating historical wounds similarly tended with curricular concessions. Thus, of the 670 stories and articles in "twenty-two readers for grades three and six published in the 1970s and early 1980s ... none had anything to do with American history since 1780."[95] The trend, documented by Huntington, accelerated well into the year 2000, when Congress, alarmed by the nation's historical Alzheimer's, made an anemic effort to correct decades of deconstruction. It allocated more funds to the Department of Education, which was a lot like letting the proverbial fox guard the historical henhouse.

Historical veracity certainly has little to do with the Texas State Board of Education's perennial haggling over a social studies and history curriculum. In the Lone Star State's 2010 political match, America's Judeo-Christian history, its authentic Founding Fathers, and the defining concepts of a "constitutional republic" and a gold standard won the day. For now, at any rate. But we shouldn't get our hopes up overmuch. Forces of commonsense might have won this particular battle; winning the overall war is a different matter. No doubt, multiculturalism, "democracy," and funny money will gain curricular ascendancy when, once again, progressives outnumber Republicans on the Board.

As a subject in South Africa's school syllabus, history was initially neglected during the transition to majority rule. The establishment of the "South African History Project" changed that. The Project aims, according to Sasha Polakow-Suransky of the *Chronicle of Higher Education*, to resurrect "the subject as a prominent field of study in the national school curriculum." Unfortunately, and following the American academy's example, the trend has been away from "the pursuit of objective historical truth," toward history from beneath.

In America, this postmodern tradition regularly lifts from obscurity heroes featured in academic works such as "Quilting Midwives during the Revolution" and "Hermaphrodites and the Clitoris in Early America." (These, incidentally, are not parodies. They were seriously intended academic dissertations, which Britain's *Times Literary Supplement* cited as an indication of how absurd certain historical studies have become.). In this tradition—and judging from the televised, raucous exchanges—the Lone Star educators would have bargained over the Texas syllabus like this:

> *Democrat didact to Republican troglodyte*: "Throw in Juan Seguín (minor "military figure of the Texas Revolution and Republic of Texas"), and we'll let you keep Thomas Jefferson (major political philosopher and American founding father)."
> *Republican troglodyte*: "Please, please, please can we have John Adams?"
> *Democrat didact*: "Only if you throw in Crispus Attucks." (Crispus Attucks, since you asked, was allegedly the first victim of the 1770 Boston Massacre. He is variously identified by historians as black, mulatto, Native American, tall, and short. By the time this reaches print there might well be textbooks upholding him as a heroic lesbian, a pioneering abortionist, or perhaps America's first martyr to "homophobia." He seems to be a veritable Rorschach

> blot upon which fashionable scribblers can project their fantasies of political correctness.)

Adapted to the public school system and its mission, the teaching of history (whether stateside or in South Africa) seeks to be more palliative than factual. The historian has been forced to turn himself into Doctor Feelgood.

In South Africa, the politically correct reconstruction of historical events aims to foster "certain values," in the words of Kader Asmal, the Minister of Education in 2000. According to Pieter Kapp, a retired professor of history at Stellenbosch University, "You have books appearing that interpret the history of South Africa only according to the perspective of the liberation struggle." Indeed, "Since 1994, tales of European conquest are slowly beginning to disappear from the nation's classrooms, giving way to epic accounts of black anti-apartheid heroes," writes Polakow-Suransky. Of course, in reality, the modern marvel that is South Africa was not the handiwork of the black nationalist movement now dismantling it, however praiseworthy that movement's struggle might have been.

The Afrikaner's "right to culture" and country has been similarly usurped, the first by a "nation-building project aimed at a single hegemonic culture"[96]; and the second, his own country, by a government which has been encouraging "Afrikaner doctors, teachers and accountants to emigrate, while various ANC government ministers enthusiastically import replacements from India, South Africa's sister country in the Commonwealth."[97] Indeed, if you imagined that successive American governments were unique in their efforts to displace their own citizens through unfettered, mass immigration, you would be wrong. The ANC comes close. However reprehensible the ANC is in encouraging white flight, as the party of the black majority—ninety-two percent of whom vote for it, compared with only four per cent of whites—it is at least showing a certain consistency in doing so. This cannot be said for America's Republican Party, which supports policies that aim to replace the historical majority it ostensibly represents and upon which it relies for reelection.

INTRA-RACIAL REPARATIONS?

There was bitter blood on Bantu lands well before the settlers arrived. The all-time PIG (Politically Incorrect Guide) to Zulu history notes correctly that the Bantu, like the Boers, were not indigenous to South Africa. They "dribbled south" from some "reservoir in the limitless north," and, like the European settlers, used their military might to displace Hottentots, Bushmen, and one another through internecine warfare. We've committed the little San people of Southern Africa (the Bushmen) to folkloric memory for their unequalled tracking skills and the delicate drawings with which they dotted the "rock outcroppings." The San were the hunters, but they were also among the hunted. Alongside the Boers, Hottentots "hunted down Bushmen for sport well into the nineteenth century.[98]

The PIG in question is Donald R. Morris's epic, *The Washing of the Spears: The Rise and Fall of the Zulu Nation*. In "the book to end all books on the tragic confrontation between the assegai and the Gatling gun," Morris places Cape Town's founder and Dutch East India Company official J. A. Van Riebeeck, on landing at the Cape in 1652, 500 miles to the north and 1,000 miles to the west [sic] of the nearest Bantu.[99] Joined by other Protestants from Europe, Dutch farmers, as we have seen, homesteaded the Cape Colony. Shaka Zulu himself considered the European clansmen to be the proper proprietors of the Cape frontier, with whom he would need to liaise diplomatically if he wished to subjugate his black brethren, the Xhosa-Nguni[100] peoples, on the southern reaches of his empire abutting the Cape. (And boy, did he subjugate them!) Indeed, the white civilization which formed south of the Orange River[101] did not encounter the black civilization in the interior for some time. And during that time, the coastal clans warred against one another, continually raiding other kraals, driving off the cattle and exterminating the victims.[102] Before the consolidation of the Zulu empire, eight hundred or so distinct Nguni Bantu clans vied for a spot under the sun in the Natal region between the mountains and the coast. Where are these lineages today?

Particularly brutal was the period spanning the early 1820s known as the *Mfecane*, "the Crushing." Up to two million natives died "in a decade that depopulated what is today the Orange Free State."[103] This death-toll was partly, but not entirely, the fault of Shaka, who destroyed the clan structure in Natal—the Zulu paramount chief was a monster of psychopathic proportions who once sated his scientific curiosity by dissecting seven hundred pregnant women. The tribal warfare caused mass migration, whereby "not a single clan remained in a belt a hundred miles wide south of the Tugela River; in an area that teemed with bustling clans only thousands of deserted kraals remained, most of them in ashes. A few thousand terrified inhabitants [hid out] in the bush or forest in pitiful bands, and cannibalism flourished,"[104] as it did whenever the kraal economy was demolished in ongoing warfare. Yes, "cannibalism, which was fully repugnant to Bantu civilization as it is our own, became common, and reached the point where entire clans depended on it and nothing else to feed themselves."[105]

Mobs on the move marked their "aimless tracks" with (DNA-rich) human bones. Was there never a duty to divine these bones for purposes other than soothsaying—say, to do the devoured justice? These days, white South Africans *supinely* accept their obligation to give up the lands they are supposed to have stolen, on the grounds that it holds ancestral remains. Should not the relatives of cannibals who gobbled up their black brethren be held to the same standards? The Bushmen have been barred by the Botswana Bantu from claiming their ancestral lands in the Central Kalahari. Where's the international uproar? Should we not be discussing intra-racial reparations?

Penetration into Natal in the early 1800s was confined to Port Natal, where a small trading post operated at the pleasure—and with the permission—of Zulu kings such as Shaka and Dingane. Port Natal settlers succored the natives. The post soon became a sanctuary to which the "detribalized natives" fled in their thousands, on the run from the daily depredations of tribal life. These natives soon came to see in the settlers "a fine defensive shield," under which they themselves could "re-establish a semblance of normal kraal life in the open."[106] How, we must ask, have the descendants of these benefactors been rewarded?

Ask the Dunns of Durban. They descend from John Dunn, a Bantuphile who settled in Natal in the mid-1800s, and to whom King Cetshwayo gave "a large tract of land along the coast north of the Tugela with full rights of a chieftain."[107] There John Dunn lived and loved like a Zulu man, with as many wives. The King's kin have sabotaged and subverted the great Cetshwayo's wishes, subjecting Dunn's descendants, Pat Dunn and her family, to "just about every 'gross violation of human rights' which Amnesty International defines"[108]—land invasion, intimidation, arson, attempted murder.

John Dunn was a white trader and adventurer. A settler. Alexander Merensky and Heinrich Grutznerwere were German missionaries. Ask their descendants how they are faring.

The year was 1865. These two missionaries built a mission station and church on a Middleburg farm in the Eastern Cape. The natives called the mission Botshabelo, "place of refuge," because the missionaries sheltered tribespeople fleeing the local Pedi chieftain and his impis. Botshabelo became known far and wide "as a witness to Christian teaching."[109] The desperate refugees were saved both spiritually and existentially—taught literacy and crafts and converted to Christianity. How have their progeny honored the memory of the righteous men who rescued them from a gory death? By laying successful claim to the historical site European missionaries built—a place that was never traditional tribal land. The graves of members of the missionary families are buried on the land. Evidently, respect for ancestral remains does not cut both ways.

RECOMPENSE OR RECONQUISTA?

He who believes he has a right to another man's property ought to produce proof that he is its rightful owner. "As the old legal adage goes, 'Possession is nine-tenths of the law,' as it is the best evidence in our uncertain world of legitimate title. The burden of proof rests squarely with the person attempting to alter and abolish present property titles."[110] It is to this potent principle that democratic rule in South Africa has taken an axe—or, rather, an assegai.

The question of land ownership deeply concerned the nineteenth century trek Boers, as they prepared to decamp from the British-ruled Cape Colony and venture north.[111] Accordingly, they sent out exploration parties tasked with negotiating the purchase of land from the chieftains, who very often acted magnanimously, allowing Europeans to settle certain areas. Against trek Boers, it must be said that they were as rough as the natives and negotiated with as much finesse. On the high veldt, at least, trek Boers did "drive organized clans off the lands they wanted, retaining only a few families of squatters on each farm to provide labor."[112] However, the narrative about the pastoral, indigenous, semi-nomadic natives, dispossessed in the seventeenth century of their lands by another such people, only of a different color—this is as simplistic as it is sentimental.

When Boer and Bantu finally clashed on the Great Fish River it was a clash of civilizations. "The Bantu viewed the land as entailed property that belonged to the clan. A chieftain might dispose of the right to live on the land, but he could not dispose of the land itself. The European mind in general could not grasp this concept and regarded a land transaction as a permanent exchange of real property." As Morris observes in his matter-of-fact way, "The Bantu view insured European encroachment and the European view future strife."[113]

Perhaps inevitably, twenty-first-century "restitution" is not dominated by individual freehold owners reclaiming expropriated land. Instead, a group of blacks scheming on a particular property will band together as a "tribe," and pool the taxpayer grants which its members have received gratis for the purpose of purchasing occupied land. "This has complicated the process," says restitution advocate Dr. Clarissa Fourie of the University of Natal, "as evidence of these rights is not as easy to assess, since there are no title deeds to substantiate these claims." This by the admission of an advocate. If unambitious, the band may claim a commercial farm as its own. If ambitious, members may "claim the sun, the moon, the stars, and the oceans."[114] "Some of the claims are on very high-value land," admits Fourie. "There is one claim that has been made which covers 129 citrus farms in the Mpumalanga Province."[115] Another shoots for central Pretoria, the capital.

The dearth of original documents deeding the claimed areas to the claimants has not stopped claims from proceeding to court. A claimant's assertion that his tribe's cattle once grazed in an area will often suffice before the bar of law to back the "historical inquiry."[116] As a leader in the Democratic opposition put it, "We are moving from the rule of law to the law of rule."

Where blacks owned freehold land and were evicted subsequent to the 1913 and 1936 Land Acts—these prohibited natives from "hiring or acquiring" land outside the "scheduled native areas"[117]—restitution ought to have been possible, based on title deeds kept on record. By now the approximately three million Africans forcibly resettled under apartheid policies ought to have been compensated financially.

It seems to me patent that land that has been farmed intensively and scientifically must never be given to men whose capacity and craving is for kraal life: a small herd of cattle and the labor of as many wives as can be afforded.[118] Considering this very reality, and where a land claim has been shown to be valid, financial compensation is the *only* just restitution.

The "tribe" or band of individuals claiming these vast tracts of land most certainly does not have a right to the installations on them. Deeply corrupt and corrupting is the notion that a claimant inherits both the land and the improvements upon it; that a successful land claim will put a claimant in possession of everything the dispossessed man has worked to build in the course of a lifetime and which has increased the value of the farmstead many times over.

Take Theo de Jager. This jolly, rotund man—the chairman of the Land Affairs committee of AgriSA, the national agricultural trade association founded back in 1904[119]—has forfeited two farms in the Limpopo Province, "northernmost province of South Africa." Lost first was the land purchased around 1998, and claimed by (ambitious) locals together with other farms in the area. When the farms failed, the farm hands burned them to the ground in a show of frustration. An American reading these words in the comfort of his Nebraska ranch house or his Manhattan brownstone might well be left incredulous at the sheer crudity of this process. But in the New South Africa it has been extremely common. De Jager picked up the shards of a broken life and bought another farm. The Lords of the Land saw that it too was good, and lunged for the man's land again.

A farming family like de Jager's has built the home and filled it with memories. Preparing to move into the homes of white private property owners is an act of conquest. The signal message conveyed by legitimizing such proceedings in law is: covet and you shall be rewarded.

Even if received opinion is accepted without question—that early Afrikaners had no right to homestead vast expanses of unoccupied land or, thereafter, repel marauders—and even if we deny that the subsequent development and capitalization of the land has benefited all the country's inhabitants in the form of employment and abundant foodstuff; even if we readily concede the justness of every single claim adjudicated in the Land Claims Court of South Africa; even if these incorrect assumptions go unchallenged—at some stage we must question the sheer waste and wholesale destruction of wealth which this supposed justice entails. Whether you believe land reform in South Africa is always and everywhere a case of returning stolen property to its rightful owners, or that it is theft plain and simple—whichever is the case: "to the extent that massive stealing becomes the order of the day," warns libertarian theorist Walter Block, "a social breakdown is the inevitable result. Not for nothing do the Ten Commandments "prohibit not only robbery, but even coveting the property of others."[120]

The Department of Rural Development and Land Reform has admitted that ninety percent of redistributed farms were "dysfunctional," to put it mildly. Dr. du Toit observes that there is not one instance of a successful land handover in the entire country.[121] At some point, wanton destruction on such a scale can only be considered unjust, if not plain criminal. A sufficient difference in degree constitutes a difference in kind. Enlarge a motorcar enough and it becomes a minivan. Depending on the number of casualties, murder bleeds into a massacre. Destroy enough land and lives and you may no longer claim to have done so in the name of restoring rights. All you have done is to mock the very idea of rights out of meaning.

CHAPTER 3

Dispossession Is Nine-Tenths of the Law

In the United States, at present, only whites can be racists since whites dominate and control the institutions that create and enforce American cultural norms and values...all white individuals are racist.

—Carolyn Pitts, American affirmative action officer*

It is imperative to get rid of merit as the overriding principle in the appointment of public servants.†

—Mario Rantho, ANC parliamentarian

KNOWN IN SOUTH Africa as Black Economic Empowerment, "BEE" is the equivalent of the racial quotas Barack Obama champions, only with many times the sting. Like affirmative action, BEE aims to take "jobs away from one group in order to compensate a second group to correct injustices caused by a third group who mistreated a fourth group at an earlier point in

---

* Frederick R. Lynch, *Invisible Victims: White Males and the Crisis of Affirmative Action* (Westport, Connecticut, 1991), p. 32

† As related in CBN Archive, *All affirmative, no action,* July 1997, http://www.cbn.co.za/archive/97-jul/schoombe.htm

history." This droll, but depressing, distillation of discriminatory, collectivist hiring practices, courtesy of Edwin Locke of the Ayn Rand Institute, doesn't do justice to South Africa's enormously ambitious BEE program. BEE, and its latest permutation, BBBEE (Broad-Based Black Economic Empowerment), makes property ownership for whites in the democratic South Africa a misnomer. The country's current rulers can and do demand that a percentage of a white-owned company be taken over by blacks, on pain of it being closed down. This goes well beyond racial quotas.

Race-based wealth distribution, and in particular racist labor litigation, is yet another unique feature of the South African democracy. This phased process requires that all enterprises, public and private, make their workforce demographically representative of the country's racial profile. By the year 2014, the transformation must have been completed. The penalties for non-compliance promise to be stiff. Currently, if a company wishes to bid for government contracts, it has to take on a black partner. Private companies operating in South Africa cannot win government contracts if they are not *co-owned* by blacks. If they want to engage in any prospecting whatsoever, all mining companies must part with a portion of the company.

BLACK DIAMONDS

For the global mining giant De Beers the term Black Diamonds has assumed new meaning. To comply with the ANC's black economic empowerment rules, the famed company, founded by Cecil Rhodes and long viewed by blacks as "a symbol of white might,"[1] has been forced to create a "black-controlled diamond mining company."[2] De Beers had already "sold" twenty-six percent of its South African business to a black-owned company—the word "sold" is in quote marks because, in line with the BEE aim of facilitating direct black ownership in the company, the white proprietor is often required to loan the "BEE partner"[3] the funds to buy him out at a convenient price. That is if "the Industrial Development Corporation, a self-funding, government-backed development bank," hasn't picked up the tab.[4] In this case, the De Beers sale came at a discount of 100 million rands.

"Private companies above a certain size are obliged to try to make their workforces 'demographically representative' (i.e. seventy-five percent black, fifty percent female, etc.) from factory floor to boardroom," explained Guest in a *Wall Street Journal* editorial. The impending requirements have done wonders to boost foreign investment in South Africa.[5] (Here the reader is invited to conjure all clichés of improbability such as: And Britney Spears will cultivate a voice. Or wear underwear.)

In Africa, the extractive view of politics prevails: People seek personal advantage from positions of power. The *Daily Mail* has recently estimated that $187 billion has been illegally removed from the continent by national rulers since the colonial powers departed.[6] "The black tycoons who made fortunes by parlaying political connections into a share of someone else's business are the most insidious effect of the new racial laws."[7] For a shakedown share of a company, oleaginous ANC officials thus regularly rent themselves out as BEE front men to the country's large companies, forced to bring on blacks so as to win government contracts. The "New South Africa" is, after all, not so new. It is being wrecked by the very "cronyism that has wrecked the rest of Africa."[8] The diamond-in-the-rough chairing Black De Beers Inc. is no other than a senior member of the ANC, Manne Dipico.[9]

Once again, the principle of expropriation, *per se*, faithfully observed by the ANC, has failed to irk commentators in the West. Rather, stealing *for the few* rather than *for the many* is what has stuck in the western commentariat's collective craw. BEE, like all state-run affirmative action subventions, has enriched the ANC's dynastic families to the exclusion of the mass of African men and women. Now that party members are rich beyond imagination, they've seen fit to extend the "racial spoils system." Enter the Broad-Based Black Economic Empowerment Act of 2003. BBBEE, a creative bit of casuistry, conflates color-coded preferential policies with the constitutional right of blacks to equality. The Act also equates global competitiveness and national unity among *all* South Africans with the exclusive promotion of the economic interests of black South Africans *only*. To this end, the relevant cabinet minister is granted sweeping powers to issue "codes of good practice" and "transformation charters."[10] And, in fact, to "make regulations with regard to any matter necessary… to ensure the proper implementation of the Act," the goal of which is to achieve "substantial change in the racial composition of ownership and management structures and of the skilled occupations of existing and new enterprises."[11]

In the course of what ANC officials refer to as the "deracialization"[12] of the economy, BBBEE offers up an Orwellian racial taxonomy: A "Black Company" is more than fifty percent owned and managed by blacks; a "Black Empowered Company" more than twenty-five percent black-owned; a "black influenced" enterprise less than twenty-five percent.[13] The BBBEE Act and its assorted charters address all sectors of the economy, requiring detailed scorecards according to which firms are rated and a timetable by which they must have placed a certain percentage of blacks in senior, middle and junior management, at the executive level, and on the board of directors. Businesses must keep paperwork documenting their pigment-driven poaching, to be submitted to a "Charter Council" as proof of compliance with the latter's dictates. Exempt from the Charter Council are enterprises employing fewer than fifty people, or making less than ten million rand.

To be fair, this is a generous exemption when compared to the draconian American Title VII of the Civil Rights Act of 1964. Like BEE, Title VII severely curtailed the contractual freedoms of individuals and enterprises. Unlike BEE, it applies to all institutions and enterprises with no more than fifteen employees engaged in interstate commerce or doing business with the federal government.[14]

Grudgingly, *The Economist* has conceded that in the process of creating a "bureaucracy that would reflect the new dispensation...many experienced white civil servants left or were pushed out, "severely hurt[ing] [the administration's] ability to deliver at every level."[15] This understates the insoluble crisis engulfing ministries, hospitals, schools and municipalities. Hiring by color, rather than merit, is all in a day's work for the government, because it has no competitors and cannot go bust—at least, not just yet. This is nice for the blacks it employs, but not as pleasant for the much larger number who depend on the state for health care, water, roads and pensions.[16] Thus, as the old guard was given the proverbial pink slip and the new, racially correct civil service ensconced instead, basic services and infrastructure began to crumble. "Public healthcare, the railways, ports and road infrastructure bear testimony to the insidious effects of racial preference on South Africa."[17] Refuse collection is erratic. The electrical grid has been degraded at every level: generation, transmission, and distribution. Since distribution is now entrusted to the local, increasingly inept, authorities, candles and paraffin lamps have made a come-back in my home town of Cape Town as well as in other cities. Daily power outages affect industries and services across the country. Rolling blackouts—"load shedding" is the local euphemism—are now as typical of Cape Town's landscape as the tablecloth of clouds that cascades over the majestic Table Mountain.

Another imported practice of dubious provenance has seen South Africa's financial institutions forced to provide loans to blacks with lower credit ratings. Shades of the American subprime fiasco. So too must debt-financing services be delivered to South African companies owned by blacks with low credit ratings. In addition, BEE mandates special blacks-only training programs, down to the amount of post-tax operating profits that must be invested in black betterment. Ultimately this is about the transfer of white-owned businesses to blacks—in financial institutions, a *minimum* of twenty-five percent black ownership was to be achieved by 2010's end.[18] Increasingly, "in South Africa, property is defined as something a black person owns," writes Afrikaner commentator Dan Roodt. "A black may own a piece of land or a business outright, whereas a white may own it only in partnership with a black, or subject to conditions such as black empowerment or training for blacks so that they may eventually take it over."[19]

In case the boardroom was not enough, the bedroom is up for grabs too. The Prevention of Illegal Squatting Act of 1951 was repealed and replaced with legislation giving squatters a legal lien on the land they invade and occupy. Born-again as "unlawful occupiers,"[20] squatters cannot be evicted without Court mediation. The lengthy, costly procedure is borne, naturally, by the owner. The interloper has a right to be apprised of the owner's intention to evict him, and be afforded the opportunity to "defend the case."[21] Woe betide an owner who attempts to evict a "household headed by women,"[22] in contravention of their "rights and needs."[23] This law, unlike BEE, can afford to be blind to the color of a man's epidermis. The reality of property ownership in the country ensures that, like prosperous businesses, farms and homes owned by white South Africans are the likeliest targets of trespassers.

Cops Call Robbers ... To Chat

Also retired by the African National Congress was the old South African Police. Instead, the ANC set about reconstructing a politically correct—and representative—force. In the renamed South African Police Service (SAPS) a dwindling number of the old law-enforcement guard labor under a form of racial *dhimmitude*, with no hope of promotion. The demotic orgy of crime reflects the capabilities of the reconstructed force. As does the unremarkable ordeal of Robert Scheepers, aged fifty-three, and his wife, Dagmar, aged fifty-seven, of Pretoria. By the time the two were attacked for the second time in four days by the same gang of armed robbers, they had resolved not to call the police. Is there any wonder? The couple had called the 911-equivalent emergency number after the first attack, which they survived because a goon's gun failed to fire. The number was out of order. The police did eventually call back, but not Mr. and Mrs. Scheepers—the intrepid SAPS contacted the robbers on the cell phone which the latter had stolen from the couple. Evidently, the purpose of the call was a congenial chat since this lot of law-enforcement officers was incapable of tracing the call. Buoyed, the robbers returned to the Scheepers' home for seconds. This time, unable to spell the street address, the 911 dispatcher sent the police to a different location.[24] The Scheepers moved out. (The robbers likely moved in.)

Hands up if you knew that, every year, millions in taxpayers' money are forked out to private security firms to protect the new South Africa's police stations. "South Africa's protectors can't protect themselves."[25]

Under the same watchful eye, pylons and poles are routinely flattened, stolen, and then smelted. Indeed, blackouts and blowouts are intricately connected to the breakdown of law and order. "Up to 100 miles of cables may be going missing every year, destined for markets such as China and India where booming economies have created insatiable demand for copper and aluminum,"[26] reports Britain's *Daily Telegraph*. "The result has been entire suburbs plunged into darkness, thousands of train passengers stranded, and frequent chaos on the roads as traffic lights fail."[27]

As *The New York Times* saw it, "[t]he country's power company *unfathomably* ran out of electricity and rationed supply."[28] (My emphasis.) Not quite. I've lived through Highveld thunder storms and Cape, South-Easter, gale-force winds. Few and far between were the blackouts. (I purchased a generator in the U.S., after experiencing my first three-day power outage.) No, Eskom, the utility that supplied most of the electricity consumed on the African continent, did not run out of juice. It just ran out of experienced, skilled engineers, expunged pursuant to BEE. "'No white male appointments for the rest of the financial year,"[29] reads an Eskom Human Resources memo, circulated in January of 2008, and uncovered by the *Carte Blanche* investigative television program. The same supple thinking went into destroying the steady supply of coal to the electricity companies. Bound by BEE policies, whereby supplies must be purchased from black firms first, Eskom began buying coal from the spot market. Buyers were to descend down the BEE procurement pyramid as follows: buy spot coal first from black women-owned suppliers, then from small black suppliers, next were large black suppliers, and only after all these options had been exhausted (or darkness descended; whatever came first), from "other" suppliers. The result was an expensive and unreliable coal supply, which contributed to the pervasive power failures.[30]

REVERSE APARTHEID

This declared discrimination on the basis of color has issued from a party that came to power promising to create a non-racial society. Instead, the ruling clique has institutionalized "apartheid in reverse." "White unemployment has risen by almost 200 percent in five years,"[31] notes an Australian television broadcaster. According to Reuters' Finbarr O'Reilly, it doubled between 1995 and 2005. "Solidarity," South Africa's oldest trade union—and the only union left which is founded on Christian, as opposed to socialist, principles—says that the number of white South Africans living below the poverty line is 450,000, namely, ten percent of the country's total white population. And even these figures are over-optimistic. BEE policies have, in practice, barred a segment of the population from the formal economy for good. The individuals most likely to be affected by the ANC's determination to make the work force reflect the population's complexion are the Afrikaners whom the ANC especially disfavors. In the years shortly after 1900, the problem of poor white Afrikaners was endemic. By and large, it resulted from the Afrikaners in question being "forced off the land by the disasters of the [Anglo-Boer] war,"[32] and having their homesteads and crops razed by the British. For a long time, successive governments' pro-Afrikaner policies eradicated the poor white Afrikaner class. Now this class is once again burgeoning. Bethlehem in Pretoria is an example of an informal settlement where Afrikaners, by and large, live in huts without sanitation or electricity.[33] Coronation Park, in Krugersdorp west of Johannesburg (where I spent the first year of my life), is another.

When he was quizzed about the pervasive "quota culture," Essop Prahada, Minister in the Presidency (whatever crony appointment that is), barked: "You cannot have transformation without pain." At the same time, Prahada has insisted that BEE is not motivated by race but by socio-economic considerations. When asked why poor whites were not eligible for BEE privileges, Prahada blasted the aforementioned Australian reporter: "You are sitting here worrying about whites. Our main concern must be the millions of *our* people living in poverty."[34] (Again, my emphasis.)

Prahada's racial solidarity is not misplaced in the democratic South Africa, where redistributive "justice" is a constitutional article of faith. The country's constitution has a clause devoted to "Limitation of Rights."[35] Apparently, the constitutional scholars who compiled the document saw no need to protect the rights of minorities "that [had] not been victims of past discrimination."[36]

The possibility that the fortunes of hitherto un-oppressed minorities might change did not occur to the occupants of the Bench. Neither did this cross the "mind" (my tongue is firmly in my cheek here) of President F. W. de Klerk in the early 1990s. De Klerk turned the screws on his white constituents, failing to fight for—and secure—a power-sharing dispensation, wherein black and white interests would be balanced.[37] Instead, he acceded to crude majoritarianism, thereby forfeiting equal treatment for white South Africans within a democratic South Africa.

Was not apartheid a form of affirmative action for the Afrikaans minority? It most certainly was. "Afrikaner nationalists implemented one of the first and most successful affirmative action programs in the form of their 'civilized labor policy' of job reservations for white Afrikaners."[38] However, I am here concerned with reality, not race. *Res ipsa loquitur* (the thing speaks for itself). Preferences for Afrikaners targeted a minority of the population. During the apartheid era, moreover, the most skilled workers were invariably Boers or Britons. This was true too in Rhodesia (now Zimbabwe), RIP. Unfair as apartheid was—and maybe in no small measure because of it—overall, such preferences for a relatively skilled minority did not destroy government and civil society. Conversely, non-merit based quotas for a preponderant segment of society still lacking in commercially useful skills is doing the trick, as the major beneficiaries of BEE form a numerical majority.[39] "One-third of all municipal councilors controlling budgets in the billions are illiterate."[40] "[B]arely one percent of black high school students pass higher grade math, and very few opt for tough subjects at university, such as science or engineering," avers Guest. "Less than two percent of chartered accountants, for example, are black."

Mathatha Tsedu, the black editor of the *Sunday Times*, South Africa's largest-circulation weekly, recently stung his subscribers by writing the following: "It pains me to say this, but my African colleagues who manage large companies or government departments tell me that to get a job done, you usually have to employ a white."[41] Alas, white males, strictly speaking, are not supposed to comprise more than ten percent of the payroll. Consequently, fifty percent of all white males are self-employed, "waging a constant struggle for survival in small businesses run from homes and garages without pension schemes, medical aid or access to capital, which is largely reserved for blacks."[42]

With *wealth distribution* usurping *wealth creation*, it is no surprise then that, by *Newsweek*'s telling, the average black household income shrank by nineteen percent between 1995 and 2000.[43] According to the Cato Institute's current estimation, "The number of people living in absolute poverty has doubled since the ANC came to power in 1994."[44] Or since democracy.

Other than to gum up commerce and retard economic growth, the pragmatic upshot of "legislating outcomes"[45] for blacks has been to increase exorbitantly the wages of a small pool of highly courted, qualified blacks—a "black managerial aristocracy"[46]—and to disenfranchise some of the ablest white workers. Or, conversely, to subjugate them. The ANC has contributed to the creation of a unique cognitive caste system. Throughout the work force, explains Roodt, white subordinates with graduate and postgraduate degrees are doing the hard-core intellectual and technical work for their black bosses. The latter often have no more than a tenth-grade diploma but are paid a great deal more than their intellectual skivvies. A black matriculant (possessor of a high-school diploma) is perfectly poised to climb the corporate structure; yet a white, in order to have a ghost of a chance at remaining employed, had better possess the Masters or the Ph.D. degree.[47] Given their pallor, promotion for whites is unlikely.

Lost in all this minute-made "justice" are the natural laws of economics. Taking from those who produce wealth to give to those who consume it is bound to decrease wealth production and increase its consumption. Lost too is the idea that wealth needs to be created; that the Good Life is won not through *gifts* but through *graft*—education, skills, merit, and hard work over generations.

AFFIRMATIVE ACTION *À LA* AMERICA

South African Black Economic Empowerment is extreme all right, but it is also extremely upfront—there is no mystery about its aims. Supported by most black South Africans, BEE is undeniably democratic, as is it constitutional. The popular will is seldom an embodiment of natural justice. In South Africa, neither is the Constitution. South Africa's Bill of Rights is contemptuous of equality before the law; it enshrines group rights and allows for compensatory and distributive "justice." The state's confiscatory powers may be used to redress "past injustices"; "...To promote the achievement of equality, legislative and other measures designed to protect or advance persons, or categories of persons, disadvantaged by unfair discrimination may be taken."

No such jerry-built justifications can be advanced for affirmative action in America, where it is both undemocratic and unconstitutional (not that this fact imposes any perceptible limits on its scope). As I write, America is caught up in the judicial jiu-jitsu of a Supreme Court confirmation, Elena Kagan's. President Obama's pick before Kagan was Sonia Sotomayor, a self-proclaimed "wise Latina" federal appellate Judge. Ballyhooed for her brilliance, Sotomayor, by her own admission, is an "affirmative action baby," whose test scores were not comparable to those of her Princeton and Yale colleagues.[48] As *The New York Times* divulged, "to get up to speed on her English skills at Princeton, Sotomayor was advised to read children's classics and study basic grammar books during her summers."[49] This revelation prompted Patrick Buchanan to ask: "How do you graduate first in your class at Princeton if your summer reading consists of *Chicken Little* and *The Troll Under the Bridge*?"[50] I am sure that Americans, who oppose minority preferences by a margin of eight to one,[51] would love to know the answer to this question. (It's fair to say, though, that the answer, whatever it might be, has precious little connection with anything our Constitution permits.)

Although the federal bureaucratic behemoth acts otherwise, the American Constitution "gave the government no license to set quotas for hiring personnel by private enterprise or admitting students to institutions of higher learning."[52] The affirmative action subterfuge has come about in the teeth of popular opposition and constitutional injunctions against unequal treatment under the law. As such, it is a betrayal of the country's founding principles.

The institutionalized American "quota culture" has been imposed by administrative fiat, courtesy of the "The Power Elite"[53]—that engorged "administrative state" under which Americans labor.[54] For the purposes of conferring affirmative action privileges, American civil servants have compiled over the decades an ever-growing list of protected groups, "as distinct from whites."[55] In addition to blacks, the list entails mainly minorities such as Hispanics—Chileans, Puerto Ricans, Cubans, Dominicans, and Mexicans—Pacific Islanders, American Indians, Asian/Indians, Filipinos, Vietnamese, Cambodians (and homosexuals).[56] It goes without saying that "those who came to this country in recent decades from Asia, Latin America and Africa" did not suffer discrimination from our government, and in fact have frequently been the beneficiaries of special government programs," averred Senator Jim Webb[‡] in a recent *Wall Street*

[‡] Previously Navy Secretary under President Reagan, and former Vietnam veteran courageous beyond even the call of U.S. Marine duty (he won the Navy Cross, the Silver Star and two Bronze Stars), Senator Webb and I once corresponded briefly. Before he became a Senator,

Journal article. "The same cannot be said of many hard-working white Americans, including those whose roots in America go back more than 200 years."[57] Ostensibly crafted to correct "the injustices endured by black Americans at the hands of their own government … not only during the period of slavery but also in the Jim Crow era that followed," affirmative action has taken a very different turn, starting in 1965, "when new immigration laws dramatically altered the demographic makeup of the U.S."[58] In short, the policies of racial redress were extended to all "people of color," and shifted "from remediation toward discrimination, this time against whites."[59]

First to forewarn about the "immigration-with-preference paradox"[60] was Frederick R. Lynch, author of *Invisible Victims: White Males and the Crisis of Affirmative Action* (1991). The perspicacious sociologist noted that once mass immigration became a bipartisan policy, millions of imported non-black minorities were—and still are—given preference over native-born American citizens."[61] No sooner do these minorities cross the border, legally or illegally, than they became eligible for affirmative action privileges.

The present ideology on immigration considers all whites, rich or poor, a privileged, "fungible monolith." This outlook brooks little or no consideration of lives lived in penury for over a century. In particular: it overlooks the descendants of poor white Southern sharecroppers who did not own slaves, but were devastated by the War Between the States both "in human and economic terms." Even now, this sizeable segment of the South has yet to recover; its attainments with respect to education and income mirror those of the region's African-Americans, with one distinction: poor whites are barred from affirmative action

---

Citizen Webb, like this writer, was a member of a beleaguered minority that had incurred the wrath of the Republican Visigoths for opposing Genghis Bush's invasion of Iraq in 2003.

programs. Much is known about the groups that inherit the earth; much less about the disinherited.

At least today we have the benefit of a study that explains, with lots of statistics, the manner in which set-in stone racial set-asides operate to the detriment of poor whites in U.S. academia. According to Princeton sociologists Thomas Espenshade and Alexandria Radford, as reported on in a 2010 column by Patrick Buchanan: When "[e]lite college admissions officers prattle about 'diversity,' what they mean is the African-American contingent on campus should be five to seven percent, with Hispanics about as numerous." Naturally, "Forty to fifty percent of those categorized as black are Afro-Caribbean or African immigrants, or the children of such immigrants."[62] Wealthy white kids can still do satisfactorily, even if they border on cretinism, as with Meghan McCain or Barbara Bush. Poor whites, on the other hand, come to a great deal of diversity-driven grief. "At America's elite schools" a tacit admissions rule exists among Ivy-League recruiters to advance the advantaged. "Lower-class whites prove to be all-around losers,' at these schools. They are rarely accepted. Lower-class Hispanics and blacks are eight to ten times more likely to get in with the same scores." In essence: "poor whites need not apply."[63]

In the U.S., the minority is targeted for affirmative action; in South Africa it is the majority. Granted, there's a world of difference between compelling minority recruitment to equal the proportion of minorities in the population, and enforcing majority recruitment to equal the proportion of the majority in the population (seventy-five percent in the case of South Africa). Nevertheless, South Africa's hollowed-out establishments are a harbinger of things to come in the U.S. If American institutions have not yet collapsed under the diversity doxology's dead weight it is because the restructuring of society underway is slower, and the complexion of the population much different. To wit, South Africa underwent an almost overnight political transformation.

One day a white, relatively well-educated minority dominated all institutions; the next a skills-deficient black majority took over. In the U.S., where the native Anglo-Protestant community and its values still prevail, the shift has been gradual.

Alas, this, as I have repeatedly stressed, mass immigration is rapidly changing. The "immigration-with-preference paradox," moreover, has also ensured a constant downward pressure on the meritocratic nature of American institutions. In *State of Emergency* (2006), Patrick J. Buchanan prognosticates that "our two largest minorities, African-American and Hispanics, which now number together seventy-nine million or twenty-seven percent of the population, are leaving school with achievement levels three, four, and five grades behind white and Asian students. [A]s their combined share of the U.S. population…rises toward 40 percent in 2050, they will use their political clout to demand equality of results: racial and ethnic quotas and affirmative action in all profession."[64]

What Would Martin Luther King Jr. Say?

Thomas Jefferson worried whether it was "desirable for us to receive at present the dissolute and demoralized handicraftsmen of the old cities of Europe."[65] Jefferson feared that immigrants under "the maxims of absolute monarchies"—and he was not talking about the monarchies of Buganda or Ethiopia—may not acclimatize to "the freest principles of the English constitution."[66] What would he say about inassimilable arrivals, welcomed into a self-loathing culture that dismisses the nation's founders and distorts its founding principles? These days, Jefferson, the Founding Father who most clearly affirmed the natural right of "all men" to be secure in their enjoyment of their "life, liberty and possessions," is mentioned mainly in the context of slavery and miscegenation.

Today, the Obama White House would be at odds with no less a Democratic luminary than President John F. Kennedy for holding, in 1962, a "dinner honoring Nobel Prize winners of the *Western Hemisphere*." Still less would President Kennedy's witty introduction have met with President Obama's approval. JFK said:

> I think this is the most extraordinary collection of talent, of human knowledge, that has ever been gathered together at the White House, with the possible exception of when Thomas Jefferson dined alone.[67]

Indeed, "What Would Jefferson Say?" is hardly an abiding concern for the custodians of cultural consensus in America. "What Would Martin Luther King Jr. Say?": now that's an entirely different question. What King—the nation's reigning philosopher-king—would say certainly matters. The historical elevation of the democratic socialist Martin Luther King Jr. above the Founding Fathers is significant, since Jefferson's libertarianism is inimical to King's egalitarianism—never the twain shall meet. The attempts by many a modern conservative to conflate the messages of the two solitudes don't pass muster. That King advocated a color-blind society is a pipe-dream exploded by historian Thomas E. Woods Jr. "Contrary to the sentiments he expressed in his famous 'I Have a Dream' speech, King favored racial quotas. In fact, he called for massive government spending [on blacks] to make up for centuries of discrimination against them—'a broad-based and gigantic Bill of Rights for the Disadvantaged.' Late in his life he grew more radical, calling for a socialist system in America."[68]

Affirmative action in lending is just the kind of program King would have commended. If jobs could be handed over to less qualified minorities,[69] why not mortgages also? Legislating away the risks of mortgage lending, and mandating that credit be extended to those who are not creditworthy, minorities overwhelmingly: now this is probably what King was getting at when he spoke of exacting payment "for centuries of discrimination."

The subprime mortgage morass that has gripped the country was precipitated, by and large, by successive administrations, egged on by ethnic interests,[70] who took the fact that "blacks were less likely to receive loans than whites"[71] as incontrovertible evidence of racial prejudice, and demanded "remedial" legislation. In view of this crisis, my original optimism that American institutions had a distance to go before buckling under the weight of affirmative admits might have been overly optimistic. That the lion's share of foreclosures is concentrated in California and Florida, followed by Texas, Georgia, and Michigan, is certainly demographically telling.[72] The rest of the country is paying its bills—and the bills of the defaulters—in the form of billions in bailouts.

Was there really a need to cripple the country even further in this winter of our discontent in order to remedy alleged root-and-branch racism in the lending industry? Not according to Woods: "[A]lthough whites are approved for mortgages more often than blacks, Asians are approved more often than whites."[73] "Are we to conclude that systematic pro-Asian, anti-white bias" pervades American society? Hardly. "When net worth and other qualifying factors are figured into the equation, the lending disparity all but disappears."[74] This is more than can be said of the laws that have encouraged home ownership for those who could ill afford it and credit for those who were not creditworthy.

You had the Federal Housing Administration (FHA) colluding with the U.S. Department of Housing and Urban Development (HUD) to provide taxpayer-subsidized home loans to illegal immigrants, no questions asked. You had the 1974 Equal Credit Opportunity Act, the 1975 Home Mortgage Disclosure Act, and the U.S. Fair Housing Act—all arrows in the quiver of the federal government and the Department of Justice, aimed at forcing banks to throw good money after bad by lending it to those with low credit ranking. "Deserving families who have bad credit histories" is how George W. Bush characterized funneling hundreds of millions of dollars per year in down payments for affirmative buyers under his American Dream Downpayment Act of 2003.[75] President Obama surely cheered his predecessor when this latter approved the "'zero-down-payment initiative,' which was much as it sounds—a government-sponsored program that allowed people to get mortgages without a down payment. More exotic mortgages followed, including ones with no monthly payments for the first two years. Other mortgages required no documentation other than the say-so of the borrower."[76]

Founded as it was on quicksand, Bush's "ownership society" subsequently metamorphosed into the bailout society. It's a bacchanalia that Barack is continuing, as he works to appease and empower multiplying voting blocks and their energetic advocates, and, in the process, construct the World's biggest debtor nation.

Thou Shalt Not Discern

Proficiency tests discriminate between the better and the lesser applicant. They are a reminder that individuals—and groups—differ in their abilities to accrue wealth. To cultivate amnesia about individual and group differences, tests have been downplayed or discarded.

Consider: Some people are richer than others. (For example, Chinese and Japanese American males have higher incomes than white American males.[77]) Others don't like it. That's envy, not inequality. The quest to reduce these differences, or to soak the rich, is a good indicator of the state of liberty, or lack thereof, in a society. Ditto the length to which a government will go to pacify the multitudes by mulcting the few, or to placate the envious by taking from those they envy. Substitute wealth with another individual difference: beauty. Is it fair that some are fairer than others? Should government, perhaps, compel supermodel Heidi Klum to subsidize plastic surgery for the congenitally ugly? And why, pray tell, is difference, rather than "inequality," deployed to describe the "unfair" beauty advantage?[78] Just as the ugly are not ugly because the comely have robbed them of looks, the same is true for the poor; they are not poor because the rich have deprived them of wealth. Be they in athletic ability or acquisitiveness or attractiveness—differences are differences, not inequalities.

When one is taught to reject the harsh reality of inequality—of not having everything one covets—then the demand for "social justice" becomes a demand for redistribution and revenge. This the rulers achieve by making the more "fortunate" fork over their fortunes to the less fortunate. Be it possessions or pulchritude, there is a sense that someone ought to pay for the pain of being without. Ultimately, egalitarianism is inimical to liberty, we must learn to live with and accept enduring and "important differences between individuals and groups."[79]

Whatever the cause of the differences yielded by a standardized test that is both statistically valid and reliable; reason dictates that someone with a higher score has more of the thing the test measures than the man with the lower score. Because, overall, blacks and Hispanics score lower on various proficiency tests, these are often considered, *post hoc*, discriminatory. A test will be discarded if it does what it's supposed to do particularly well—screen out less able candidates—and if more of those candidates are black than white. Take the Prudential insurance company. It used to administer to job applicants a ninth-grade reading test. Because blacks were less likely than whites to pass this onerous test, the courts ruled that Prudential may not require its applicants to pass it.[80] The case, naturally, set a precedent for posterity.

Across the American workplace, the importance of "meritocratic criteria" such as test scores or "minimum credentials" has been downplayed, if not downright eliminated as "inherently biased against minorities."[81] In 2003, Frank Ricci, a firefighter from New Haven, Connecticut, was denied a promotion because he bested all the blacks in the department on a test seventy seven other candidates took. The test determined that Ricci was more suited than his less-qualified colleagues to fighting fires and dousing departmental flames. City officials didn't like the results, so they voided the test, and put the promotion on hold until a less sensitive test could be developed—one that better screened-out proficiency and ability. In government, such confidence-inspiring measures as dropping entrance exams have been taken too. The U.S. government hasn't had an entrance test since 1982. It abandoned both the Federal Civil Service Entrance Examination and the Professional and Administrative Career Examination (PACE) because blacks and Latinos were much less likely to pass either of them[82] In academia, law schools have lowered the bar in admissions and on the bar exam. Universities run a "dual admissions system"; "one admissions pool for white applicants and another, far less competitive, pool for minorities."[83]

When given the opportunity to exercise their democratic will, the American people have passed popular proposition ballots banning state governments from any race or gender consideration in hiring, contracting or educational policies. All the same, the decades-old race racket just went underground. Byzantine college bureaucracies, teeming with scheming academics, have simply used subterfuge to thwart the popular will. The sclerotic, California university system is one such example.

The UCLA Race Racket

Ask Senator John McCain to free-associate and in response to "illegal aliens" he'll blurt "God's children," and vice versa. This apparently irresistible combination surfaced again in his 2008 convention address: "Everyone has something to contribute and deserves the opportunity to reach their God-given potential," McCain bleated. "[F]rom the boy whose descendents [*sic*] arrived on the *Mayflower* to the [likely illegal] Latina daughter of migrant workers. We're all God's children and we're all Americans."[84]

God, no doubt, moves in mysterious ways. But McCain needs to be reminded that the boy whose forefathers settled the country he professes to love has not been in the good graces of government for quite some time. The Latina daughter of illegal migrants is another matter entirely. She's benefiting big-time—at least at a top government school like the University of California, Los Angeles.

Before Californians passed Proposition 209, in 1996, it was standard practice at the University of California campuses in Los Angeles to admit minorities with low scores, while denying admission to whites and Asians with top grades and test scores. "Prop. 209" was meant to ensure that race would no longer be a deciding factor in who gets into top government schools. It was introduced by Ward Connerly, president of the American Civil Rights Institute. Connerly is the force behind the drive to rid America of the invidious "race preferences, set-asides, and quotas," and also the man who has placed the issue on the ballot in states such as Nebraska, Arizona, and Colorado. The libertarian Connerly's stated aim is to restore the primacy of individual merit to American institutions. Or, as he told an unsympathetic correspondent for the public broadcaster: "to do what's best for the country." Alas, never underestimate the tenacity of diversity devotees. The preachers and practitioners of "benevolent" discrimination were not about to relinquish the color-coded preference system they had worked so hard to institutionalize.

Undaunted, Californian university administrators proceeded to fashion an admissions process that utilized "stealthy surrogates for race." As Manhattan Institute scholar Heather Mac Donald has documented in detail, "Tutors in the university's outreach programs [teach] students to emphasize their social and economic disadvantages in their application essay."[85] Minority applicants have become adept at belaboring the pigment burden in the essay section of the admissions process.[86] Evidently, administrators are equally good at picking up cues that help them color-pick candidates.

"For several decades," chronicles Mac Donald in *Elites to Anti-Affirmative-Action Voters: Drop Dead*, "the university had divided its applicants into two categories: it admitted one half only by objective tests of academic merit, such as standardized test scores and honors classes; it evaluated the other half subjectively, weighing such factors as race, economic status, or leadership. From this tier, where racial preferences had free rein, the vast majority of blacks and Hispanics were drawn." Consequently, "[t]he median SAT score of blacks and Hispanics in Berkeley's liberal arts programs was 250 points lower (on a 1,600-point scale) than that of whites and Asians."[87] Due to the high dropout rate of affirmative-action beneficiaries—and to prevent further attrition—UCLA had also created a bunch of BS majors. Examples are Critical Race Theory and Black Studies.

After "Prop. 209" passed, the number of "underrepresented minorities" accepted at UCLA dropped by half. Consequently, energetic ethnic advocates framed the piecemeal retreat from affirmative action as a grave injustice. To increase artificially the Lilliputian number of minorities, admission standards were thus lowered for all students. For example, the importance of LSAT scores was diminished in the admission to UC Berkeley Boalt Hall School of Law. Similarly, students graduating with top marks from failing schools that award As purely for showing up were considered just as eligible as—if not more so than—students graduating with honors from highly competitive secondary schools. In an attempt to net yet more minorities, "all students in the top four percent of their high school class, regardless of their standardized test scores,"[88] were accepted.

But UC Berkeley was not quick enough to adopt bush-college standards. The measures taken by California university campuses failed to yield the critical mass of minorities for which ethnic lobbies were clamoring. So the university, "incredibly," began ignoring altogether "its applicants' objective academic rankings," and considering a "holistic" method of assessment. Academic scores are currently "contextualized." To wit, an applicant with a lower SAT score who mentions having taken a bullet or quit a gang will be given preference over a high-scoring applicant burdened by a two-parent family.

The accommodation of elites to racial preferences has been studied extensively by Lynch, who found that when polled, corporate, political and academic elites mostly foreswear quotas and affirmative action, but seldom resist their implementation. Lynch explains this paradox in terms of the need to ward off "legal action by government agencies or lawsuits by members of minority groups."[89] But developing the ability to ward off the Reverends Jesse Jackson and Al Sharpton also confers a powerful evolutionary advantage.

Republicans, the consummate drag queens of politics (no offense to drag queens), are no different. These days McCain, a Johnny-come-lately to conservatism, disavows affirmative action—sort of. But in 1998 he supported it. And in 2003, the Bush administration filed a brief challenging racial preference in student admissions at the University of Michigan. The university was awarding candidates twenty points out of 150 for having the right complexion (non-white) and only twelve points for the right cerebral cortex (a perfect SAT score).

Bush's was a most unusual brief because, as it transpired, the administration's challenge was a cover for the kind of racket run at UCLA. Race, the administration's Solicitor-General Theodore Olson conceded, could be a factor in admissions under certain conditions. Racial cue cards in the form of "a statement people can make about whether they've overcome hardship" were quite kosher.

Barack Obama's honest support for affirmative action may be more irksome. But is there really a dime's worth of difference between the parties?

To Hell with Honky

Optimists (or ignoramuses) like to point out that while the government, most American undergraduate institutions, as well as law schools and medical schools have somehow stumbled into the practice of affirmative action, any public institution so doing exposes itself to Fourteenth Amendment due process and equal protection claims. But such claims just won't fly. "White males," contends Lynch, "very rarely win in reverse discrimination lawsuits; the [landmark] *Bakke* and *Johnson* cases have been exceptions, not the rule … elites and their institutions clearly have the upper hand."[90] The "spiral of silence"—spurred by the belief, uncontested by the media, that affirmative action is widely supported by the public—has been compounded by the fact that with few exceptions, jurists, journalists, politicians, pundits and social scientists have ignored the impact of these systemic practices on white men, treating it as a look-away issue.

The media monolith rarely covers quotas except to mock the men who complain about them. In seeking redress in the courts against the "Jim Crow liberals of New Haven" who punished him for excelling, the aforementioned Frank Ricci had done the unthinkable. He had not petitioned *for* special favors but *against* them. Yet petition he had. For asking that the city accept inequality of outcomes, the dyslexic Ricci, who came sixth among seventy seven test takers, was libeled by liberals. Having embraced the role of the state as socialist leveler, some libertarians even called Ricci a sore loser for wanting to win. After all, did the city not toss out the test results for winners and losers; white and black alike?[91] "Elites are ... aware that the odds for legal action by individual white males are small and that the chances of white males winning a reverse discrimination lawsuit are even smaller."[92] They know that, rather than confront the system, Anglo-American males, like their South African counterparts, are inclined to "suck it up" and go gentle into that good night. This, and the clandestine, top-down nature of the policy, accounts for why business has forged ahead with affirmative action programs. Across the U.S., job fairs are held from which whites are excluded.[93] Hollywood studios, major newspapers and automakers provide special slots for non-white workers.[94] The Mead Corporation, Xerox, and Corning all calculate executive bonuses partly on the basis of how many non-whites have been hired or promoted.[95] "In its own executive searches Kentucky Fried Chicken keeps separate lists of white and black candidates and then hires from each list."[96] Care is taken not to pit blacks against whites, sparing them the competition.

It is no surprise, then, that race-based affirmative action *à la* South Africa has avid backers among American elites, who see nothing wrong with the fact that many Africans are being propelled into key positions by fiat, not talent. "South Africa," puled *Time* magazine, "depends on a successful *handover* [emphasis added]. If it fails, the country will remain one of the most unequal in the world, and economic growth is likely to stagnate as crime and poverty grow."[97] This is a *non sequitur*, as it assumes causes not in evidence, namely, that continued white dominance of the economy will also undermine it. (Zimbabwe is a test case for that assumption, now, isn't it?!) The assumptions that *Time* makes are economically and morally inverse and perverse, and certainly empirically so. The only empirical certainty of a "handover" is the creation of vast bureaucracies for monitoring and enforcement in government, educational institutions and business.[98] Writes George Bornstein:

> Thomas Sowell studied the effects of affirmative action programs under a variety of names in almost twenty countries, including the oldest modern ones in India, as well as in China, Britain, Nigeria, Indonesia, Israel, Canada, Pakistan and the former Soviet Union and its successor states. After initial success, such programs tend to stall. New opportunities harden into permanent entitlements. Sowell did not find a single affirmative action program that ever disappeared because it had succeeded.[99]

The American founders, the followers of John Locke, understood that if individuals were to flourish, life, liberty and property would have to be protected. Wealth redounds to all members of society, irrespective of color or creed, when all are free to produce and trade safely and fearlessly. Individual differences in the capacity to accrue wealth are not the source of South Africa or America's undoing, but the coercive efforts to eradicate these differences will be.

Civil Wrongs

In a free society—one not silhouetted by the State—honored is the right of the individual to associate and disassociate, invest and disinvest, speak and misspeak at will. Contrary to the civil servant, the private person's "refusal to deal"[100] ought to be sacrosanct. I therefore second Richard Epstein, of *Forbidden*

Grounds: *The Case Against Employment Discrimination Laws* fame, that, "Voluntary affirmative action is perfectly acceptable by private firms, but far more problematic when undertaken by government." As do I concur with Epstein's cleverly and closely argued case against the federal Frankenstein's "unconstitutional interference" with intrastate businesses under, first, the guise of regulating interstate commerce, and then, cloaked as "an employment discrimination statute such as Title VII."[101] Where we depart from Epstein, an impassioned and ingenious opponent of antidiscrimination laws, is in his concession that federal power extends to enforcing the Fourteenth Amendment's injunction against discrimination in the states. The Bill of Rights, very plainly, did not grant the federal government any powers. Prior to the ratification of the Fourteenth Amendment, the federal government had no authority to enforce the Bill of Rights in the states. The Fourteenth reversed this preordained scheme by placing the power to enforce the Bill of Rights in federal hands, where it was never meant to be. As Felix Morley observed in *Freedom and Federalism*, the Fourteenth nullified "the original purpose of the Bill of Rights, by vesting its enforcement in the national rather than in the state governments,"[102] with the result that the Ninth and Tenth Amendments were sundered.

In the encroaching American State, the right of free association has been circumscribed by crippling codes of hiring, firing, renting, and money lending. The culprit is the Civil Rights Act of 1964, the "most radical law affecting civil rights ever passed by any nation."[103] Through it, incontinent legislators have marked their territory by invading ours. There can be no doubt that civil rights laws coerce individuals, often against their better judgment, into involuntary associations, as is it indisputable that under antidiscrimination law private property owners have lost a great deal of control over what is rightfully—and naturally—theirs. Yet conservatives, no less, reach for the smelling salts each time an attempt is made to explore the effects on liberty of this overarching and overreaching bit of legislation.[104]

"Far and away the most egregious form of government interference with the contractual rights of private persons and organizations is carried out in the name of affirmative action—the laws and regulations enacted since 1964 under the capacious category of 'civil rights,'" observers Richard Pipes in *Property and Freedom: The Story of How Through The Centuries Private Ownership has Promoted Liberty and the Rule of Law*. "Initially conceived as a means of enforcing principles of nondiscrimination in regard to black citizens mandated by the Fourteenth and Fifteenth Amendments, [affirmative action] was soon extended to other groups ... and ultimately turned into a vehicle for reverse discrimination against whites and males."[105]

The test for discrimination in the U.S. is underrepresentation. If an employer has failed to recruit minorities in proportion to their numbers in the vicinity, then he can be found legally liable for discrimination. His intent is considered irrelevant: intent be damned. Yet defenders of the Civil Rights Act of 1964 insist that all the Act did was to "mandate equal treatment of individuals."[106]

Not quite. Here's an excerpt from Title VII:

> Nothing contained in this title shall be interpreted to require any employer ... to grant preferential treatment to any individual or any group because of the race, color, religion, sex or national origin of such individual or group on account on an imbalance which may exist with respect to the total number or percentage of persons of any race, color, religion, sex or national origin employed by an employer.[107]

Nothing in the act requires racial and ethnic quotas, but then, nudge-nudge, wink-wink, nothing prohibits it, does it? As Pipes concedes, the Act, "and several executive orders" signed by

President Johnson," provided the "legislative basis for affirmative action."[108] First came Title VI, which severely curtailed the contractual freedoms of individuals and enterprises in all institutions receiving federal financial assistance. Title VII followed with restrictions on the freedom of association of "trade unions, employment agencies, and all enterprises with more than fifteen employees engaged in interstate commerce or doing business with the federal government, among others."[109]

Above all, civil rights laws have been enforced strictly in favor of protected classes, in a manner that flouts equal treatment before the law.[110] The claim that this was not their original design is unconvincing. For if, as a condition of letting you live unmolested, an all-knowing central planner retains a lien on your life and on what you acquire in the course of sustaining that life—you own diddly-squat. Can there be any doubt that civil rights law and other loot-and-distribute legislation render ownership symbolic, subject to the whims and "wisdom" of the sovereign of the day?

In addition to curtailing freedom of association and private property rights, as well as messing with the concept of merit, Title VII facilitated a segue from equality under the law to equality of outcomes for protected species; "from individualistic ideals to the collectivist philosophy of proportional representation."[111] This is in line with a regrettable shift over "the past two centuries," from "equality before the law, through equality of opportunity, to equality of result."[112]

Inherent in private property is the right to include or exclude. If a private school wishes to privilege African-American albinos, that's the prerogative of private property. Similarly, white people ought to be able to exclude blacks; and blacks, whites. Wait a second; blacks are permitted to oust whites from their associations. Blacks-only clubs are viewed as objects of ethnic pride; whites-only cliques are said to signify Nazism on the rise.

In this context, meditating on the meaning of rights might be appropriate. Sometimes the law of the state coincides with the natural law. More often than not, natural justice has been buried under the rubble of legislation and statute. This is the case with antidiscrimination law: "[T]he observation that every private person is entitled to deal with whomever he wants on whatever terms he sees fit" is perfectly consistent with a commitment to equality under the law.[113] This is because "the universal liberty to own and contract" with whomever one pleases is a natural right which antedates the state. The right to be employed, housed, educated, and loaned money to—these are ersatz rights manufactured by the state. So why exactly is the right "to own and contract" (property and freedom of association) a universal liberty, but not the right to avail oneself of another's business, rental apartment and school? Simply this: the former imposes no obligations on other free individuals; the latter enslaves some in the service of others.

In an attempt to shape society in politically pleasing ways, private property owners have been coerced into liking, hiring or renting against their will. Denunciations aside, quotas are a perfectly logical, if diabolical, extension of the regulation of private property courtesy of the Civil Rights Act. This was certainly not what James Madison meant when he wrote in the *Federalist Papers*—the key to the Constitution—that the first object of government was the protection of the "diversity in the faculties of men, from which the rights of property originate."[114] The Father of the Constitution also warned of the dangers to the nation of factions that would institute "… an equal division of property, or … any other improper wicked project."[115] Never did Madison imagine that government would emerge as the primary faction propelling such usurpations.

TOWARD A MERIT-BASED SOCIETY

What South Africa has become today, America is on the verge of becoming, unless it returns to the principles from which its greatness sprang. Sadly, it is already too late for South Africa. Americans, however, must once again embrace a merit-based individualism. Enforced by legal fiat, preferential treatment that pays tribute to a type, not to the individual, flouts justice in every respect, and is profoundly un-American.

As we have established, in the U.S., the government already presides over an elaborate system of reverse-racism laws. Being black guarantees special privileges. The coolness of being black and the considerable leverage the identity affords those who cultivate it is why celebrities like Obama, Halle Berry, and Alicia Keys have chosen to identify with the fathers who abandoned them over the (devoted, liberal, white) mothers who reared them. Berry, Keys, and Obama have embraced this politicized racial identity. To do so is smart, because in America, black is indeed beautiful. Yet in an America that has placed Obama in the Oval Office, the prevalence of alleged deep-seated racism is still inferred, *post haste* and *post hoc*, from the fact that African-Americans lag behind Anglo-Americans in academic achievements and socio-economic status.

In a court of law, statistical data is taken as both proxy for and proof of discrimination. Creedal multiculturalism simply doesn't admit of the possibility that aptitudes and abilities may vary by culture or ethnicity, as well as from one individual to another.[116] According to this view—pervasive in bureaucracy-stiffened business and government agencies and in teaching institutions—racial and ethnic groups must be reflected in academia and in the professions in proportion to their presence in the larger population, if justice is to be achieved. (Although the NBA or the 100-meter dash will not be forced to better reflect America.) The absence of such perfect representation is blamed on endemic white racism. But in professions and academic pursuits where mathematical precocity is a factor, white Americans trail Asian-Americans. And white Gentiles lag behind Ashkenazi Jews. By logical extension, these realities must imply a systemic bias against whites in the U.S., which is nonsense on stilts.

Malaysian governments certainly adopted this illogic toward their Chinese population, whose starting status as indentured laborers didn't stop it from rising to dominate business, the academy, and the professions. To achieve "racial balance," pro-Malay affirmative action laws were mandated in all government-controlled institutions. This is the same logic to which Hitler had awoken. In proportion to their numbers, Jews were grossly overrepresented in Germany's economic, professional, and cultural life, a reality Hitler sought to amend. He used the state apparatus to find a "Final Solution" to the Jewish advantage. Indeed, be they apartheid, affirmative-action, or the "Final Solution," policies of racial discrimination have *generally* issued from the state. It's hardly hyperbolic to say that Hitler's "Final Solution" was a *reductio ad inferno* of affirmative action for Aryans. Not for nothing were the Chinese of Malaysia and Southeast Asia referred to by King Rama VI of Thailand (reigned 1910-1925) as "The Jews of the East."[117] The pogroms waged against them, and the persecution of the over-achieving Indians of East Africa—these were condoned, if not facilitated, by respective governments.

But here's the paradox of state-mandated racial preferences; individuals will do business with people they dislike, even circumvent the law, if such circumvention turns out to be lucrative. Thus, despite the Malay disdain for the Chinese, Malaysians are more likely to patronize Chinese professionals and businesses. Malay-owned-and-run banks make more loans to the more creditworthy Chinese, Indians and owners of foreign enterprises.[118] Ditto black-owned banks in the U.S. Since they are "under less pressure than white-owned banks to consider race and ethnicity," explains Steven Farron in the *Journal of Libertarian Studies*, they "direct a considerably smaller proportion of their investment to black neighborhoods, black-owned business and black individuals than do white-owned banks."[119]

Despite the incinerating antipathy toward Jews in Nazi Germany—antipathy far in excess of the alleged racism African-Americans complain of nowadays—Jews remained active in the German economy until the state shipped them off to the ghettos and the death camps. Writes Farron: "Even though collective German public opinion regarded Jewish overrepresentation in the professions as a serious problem, the aggregate German individual preferred employing Jewish lawyers and doctors despite the impediments placed in their way. After her suicide attempt, Eva Braun, the Führer's mistress, was treated by a Jewish doctor."[120] Wallach's famous drapes adorned both the Göring and Hitler abodes. And Nazi party members purchased goods overwhelmingly at Jewish stores.

In Apartheid South Africa, white industrialists—miners especially—"put continual pressure on the South African government to allow them to use more black labor."[121] Afrikaner farmers also chose overwhelmingly to ignore racial job quotas, despite their own racist predilections, and also despite high unemployment among rural Afrikaners. Well before the official dismantling of apartheid laws (carried out, incidentally, by the white minority government), the agricultural sector, skilled and managerial jobs included, came to be dominated by blacks. As was the semi-skilled labor market—clothing, furniture, millinery, sheet metal, construction, mining, baking. Clearly, whites, acting as individuals, chose to subordinate ethnic advancement to optimize their livelihood.

Free market economists (the only kind worth consulting) have long since insisted that the rational, self-interest of individuals in private enterprise is *always* not to discriminate. "The market is color-blind," said Milton Friedman. "No one who goes to the market to buy bread knows or cares whether the wheat was grown by a Jew, Catholic, Protestant, Muslim or atheist; by whites or blacks."[122] As Thomas Sowell put it so well, "prejudice is free, but discrimination has costs."[123] And as expounded by Professor Farron:

> [P]eople demand that their governments restrict the economic and occupational success of specific ethnic or racial groups. However, when the same people act as individuals or business owners, they actively resist and/or circumvent these restrictions. The reason is a fundamental economic principle ... If an individual or business, while engaging in economic activity—hiring, money lending—considers any non-economic factors, the person or business will suffer economically... When individuals buy products or services, few practice discrimination, no matter how desirable they think it is and no matter how eagerly they want their government to enforce it.[124]

Arguably, however, the good economists, while certainly not wholesale liars as are their Keynesian counterparts, are still offering up a half-truth. Rational self-interest does indeed propel people, however prejudiced, to set aside bias and put their scarce resources to the best use. But to state simply that "discrimination is bad for business"[125] is to present an incomplete picture. This solecism stems from the taint the word "discriminate" has acquired. The market, by which we mean the trillions of capitalist acts between consenting adults, is discriminating as in discerning—it is biased toward productivity. Hiring people on the basis of criteria other than productivity hurts the proprietor's pocket. Thus, we can be fairly certain that, *absent affirmative-action laws, the market would reflect a bias toward productivity*. In other words, what the good economists are loath to let on is that a free market is a market in which groups and individuals are differently represented. Parity in prosperity and performance can be achieved only by playing socialist leveler.

In America, a return to the republic of private-property rights, individual freedoms, and radical decentralization is predicated on rejecting infringements on property. This entails not compelling property owners to part with their real estate or rightful revenues in the name of affirmative action. And in turn, this entails recognizing what is flippantly called political correctness for the codified and legalized theft and coercion it really is.

In South Africa, the pool of haves is destined to be drained, or shrink to an unsustainable size. Driving this development is the Marxist-Leninist zero-sum analysis that sees wealth as having been attained at someone else's expense. Propelled as it is by envy, this false and dangerous proposition has brought about the persecution of "ethnic minorities ... which have achieved prosperity from poverty—Jews in Europe, Levantines and Indians in Africa, Chinese in south-east Asia."[126] And now, Europeans in South Africa.

CHAPTER 4

Mandela, Mbeki, and Mugabe Sitting In A Baobab Tree K-I-S-S-I-N-G

> *When we gained power, the country was at the edge of the abyss; since, we have taken a great step forward.*
>
> —Anonymous African government minister

> *Our party must continue to strike fear in the hearts of the white man, our real enemy.**
>
> —Robert Mugabe

THE WEST HAS already abetted the destruction of one other western outpost in Africa: Zimbabwe. Conveniently, the American chattering class has reduced Zimbabwe's collapse to the shenanigans of one man: Robert G. Mugabe.[1] In lengthy policy papers and assorted disquisitions (including a State Department Human Rights Report[2]), politicians and pundits alike have expounded over the years on the tragic tribulations of Zimbabwe. Strong language (and active verbs) are routinely deployed to implicate Mugabe and his Zanu-PF party henchmen for banning

---

* As related in "Zimbabwe's Whites Face Genocide" by Samuel Francis, *Middle America News,* August 2002, p. 23.

political protest, suppressing "freedom of speech, press, assembly, association, and academic freedom,"[3] rigging elections, rounding up and torturing opposition leaders, to say nothing of detaining them without trial, and displacing people in their hundreds of thousands by turning them out of their shanties.

The Marxist Mugabe did all that and more. He instituted a Soviet-style command economy, nationalizing industries, the press included, and turning what was once Africa's breadbasket into its dustbowl. This entailed abolishing private property and distributing the commercial, white-owned farms that fed the country—"employed one-third of the wage earning labor force"[4] and generated all its exports—to rabble, who looted them and then let them fall into disrepair. Like a house of cards, farm-dependent industries soon collapsed. Famine and widespread starvation ensued, making Zimbabwe aid-dependent. Mugabe responded by fixing prices, which caused severe shortages and killed off what little economic activity that still took place in that country. "The population of thirteen million Zimbabweans was ten percent poorer by the end of the 1990s than at the beginning."[5] Because fewer Zimbabweans are now capable of substantial production, the amount of goods in the Zimbabwean economy keeps decreasing. But while the economy contracts, the money supply keeps increasing, as Mugabe continues to print money promiscuously. The result has been hyperinflation which, at the time of writing, stood at a staggering five sextillion percent.[6] The natural laws of economics cannot be suspended by man, but Mugabe is no ordinary mortal. The torqued-up tyrant bolstered his economic planning with the attendant massacres, slaughtering his political opponents, among whom were free traders. Rigging elections was another of Mugabe's pastimes, and still is. Zimbabwe's infrastructure is falling apart. The smell of sewerage hanging over the capital Harare is more than metaphoric—the treatment facilities, like the power grid, are no longer maintained.

The *dirigiste* direction in which Mugabe took Zimbabwe has met with circumscribed condemnation in the West. Commentators have not protested the evils of property confiscation under Mugabe—they did not cavil over the fact that land transactions were not "conducted on a willing-seller willing-buyer basis."[7] Rather, the chattering class in the West fumed that prime, commercial farmland has ended up in the hands of Mugabe's cronies, rather than being "fairly" redistributed to all black Zimbabweans.[8] Similarly, when Mugabe first lunged in the 1990s for land that was not his, Britain, the United States, the World Bank, and the International Monetary Fund had not been terribly exercised. Land grabs *per se* were fine, so long as "fair payment" was offered. The process "lacked transparency," one pointy-head snorted, as though theft—expropriating from Peter in order to lavish on Paul—transparent or clandestine, was ever above board.

At some point in the reams of repudiations and recommendations issued authoritatively about Zimbabwe, American writers will shift mysteriously to the passive voice. Text is layered with oblique references to a Zimbabwe where all was sweetness and light. One is told that once-upon-a-time this helter-skelter of a society used to export food. That not so long ago, life expectancy, now thirty-three years, was sixty years; that in that bygone era, unemployment, now over eighty percent, was extremely low. Veiled vocabulary describes a Zimbabwe that had the "best health care system in Africa," and the highest literacy rates. Mugabe reversed all that, we are told. But who was the Prince among Men who presided over the good times before Zimbabwe's Dantean descent into hell? Chroniclers of Zimbabwe seldom overburden themselves with the inconvenient details.

Enter the phantom Ian Smith, prime minister of Rhodesia, RIP, whose rule brought about economic prosperity that benefited all his compatriots. A native of Rhodesia, Smith became the leader of the former British colony, declaring its independence from Britain in 1965. Smith resisted the tide of black nationalism sweeping Africa and insisted that "there would be no majority rule, 'not in a thousand years,' in Rhodesia. Black Africans, Mr. Smith said, were not ready for self-government."[9] For opposing raw democracy—Smith insisted that the white man had "built [Rhodesia], and intends to keep it"[10]—this Anglo-African was ostracized by the international community, which refused to recognize his minority white rule, and punished Rhodesians with boycotts and sanctions.

To be fair, the U.S.'s policy toward Rhodesia had been slightly more nuanced during the Cold War, given that America equated African majority rule with Marxism. Anticommunist crusader Ronald Reagan pursued a foreign policy of "constructive engagement"[11] with South Africa. For this he was maligned by many an American academic, who more often than not also rooted for the proxies of Cuba and the Soviet Union in the region. U.S. Secretary of State Henry Kissinger promised apartheid-era South Africans to "curb any missionary zeal of my officers in the State Department to harass you,"[12] for which he, in turn, was castigated by Christopher Hitchens.[13] But once Jimmy Carter was elected, Marxism was no longer considered an impediment to mob rule. The U.S. joined the UN, the United Kingdom, and the rest of the international community in a commitment to ensconce Mugabe. Acting in cahoots with the United Nations and, yes, South Africa, the U.S. eventually pressured Smith to concede to majority rule. However, Smith's 1978 power-sharing negotiations with moderate black leaders did nothing to assuage the unholy alliance acting with the international community's acquiescence. The West would not rest until Smith ceded power to Mugabe and his nationalist guerrillas.

The Lancaster House accords paved the way for "the transition from Smith's evil regime to the independent black-run nation of Zimbabwe"[14], writes Keith B. Richburg in his remarkable "journalistic *tour de force*," *Out of America: A Black Man*

Confronts Africa. Remarkable, because, were this *Washington Post* reporter not a black man, he'd be labeled a racist by America's liberal literati. A racist, or a self-hating African, or both. Having experienced Africa, and then daring to describe its horrors in doleful detail, Richburg got down on his knees and thanked God that "his nameless ancestor, brought across the ocean in chains and leg irons,"[15] made it out to America. Remarkable yet, because despite witnessing every atrocity imaginable north of Zimbabwe during his tenure as the paper's Africa bureau chief, Richburg—bystander as thousands of bloated, disemboweled bodies floated down the Kagera River into Lake Victoria from Rwanda; witness as ordinary moms and pops in Nairobi laughed and lopped off the limbs of a petty thief; friend to colleagues "shot, stabbed, beaten to death by mobs"[16]—despite all that, Richburg still held out hope for Zimbabwe in the mid-1990s. By then, Mugabe had been killing to consolidate power for a considerable time.

ONE MAN, ONE VOTE, ONE TIME

Elections across Africa have traditionally followed a familiar pattern: Radical black nationalist movements take power everywhere, then elections cease. One man, one vote, one time. Or, if they take place, they're rigged. When Mugabe was elected leader for life in 1980, he celebrated Britain's vote of confidence by eliminating over 10,000 innocent Ndebele in Matabeleland, with whose leader, Joshua Nkomo, Mugabe refused to share power. Nkomo, who had much the same status then which Morgan Tsvangirai has now, refused to accept the 1980 election results and his supporters, from the Ndebele tribe, retreated to their stronghold of Matabeleland, and launched a low-level campaign of terror"[17] aimed at the still-substantial white population. The Ndebele death toll remains indeterminate because, as Richburg wryly observes, "Zimbabwe had graduated into the ranks of an independent black African country, and one of the criteria for membership in the club is that you stop counting the bodies."[18]

Certainly, members of "Africanist circles abroad"[19] chose to discount the rising body count and the one-party putsch in Zimbabwe. On college campuses across the U.S., Mugabe was a hit, never a hit man; his liberation war was not to be tarnished by the inevitable reality unfolding on the ground. "Peace has come to Zimbabwe, Third World's right on the one," belted singer Stevie Wonder on the 1980 platinum album, "Hotter than July." Youngsters around the U.S. retorted: "Now's the time for celebration', Cause we've only just begun." Naturally, vanity diplomacy was a favored pastime of the West's "Sexy Beast," Mugabe. The revolutionary freedom fighter was spokesperson and cherished idol of the anti-apartheid growth industry abroad. It took decades and piles of dead bodies before Robert Mugabe lost luster in the eyes of the American mainstream media. By the time the megalomaniac Mugabe was knighted by Queen Elizabeth II (1994)—and given honorary doctorates from the Universities of Edinburgh (1984), Massachusetts (1986), and Michigan (1990)—he had already done his "best" work: slaughtering all those innocent Ndebele in Matabeleland (1983). Western conventional wisdom was no wiser. (And the UN responded invariably by … condemning Israel.)

As the dictator Mugabe hangs on to power for dear life, reasonable people are being persuaded by the pulp press that if not for this one megalomaniac, freedom would have flourished in Zimbabwe, as it has, presumably, in Angola, Congo, Congo-Brazzaville, Ethiopia, Eritrea, Liberia, Sierra Leone, Somalia, Sudan, and the rest of strife-torn Africa south of the Sahara. Reasonable people are also expected to infer from popular analysis that once Mugabe is dislodged, dies, or agrees to divvy power, the leader of the Zimbabwean opposition party will not deign to commandeer the state's security forces to subdue his opposition as his predecessor has done. The pundit peanut gallery's latest modish messiah is the aforementioned Morgan Tsvangirai of the Movement for Democratic Change (MDC). Thus, late in 2007, when Mugabe passed a new bill designed to "move majority control of foreign-owned companies operating in the country to black Zimbabweans,"[20] nobody noticed that members of the MDC, the party of Mr. Tsvangirai, protested—but not against state-sanctioned theft. Like its western supporters, the MDC faulted the measure for failing to empower the people sufficiently.[21]

The MDC's rickety political plank promises indubitably what the majority of Zimbabweans want, including "equitable" land reform. A euphemism for land distribution in the Mugabe mold, this concept is anathema to private property rights. The latter are nowhere to be found in the MDC's agenda for Zimbabwe.[22] Conversely, the right to housing, food, education, health care, and enriching employment, *ad infinitum*, makes Zimbabwe's opposition party's platform almost as ambitious as Barack Obama's, down to the Manna From Heaven Healthcare windfall he has implemented. Like the American Democrat, Mr. Tsvangirai is promising Zimbabweans everything they want. Similarly, the leader of the Movement for Democratic Change doesn't seem to understand that his country is bankrupt and that, unlike the mighty U.S.A., Zimbabwe has no line of credit. Or that, as the great American writer Henry Hazlitt put it, "Government has nothing to give to anybody that it doesn't first take from somebody else." Or that there are precious few left in Zimbabwe from whom to take. The shortages and queues, courtesy of communism, exist in Zimbabwe as they did in the Soviet Union. Jokes from *Hammer & Tickle*, a book of black humor under Red rule, are not out of place in Zimbabwe:

> The problem of queues will be solved when we reach full Communism. How come? There will be nothing left to queue up for.[23]

Contrary to convictions in the West, any improvement experienced subsequent to the dethroning of the dictator Mugabe will be due to the West's renewed investment in Zimbabwe and not to the changing of the guard. For even if Mr. Tsvangirai proves no dictator-in-waiting, there is nothing in his political platform to indicate he will not continue to rob Peter to pay Paul until there is nobody left to rob. Entirely absent from Mr. Tsvangirai's "philosophy" is an understanding that only the rule of law and the protection of individual liberties, private property—especially of wealth-creating whites—can begin to reduce the dizzying scale of Zimbabwe's problems. Without these building blocks and bulwarks of prosperity and peace—Zimbabwe cannot be rebuilt.

The seductive narrative about Zimbabwe gets this much right: There is nothing new about "Robert Mugabe's feared militiamen"[24] and their "rampage through Zimbabwe's last productive farms," as they threaten "to drive the country to starvation with a campaign not just to reclaim white-owned land but to destroy the farming system."[25] Still less novel is the meaningless game of musical chairs enacted throughout Africa like clockwork. The Big Man is overthrown; another Alpha Male jockeys his way into his predecessor's position and asserts his primacy over the people and their property. Westerners whooping it up for Tsvangirai are hip to the former, but not to the latter.

Mobutu Sese Seko ruled Zaïre ruthlessly, only to be overthrown by Laurent Kabila. Under Kabila nothing changed except Zaïre's name; it became the Democratic Republic of the Congo. Sandwiched between Nigeria's Strongman Sani Abacha and Olusegun Obasanjo was one more general. Then military rule was abolished and Umaru Yar'Adua elected. Yar'Adua died in May 2010. Ethnic violence continues unabated; instead of extracting oil from the earth, Nigeria's factions quarrel and kill over crude. Kenya's President Mwai Kibaki was opposed by one Raila Odinga. The latter, now Prime Minister, is of the Kalenjin clan; the former of the Kikuyu. Even in one of Africa's success stories it all comes down to tribal rivalries. A coalition was finally formed after Kenyan blood was spilled, and public office is now being scavenged by two thieves and their posses, instead of one. Kenneth Kaunda oversaw the transition from a one-party state to the multi-party Zambia. But once the new Big Man on the block, Frederick Chiluba, was faced with an election, he banned the opposition parties—and Kaunda. In Côte D'Ivoire, stability ended with Félix Houphouët-Boigny's reign, after which a succession of leaders have consolidated power by siccing Christians onto Muslims. While General Yoweri Museveni, president of Uganda, preys—in league with Rwandans—on the Congolese, Joseph Kony, a Ugandan Homie, butchers his compatriots. The reputation of the Janjaweed militia of Sudan precedes it.

The good news now is that Zambians, under their latest leader Rupiah Bwezani Banda, are no longer dying in large numbers through ethnic clashes. The bad news is that they're dying in large numbers from hunger instead. "Even when regimes have changed hands, new governments, whatever promises they made on arrival, have lost little time in adopting the habits of their predecessors,"[26] observes historian Martin Meredith. One can only hope that Zimbabwe's Tsvangirai measures up to Zambia's relatively benign Levy Mwanawasa, Banda's predecessor, who died in 2008.

Of the forty-four countries of sub-Saharan Africa, *The Economist*'s democracy index lists twenty-three as authoritarian and thirteen as hybrids. Only seven, including South Africa, hold *notionally* free elections.[27] In all, Meredith singles out only South Africa and Botswana as well-managed African democracies.[28] Still,

Sideshow Bob Mugabe's epic villainy was, evidently, nothing but a detail of history. An anomaly in the annals of Africa south of the Sahara. There were no lessons to be learned relevant to averting the destruction of another—this time the last—Western outpost in Africa.

Juxtaposing the malevolent Mugabe with his eternally suffering people affords the wags of the West yet another bogus bifurcation: the long-suffering African people vs. their predatory politicians. While ordinarily Africans do seem to be caught eternally between Scylla and Charybdis, the government of Zimbabwe—and others across Africa—doesn't stand apart from the governed; it reflects them. Consider: Early on, Mugabe had attempted to heed "a piece of advice that Mozambiquean president Samora Machel" had given him "well before independence. Machel told him simply, 'Keep your whites.'"[29] Mugabe kept his whites a little longer than he had originally envisaged, thanks to the Lancaster House agreements. These had "imposed a ten-year constitutional constraint on redistributing land. ... But in the early 1990s, with the expiration of the constitutional prohibition, black Zimbabweans became impatient."[30] Despite this, as Richburg notes, "Mugabe remained ambivalent, recognizing, apparently, that despite the popular appeal of land confiscation, the white commercial farmers still constituted the backbone of Zimbabwe's economy."[31] Restless natives would have none of it. Armed with axes and machetes, gangs of so-called war veterans proceeded to fleece farmers and 400,000 of their employees without so much as flinching. In the land invasions of 2000, 50,000 of these squatters "seized more than 500 of the country's 4,500 commercial farms, claiming they [were] taking back land stolen under British colonial rule."[32] They assaulted farmers and their families, writes Meredith, "threatened to kill them and forced many to flee their homes, ransacking their possessions. They set up armed camps and roadblocks, stole tractors, slaughtered cattle, destroyed crops and polluted water supplies."[33]

The "occupation" was extended to private hospitals, hundreds of businesses, foreign embassies, and aid agencies. The looting of white property owners continues apace—even as, in 2009, a power-sharing agreement to divide what remains of Zimbabwe between Mugabe, Tsvangirai, and another nascent player, Arthur Mutambara, was brokered. At the time of writing, another seventy-seven of the country's 400 remaining white-owned commercial farms had been invaded and occupied.[34] A unity government has meant that Mugabe and partner are seizing white-controlled farms in unison.

This may come as news to the doctrinaire democrats who doggedly conflate the will of the people with liberty, but these weapons-wielding "mobs of so-called war veterans" converging on Zimbabwe's remaining productive farms express the democratic aspirations of most black Zimbabweans. And of their South African neighbors, a majority of whom "want the land, cars, houses, and swimming pools of their erstwhile white rulers."[35] Sooner or later," *The Daily Mail*'s Max Hastings has surmised,

> [M]ost African leaders find it expedient to hand over the white men's toys to their own people, without all the bother of explaining that these things should be won through education, skills, enterprise and hard labor over generations.[36]

That's what Mugabe discovered.

In quick succession, Tsvangirai withdrew from Zimbabwe's runoff presidential election and sought shelter at the Dutch embassy. "We can't win; save yourselves" was his message to his supporters. To suppress the results of the latest elections, Mugabe and his blood-besmirched junta continued to do what they do best: kneecap—and when necessary kill—members of the opposition. Across the Limpopo River, Mugabe's pals—first Thabo Mbeki, and then Jacob Zuma—kept their lips zipped. At the time, the former South African president, Mbeki, chaired a special session of the United Nations Security Council, during which he ventured that there was no crisis in Zimbabwe. Western analysts had therefore hastily deduced that Mbeki, who was president of South Africa from 1999 until 2008, was "a sidekick to the man who ruined Zimbabwe."[37] How deeply silly. Whatever one may think of Mbeki, the man led the most powerful country on the continent; Mugabe the least powerful. The better question is: Given the power differential between the two, why would Mbeki, and Mandela before him, succor Mugabe? Was Mandela Mugabe's marionette too? Yet another preposterous proposition.

THE CHE GUEVARA OF AFRICA

A liberal commentariat that hangs its hopes on one Mr. Tsvangirai is not that different from fashionable celebrities in search of a *cause célèbre*, the Che Guevara of Africa. To some extent, Mandela's legend has been nourished—even created—by sentimental Westerners. The measure of the man whom Oprah Winfrey and supermodel Naomi Campbell have taken to calling "*Madiba*"—Mandela's African honorific; Winfrey and Campbell's African affectation—has been determined by the soggy sentimentality of our MTV-coated culture. "*Madiba*'s" TV smile has won out over his political philosophy, founded as it is on energetic income redistribution in the neo-Marxist tradition, on "land reform" in the same tradition, and on ethnic animosity toward the Afrikaner.

Guru and gadfly, sage and showman, Nelson Rolihlahla Mandela is not the focus of this monograph. Boatloads of biographical stuffing can be found in the odes penned to the man. Concentrating on Mandela, moreover, in a narrative about South Africa today would be like focusing on Jimmy Carter in an account of America of 2010. Going against the trend of hagiography as we are, it must be conceded that, notwithstanding

Mandela's agreement with the "racial socialism"[38] currently contributing to the destruction of South Africa, his present role in his country's Zimbabwefication is more symbolic—symbolic such as his belated, tokenistic condemnation of Mugabe to an intellectually meaty crowd of "moody models, desperate divas and priapic ex-Presidents,"[39] who convened to celebrate Nelson's ninetieth. The focus of our attention is, then, not the aging leader but his legacy, the ANC. Or "The Scourge of the ANC,"[40] to quote the title of the polemical essay by Dan Roodt.

The patrician Mandela certainly deserves the sobriquets heaped on him by the distinguished liberal historian Hermann Giliomee: "He had an imposing bearing and a physical presence, together with gravitas and charisma. He also had that rare, intangible quality best described by Seamus Heaney as 'great transmission of grace.'"[41] Undeniably and uniquely, Mandela combined "the style of a tribal chief and that of an instinctive democratic leader, accompanied by old-world courtesy."[42] But there's more to Mandela than meets the proverbial eye.

Cut to the year 1992. The occasion was immortalized on YouTube in 2006.[43] Mandela's fist is clenched in a black power salute. Flanking him are members of the South African Communist Party, African National Congress leaders, and the ANC's terrorist arm, the Umkhonto we Sizwe (MK), which Mandela led. The sweet sounds of the MK anthem mask the ditty's murderous words:

> Go safely mkhonto
> Mkonto we Sizwe
> We the members of the Umkhonto have pledged ourselves to kill them—kill the whites

The catchy chorus is repeated many times and finally sealed with the responsorial, "*Amandla*!" ("Power"); followed by "*Awethu*" ("to the People"). Mandela's genial countenance is at odds with the blood-curdling hymn he is mouthing. The "kill the whites" rallying cry still inspires enthusiasm at funerals and at political gatherings across South Africa, and has been, in practice, a soundtrack for the epic murder campaign currently being waged—however seldom it is acknowledged—against the country's Boers. This is a side of the revered leader the world seldom sees. Or, rather, has chosen to ignore. Indeed, it appears impossible to persuade the charmed circles of the West that their idol (Mandela) had a bloodthirsty side, that his country (South Africa) is far from a political idyll, and that these facts might conceivably be important in assessing him.

Thanks to the foreign press, an elusive aura has always surrounded Mandela. At the time of his capture in 1962 and trial in 1963 for terrorism, he was described as though in possession of Scarlet-Pimpernel-like qualities—materializing and dematerializing mysteriously for his spectacular cameos. The reality of his arrest and capture were, however, decidedly more prosaic. (At the time, the writer's father had briefly sheltered the children of two Jewish fugitives involved with the ANC's operations. The family home was ransacked, and the infant Ilana's mattress shredded by the South African Police.) About the myth of Mandela as a disciplined freedom fighter, the *Pittsburgh Tribune-Review* writes wryly:

> [A]s a newly qualified attorney [Mandela] was known as a big spending ladies' man rather than as a focused political activist. To the horror of his African National Congress (ANC) colleagues, he even fancied becoming a professional boxer, so some of the ANC sighed with relief when he went to jail.[44]

Nor was the ANC very good at terrorism—it certainly had nothing on the ascetic, self-sacrificing Salafis who man al-Qaeda. "Without East European expertise and logistics, not to forget

Swedish money, [the ANC] would never have managed to make and transport a single bomb across the South African border,"[45] avers Roodt. There was certainly precious little that would have dampened Joseph Lelyveld's enthusiasm for "The Struggle." But when the former (aforementioned) *New York Times* editor went looking for his exiled ANC heroes all over Africa, he found nothing but monosyllabic, apathetic, oft-inebriated men whom he desperately tried to rouse with revolutionary rhetoric.

In any event, the sainted Mandela was caught plotting sabotage and conspiring to overthrow the government. "Mandela ... freely admitted at his trial, 'I do not deny that I planned sabotage. I planned it as a result of a calm and sober assessment of the political situation'"[46] Confirms Giliomee: "Under the leadership of Nelson Mandela, the armed wing of the ANC, Umkhonto we Sizwe, embarked on a low-key campaign of sabotage."[47] For that he was incarcerated for life. In 1967, the U.S. had similarly incarcerated the Black Panther's Huey Newton for committing murder and other "revolutionary" acts against "racist" America. The FBI under J. Edgar Hoover proceeded to hunt down his compatriots who were plotting sabotage and assassination. Were they wrong too? The South African government later offered to release Mandela if he foreswore violence. Mandela—heroically, at least as *The New York Times* saw it[48]—refused to do any such thing; so he sat. At the time, the Pentagon had classified the ANC as a terrorist organization. Amnesty International concurred, in a manner; it never recognized Mandela as a prisoner of conscience due to his commitment to violence.[49] In 2002, "ANC member Tokyo Sexwale ..., was refused a visa to the United States as a result of his terrorist past."[50]

Mandela has not always embodied the "great transmission of grace."[51] The man who causes the Clintons, rocker Bono, Barbra Streisand, Richard Branson, and even Queen Beatrix of the Netherlands to fall about themselves, was rather ungracious to

George W. Bush. In 2003, Bush had conferred on Mandela the nation's highest civilian honor, the Medal of Freedom. Mandela greedily accepted the honor, but responded rudely by calling America "a power with a president who has no foresight and cannot think properly," and "is now wanting to plunge the world into a holocaust … If there is a country that has committed unspeakable atrocities in the world, it is the United States of America. They don't care for human beings."[52] If the then eighty-five-year-old Mandela was referring to the invasion of Iraq, he must have forgotten in his dotage that he had invaded Lesotho in 1998.[53] Pot. Kettle. Black.

Rebranding Socialism

History is being extremely kind to "*Madiba*." Since he came to power in 1994, approximately 300,000 people have been murdered.[54] The "Umkhonto we Sizwe" rallying cry is, indubitably, emblematic of the murderous reality that is the democratic South Africa. For having chosen not to implement the ANC's radical agenda from the 1950s, Mandela incurred the contempt of oddball socialist scribes like the Canadian Naomi Klein.[55] Were Ms. Klein—the author of *No Logo: Taking Aim at the Brand Bullies*—more discerning, she'd have credited Mandela for brilliantly rebranding socialism.

His crafty Third-Way politics aside, Mandela has nevertheless remained as committed as his political predecessors to race-based social planning.

> An important element of our policy," he said at the fiftieth ANC Conference, on December 16, 1997, "is the deracialisation of the economy to ensure that … in its ownership and management, this economy increasingly reflects the racial composition of our

> society … The situation cannot be sustained in which the future of humanity is surrendered to the so-called free market, with government denied the right to intervene … The evolution of the capitalist system in our country put on the highest pedestal the promotion of the material interests of the white minority.[56]

Wrong, "Madiba." If anything, capitalism undermined the country's caste system; and capitalists had consistently defied apartheid's race-based laws because of their "material interests." Why, the "biggest industrial upheaval in South Africa's history,"[57] the miner's strike of 1922, erupted because "the Chamber of Mines announced plans to extend the use of black labor. By 1920 the gold mines employed over twenty-one thousand whites … and nearly one hundred and eighty thousand blacks."[58] White miners were vastly more expensive than black miners, and not much more productive.

> One of the mining chiefs, Sir Lionel Phillips, stated flatly that the wages paid to European miners put the economic existence of the mines in jeopardy. … Production costs were rising so the mining houses, entirely English owned and with no great sympathy for their increasingly Afrikaner workforce, proposed to abandon existing agreements with the white unions and open up for black workers…jobs previously reserved for whites.[59]

A small war ensued. Bigotry led to bloodshed and martial law was declared. Although a defining event in the annals of South African labor, the General Strike exemplified the way South African capitalists worked against apartheid to maximize self-interest. Mandela clearly looks at business through the wrong end of a telescope.

Problematic too is Mandela's Orwellian use of the world "deracialisation," when what he was in fact describing and prescribing is racialization—a coerced state of affairs whereby the economy is forced, by hook or by crook, to reflect the country's racial composition. Duly, the father of the Rainbow Nation also fathered the Employment Equity Act.[60] It has seen the ANC assume partial ownership over business. Mandela's comrade-in-arms, the late Joe Slovo, once dilated on the nature of ownership in the New South Africa. In an interview with a liberal newsman, this ANC and Communist Party leader suggested an alternative to nationalization which he dubbed 'socialization.'" With a wink and a nod Slovo explained how the state would—and has since begun to—assume control of the economy "without ownership":

> The state could pass a law to give control without ownership—it can just do it. It can say the state has the right to take the following decisions in Anglo American [the great mining company]. You can have regulations and legislation like that, without ownership.[61]

All of which is under way in South Africa. Mandela, moreover, has provided the intellectual seed-capital for this catastrophic "racial socialism."[62] (And who can forget how, in September of 1991, "Mr. Mandela threatened South African business with nationalization of mines and financial institutions unless business [came] up with an alternative option for the redistribution of wealth"?[63])

If the values that have guided Mandela's governance can be discounted, then it is indeed possible to credit him with facilitating transition without revolution in South Africa. Unlike Mugabe, Mandela did not appoint himself Leader for Life, and has been the only head of state on the Continent to have ceded power voluntarily after a term in office. If not aping Africa's ruling rogues is an achievement, then so be it.

Granted, Mandela has also attempted to mediate peace around Africa. But, "not long after he was released from prison," notes *The New Republic*'s assistant editor James Kirchick, "Mr. Mandela began cavorting with the likes of Fidel Castro ('Long live Comrade Fidel Castro!' he said at a 1991 rally in Havana), Moammar Gaddafi (whom he visited in 1997, greeting the Libyan dictator as 'my brother leader'), and Yasser Arafat ('a comrade in arms')."[64] One has to wonder, though, why Mr. Kirchick feigns surprise at—and feels betrayed by—Mandela's dalliances. Mandela and the ANC had never concealed that they were as tight as thieves with communists and terrorist regimes—Castro, Gaddafi, Arafat, North Korea and Iran's cankered Khameneis. Nevertheless, and at the time, public intellectuals such as Mr. Kirchick thought nothing of delivering South Africa into the hands of professed radical Marxist terrorists. Any one suggesting such folly to the wise Margaret Thatcher risked taking a handbagging. The Iron Lady ventured that grooming the ANC as South Africa's government-in-waiting was tantamount to "living in cloud-cuckoo land."[65]

In *The Afrikaners*, Giliomee also commends Mandela for his insight into Afrikaner nationalism. Mandela, Giliomee contends, considers Afrikaner nationalism "a legitimate indigenous movement, which, like African nationalism, had fought British colonialism."[66] This is not persuasive. Forensic evidence against this romanticized view is still being recovered from the dying Afrikaner body politic. Judging by the ANC-led charge against the country's Afrikaner history and heroes—landmarks and learning institutions—Mandela's keen understanding of the Afrikaner was not transmitted to the political party he created. Of late, local and international establishment press has showered Mr. Mandela with more praise for serving as the mighty Springboks' mascot.

The Springboks are the South African national rugby team, and the reigning world champions. Not that you'd guess it from the film "Invictus," Clint Eastwood's "over-reverent biopic," but

Mandela has never raised his authoritative voice against the ANC's plans to force this traditionally Afrikaner game to become racially representative. Conversely, the absence of pale faces among the "Bafana Bafana," South Africa's equally celebrated national soccer team, has failed to similarly awaken the leader's central planning impulses. Has Mandela piped up about the ANC's unremitting attacks on Afrikaans as the language of instruction in Afrikaner schools and universities? Or about the systematic culling of the white farming community? Has that paragon of virtue, Mandela, called publicly for a stop to these pogroms? Cancelled a birthday bash with "the hollow international jet set"—"ex-presidents, vacuous and egomaniacal politicians, starlets, coke-addled fashion models, intellectually challenged and morally strained musicians"[67]? Called for a day of prayer instead (oops; he's an ex-communist)? No, no, and no again.

Bit by barbaric bit, South Africa is being dismantled by official racial socialism, obscene levels of crime—organized and disorganized—AIDS, corruption, and an accreting kleptocracy. In response, people are "packing for Perth," or as Mandela would say, the "traitors" pack for Perth. The South African Institute of Race Relations (SAIRR) was suitably dismayed to discover that close to one million whites had already left the country; the white population shrank from 5,215,000 in 1995 to 4,374,000 in 2005 (nearly one-fifth of this demographic).[68]

Chief among the reasons cited for the exodus are violent crime and affirmative action.[69] Alas, as the flight from crime gathered steam, the government stopped collecting the necessary emigration statistics.[70] (Correlation is not causation, but ...) The same strategy was initially adopted to combat out-of-control crime: suppress the statistics. The exact numbers are, therefore, unknown. What is known is that most émigrés are skilled white men.[71] Also on record is Mandela's message to them: He has accused whites of betraying him and of being "traitors" and "cowards."[72] Had "*Madiba*" wrestled with these defining issues, perhaps he'd be deserving of the monstrous statues raised in his honor. These too are in the socialist realist aesthetic tradition.

SALUTING THE ALPHA MALE

Back to the original question: Why have the leaders of the most powerful country on the continent (Mandela and Mbeki) succored the leader of the most corrupt (Mugabe)? The luminaries of Western café society were not the only ones to have given Mugabe a pass. So did blacks. "When Mugabe slaughtered 20,000 black people in southern Zimbabwe in 1983," observes columnist Andrew Kenny, "nobody outside Zimbabwe, including the ANC, paid it the slightest attention. Nor did they care when, after 2000, he drove thousands of black farm workers out of their livelihoods and committed countless atrocities against his black population. But when he killed a dozen white farmers and pushed others off their farms, it caused tremendous excitement."[73]

When he socked it to Whitey, Mugabe cemented his status as hero to black activists and their white sycophants in South Africa, the US, and England.

"Whenever there is a South African radio phone-in programme [sic] on Zimbabwe, white South Africans and black Zimbabweans denounce Mugabe, and black South Africans applaud him. Therefore, one theory goes, Mbeki could not afford to criticise [sic] Mugabe,"[74] who is revered, never reviled, by South African blacks.

Left-liberal journalist John Pilger and classical liberal columnist Andrew Kenny concur: bar Zimbabweans, blacks across Africa and beyond have a soft spot for Mugabe. While issuing the obligatory denunciations of the despot, Pilger makes clear that Mugabe is merely a cog in the real "silent war on Africa," waged as it is by bourgeois, neo-colonial businessmen and their brokers in western governments. From his comfy perch in England, this

Hugo Chávez supporter preaches against colonialism and capitalism. Writing in the *Mail & Guardian Online,* Pilger untangled the mystery of Mbeki and Mugabe's cozy relationship: "When Robert Mugabe attended the ceremony to mark Thabo Mbeki's second term as President of South Africa, the black crowd gave Zimbabwe's dictator a standing ovation." This is a "symbolic expression of appreciation for an African leader who, many poor blacks think, has given those greedy whites a long-delayed and just come-uppance."[75]

South Africa's strongmen are saluting their Alpha Male Mugabe by implementing a slow-motion version of his program. One only need look at the present in Zimbabwe "if you want to see the future of South Africa," ventures Kenny.[76] When Mugabe took power in 1980, there were about 300,000 whites in Zimbabwe. Pursuant to the purges conducted by the leader and his people, fewer than 20,000 whites remain. Of these, only 200 are farmers, five percent of the total eight years ago."[77] Although most farmland in South Africa is still owned by whites, the government intends to change the landowner's landscape by 2014. "Having so far acquired land on a 'willing buyer, willing seller' basis, officials have signaled that large-scale expropriations are on the cards."[78]

> In South Africa, the main instrument of transformation is Black Economic Empowerment (BEE). This requires whites to hand over big chunks of the ownership of companies to blacks and to surrender top jobs to them. Almost all the blacks so enriched belong to a small elite connected to the ANC. BEE is already happening to mines, banks and factories. In other words, a peaceful Mugabe-like program is already in progress in South Africa.[79]

Except that it's not so peaceful. South Africans are dying in droves, a reality the affable Mandela, the imperious Mbeki, and their successor Zuma have accepted without piety and pity.

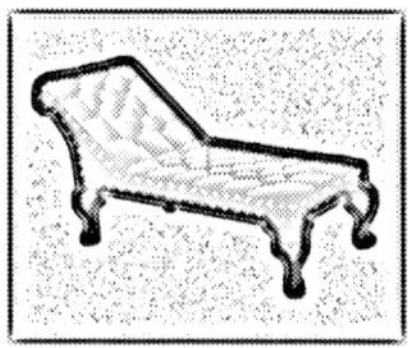

CHAPTER 5

The Root-Causes Racket

The central conservative truth is that it is culture, not politics, that determines the success of a society. The central liberal truth is that politics can change a culture and save it from itself.

—Daniel Patrick Moynihan

Did we ever seriously intend to bring about a democratic dispensation in South Africa, with its checks and balances and accountability? Or was it about settling old colonial scores?

—Breyten Breytenbach

THE IT GIRL of foreign Aid can be quite the village scold. Actress Angelina Jolie was asked by CNN's Anderson Cooper (not quite in these words) why she thought Africans butcher, mutilate, and rape their compatriots with clockwork predictability. Why do grown, Sierra Leonean men hack off the arms of small Sierra Leonean girls and rape them to shreds? Why is this repeated in Uganda, Sudan, the Congo, Rwanda, Somalia—you name them? "We have...we colonized them,"[1] stammered Jolie. She also offered up this tautology: It's "from the violence"—"they had their limbs cut off from the violence." Or if you find that last redundancy meaningless, Jolie whipped another rabbit from her hat: blame "drugs, perhaps."

When discussing crime and culpability (punishment is altogether problematic), the likes of Angelina Jolie prefer the passive voice. In the progressive's universe, crimes are *caused*, not *committed*. Evil actions don't *incriminate*, they *mitigate*. Perps don't *do* a crime, but are *driven* to their deeds by forces beyond their control. Or so the experts tell us. As a popular television ad blares, "Genocide is ravaging Darfur." In truth, Arab gangsters with genocide on their minds—the Janjaweed—are ravaging African Darfurians. (Muslim racial violence gets the same sympathetic treatment from mainstream opinion makers that black African racial violence does.)

Indeed, Angelina was parroting a widely shared misperception. In their capacities as U.N. goodwill ambassadors, or *Time* magazine "Persons of the Year"; in the free access they enjoy to popes and presidents, Brangelina (Jolie plus Brad Pitt), Bono, and their enablers in the media (such as the aforementioned Anderson *Vanderbilt* Cooper) are dictating the cultural and political script *vis-à-vis* Africa. To cite columnist Peggy Noonan: "These people have read an article and now want to tell us the truth, if we can handle it." According to these self-styled social reformers, underdevelopment and poverty; perennial genocides, and spiraling crime—these are indirectly our doing. Or so the sanctimonious stars claim when they let down their guard. When it comes to development aid, we're stingy and indifferent. If *colonialism* was our original sin; *capitalism* is our cardinal sin. Our voracious system of production is a zero-sum game. To wit, the standards of living we enjoy come at the expense of Africa's poor. Or so these professional do-gooders will typically claim. In short, the West is responsible for African misdeeds and misadventures.

The paradox at the heart of the root-causes fraud is that causal explanations are invoked only after *bad deeds* have been committed or failure is a *fait accompli*. *Good deeds* and success have no need of mitigating circumstances. Confronted with people who perpetrate evil and live chaotic lives, lefties will toss free will to the wind. They acknowledge human agency only if and when adaptive actions are involved. (And even then only half-heartedly, as left-liberals are forever exalting man's basest instincts and debasing his most exalted. Trust a liberal to see God in cop killer Mumia Abu-Jamal and the devil in the Pope.)

American pseudo-intellectuals—that generally means the tele-experts—have been tireless in developing the "science" of excuse-making, where misbehavior is medicalized or politicized and aggression seen, invariably, as a symptom of oppression (for which the putative oppressor should be blamed). Their exculpatory idiom in the case of the common criminal is "Daddy didn't love me." In the case of the Jihadist *du jour* it's "America loves Israel more than me." And the Boer killer is a "victim" of apartheid.

Placing bad behavior beyond the strictures of traditional morality makes it amenable to "therapeutic" or state interventions; pharmacology or foreign aid, take your pick. In the case of South African criminals, *Time* magazine exemplifies the root-causes reasoning, having asserted, in a 2004 article, that unless a successful handover takes place in South Africa, crime will persist.[2] By *Time*'s reasoning, crime is caused by *deprivation* and not *depravity*. Therefore, accelerating race-based wealth distribution will remove the reasons for crime.

Here we arrive at the crux of the transformation underway in South Africa. "Even assuming that…improvements were possible under conditions of hard-core affirmative action, it must be admitted that criminal justice treats the symptom and not the cause of social violence."[3] Better policing, more efficient courts and more secure prisons—these are valiant but vain efforts. Violent crime cannot be easily curtailed, not now that an entirely different set of values and norms has permeated South African institutions and society at large. The point can be illustrated by way of an American example:

During the neoconservative-dominated Bush administration, Americans were lectured that the democratic impulse was universal and a democratic heart throbbed in every thorax. With enough "persuasion" (and a little shock and awe), Afghani and Iraqi alike could be fashioned into global democrats, citizens of the world. Struck by historical and philosophical Alzheimer's, leaders like Condoleezza Rice took to comparing the carnage in Iraq to the constitutional cramps of early America. This unlikely comparison was made by those who take for granted, or don't know, their own philosophical heritage, and are ignorant of the history of others. Then as now, there exists no philosophical connection between the feuding Mohammedans (Iraqis) and the heirs to Baron de Montesquieu's classical liberalism (early Americans). Faction fighting in Iraq is as old as the sand dunes, and tyrants as constant as the Tigris. Similarly, the new dispensation emerging in South Africa has very little to do with the birth pangs of a fledgling Western democracy, and a great deal in common with age-old enmities seen elsewhere in Africa.

Western civilization, and the legal philosophy of liberalism that evolved within it, may be defined in terms of the continuous development—revived in western Europe, circa A.D. 700—of certain distinctive institutions, beliefs and values, including "certain ideas concerning the nature of reality and of man,"[4] to borrow from James Burnham. These ancient traditions cannot easily be grafted onto other cultures. Where they have taken root, it seems to have been the result of *colonization* and imperialism more than *emulation*.

The ideas of human rights—the dignity of the individual and the respect for diversity—are distinctly Western, an outgrowth of the Enlightenment. "European mores are unavoidably the basis of modern life."[5] If not for Africa's bumptious encounter with the West, these concepts would still be as alien there as the jejune

Jolie (who claims "she has found her place among these people in need," but face it; even if Jolie chose to relocate to a mud hut, wear grass skirts, and carry groceries on her head, she'd still be immune to every cruel contingency plaguing Africans). The same goes for the ever-endangered democratic institutions which the West has planted in that continent's blood-soaked soil. The fate of South Africa and Iraq gives rise to the depressing thought that perhaps liberal civilization has spread about as far as it's going to do in the foreseeable future.

THE COLONIALISM CANARD

"Pseudo-scholars such as Edward Said and legions of liberal intellectuals have made careers out of blaming the West for problems that were endemic to many societies both before and after their experiences as European colonies,"[6] observed Australian historian Keith Windschuttle.

The truth is that colonization constituted the least tumultuous period in African history. This is fact; its enunciation is not to condone colonialism or similar, undeniably coercive forays, only to venture, as did George Eliot in *Daniel Deronda*, that "to object to colonization absolutely is to object to history itself. To ask whether colonization in itself is a good or bad is the same as asking whether history is a good or bad thing[7]

"The decolonization process" in Africa "was substantially completed by the end of the 1960s," attests Lawrence E. Harrison, in *Culture Matters: How Values Shape Human Progress*. Yet half of the more than 600 million people south of the Sahara live in poverty. In at least eighteen countries life expectancy is below fifty years, and half or more of women are illiterate. In at least thirteen countries, half or more of the adult population is illiterate.[8] Since the colonial powers decamped, economic conditions have declined across the Dark Continent. Democratic institutions have been slow or have failed to emerge.[9]

Four decades since decolonization, colonialism, dependency and racism no longer cut it as explanations for Africa's persistent and pervasive underdevelopment. These highly politicized, Marxist-Leninist constructs describe underdeveloped nations as having been "bilked by rich capitalist countries."[10] According to these socialist, zero-sum formulations, one person's plenty is another's poverty. The corresponding antidote invariably involves taking from one and giving to the other—from rich to poor; from North to South. The notion, however, of a preexisting income pie from which the greedy appropriate an unfair share is itself pie-in-the-sky. Wealth, earned or "unearned," as egalitarians term inheritance, doesn't exist outside the individuals who create it; it is a return for desirable services, skills and resources they render to others. Labor productivity is the main determinant of wages—and wealth. People in the West produce what they consume—and much more; they don't remove, or steal it from Third Worlders. Wrote seminal development economist, the late Lord Peter Bauer: "Incomes, including those of the relatively prosperous or the owners of property, are not taken from other people. Normally they are produced by their recipient and the resources they own."[11]

The concept of a wealth gap is an extension of the politically contrived construct of exploitation—rich of poor, North of South. Politicians are perpetually promising to do their level best to level the playing field. However, David Dollar and Aart Kraay, authors of a study titled *Growth Is Good for the Poor*, offer evidence that when average incomes rise, the average income of the poorest fifth of society rise proportionately. Their study spanned four decades, used a sample of ninety two countries, and yielded results that hold across regions, periods, income levels and growth rates.[12] Just as there is no such thing as a preexisting income pie, the same is true for economic growth—it is not static. Nor is it confined to those who generate it. Rather, economic growth redounds to all.

The colonialism humbug, unhelpful in explaining and hence helping the Third World, was once "conventional wisdom that brooked no dissent." Now, promised Harrison, it is rarely mentioned in intellectually respectable quarters. "For many, including some Africans, the statute of limitation on colonialism as an explanation for underdevelopment lapsed long ago," he notes. "Moreover, four former colonies, two British (Hong Kong and Singapore) and two Japanese (South Korea and Taiwan) have vaulted into the First World."[13]

A former USAID official,"[14] now at Harvard, Harrison, author of *Underdevelopment is a State of Mind*, knows what he is talking about: "Over the years, the development assistance institutions have promoted an assortment of solutions," from land reform, to sustainable, and culturally sensitive, development. Billions of dollars later, "rapid growth, democracy and social justice" remain rare in Africa.[15]

Another process that has eluded Africa is detribalization.

The beginning of the English nation began with Anglo-Saxon colonizers who massacred the Britons, recounts historian Kenneth M. Newton. "The descendants of these Anglo-Saxons went on to colonize America, replacing the 'Red Indians.'" "The "bloody nature of the various colonizations in the past" notwithstanding, in the case of England, what emerged was "a distinct identity for a people descended from diverse ethnic groups that had previously tended to slaughter each other."[16] That nation produced Shakespeare, Newton, and George Eliot. The American founding fathers were sired and philosophically inspired by the same Saxon forefathers—and the ancient rights guaranteed by the Saxon constitution. They went on to forge a constitution that transcended their tribe.[17] Would that Africans were, at least, more economically interconnected; if that ever happened, they'd be less likely to keep cannibalizing one another as they do. But tribe burrows deep in Africa's marrow and infects its lymphatic system.

Africa BC/AC (Before and After Colonialism)

From their plush apartments, over groaning dinner tables, pseudo-intellectuals have the luxury of depicting squalor and sickness as idyllic, primordially peaceful and harmonious. After all, when the affluent relinquish their earthly possessions to return to the simple life, it is always with aid of sophisticated technology and the option to be air-lifted to a hospital if the need arises. (By the looks of it, "climageddon" has not restricted Al Gore's fluids and food intake.) Is there any wonder, then, that "the stereotype of colonial history" has been perpetuated by the relatively well-to-do intellectual elite? Theories of exploitation, Marxism for one, originated with Western intellectuals, not with African peasants. It is this clique alone that could afford to pile myth on myth about a system that had benefited ordinary people.[18]

What is meant by "benefited"? Naturally, the premise taken here is that development is desirable and material progress good. British colonists in Africa reduced the state of squalor, disease and death associated with lack of development. To the extent that this is condemned, the Rousseauist myth of the noble, happy savage is condoned. Granted, Africa's poor did not elect to have these conditions, good and bad, foisted on them. However, once introduced to potable water, sanitation, transportation, and primary healthcare, few Africans wish to do without them. Fewer Africans still would wish to return to Native Customary Law once introduced to the idea that their lives were no longer the property of the Supreme Chief to do with as he pleased.[19] It "is an absurdity to assert that cannibalism, slavery, magical therapy, and killing the aged should be accorded the same 'dignity' or 'validity' as old-age security, scientific medicine, and metal artifacts," notes anthropologist George Peter. "All people prefer Western technology and would rather be able to feed their children and elderly than kill them."[20] And the West largely eliminated "many of the worst endemic and epidemic diseases in West Africa."[21] Ask Moeletsi Mbeki, the brother of South Africa's former president Thabo Mbeki. He has said that "the average African is poorer [today] than during the age of colonialism."

Even so—and whether they stay or go—the blame for all the ills of this backward and benighted region falls on Westerners. One dreadfully off-course notion has it that the colonial powers plundered Africa and failed to plow back profits into the place. This manifest absurdity is belied by the major agricultural, mineral, commercial and industrial installations throughout the continent. The infrastructure in Africa was built by the colonial powers. Far from draining wealth from less developed countries," as Bauer richly documented, "British industry helped to create it there."[22]

Another widely canvassed, equally implausible, accusation is that the West, which was streaks ahead of sub-Saharan Africa and Southeast Asia well before colonization, got rich on the backs of poor nations. How then do we explain the fact that the Scandinavian countries, Switzerland and Australia have achieved some of the world's highest living standards? After all, none of these nations had any colonies (except Australia, which after World War I acquired sovereignty over the former German territory consisting of what is now Papua New Guinea). They were rich without any meaningful ties to the undeveloped world. The wealthiest and most advanced countries were themselves colonies once: North America and Australia. As Bauer conclusively proved, the West's human resources, and not any exploitation of the backward world, account for its innovation and achievements. The West is what it is due to human capital—people of superior ideas and abilities, capable of innovation, exploration, science, philosophy. Human action is the ultimate adjudicator of a human being's worth; the aggregate action of many human beings acting in concert makes or breaks a society. Overall, American society is superior to assorted African societies because America is inhabited by the kind of individuals who make possible a thriving civil society.

Much less is it legitimate to claim that contact with entrepreneurial Europeans and Asians has enervated Africa. Regions that have had the greatest commercial contact with the West are far and away more developed than regions that had little such contact. Compare the people of West Africa, parts of East and Southern Africa, and the inhabitants of Africa's ports, with desert and rainforest dwellers like the Bushmen and pigmies. Or with never-colonized Liberia, Afghanistan, Tibet and Nepal.

We can't lay the blame for Africa's tragedy on the much-deplored exploitation of natural resources either. Most natural resources are useless lumps of nothing. Without the ingenuity of men—Briton or Bantu—iron, aluminum, coal and oil would lie purposeless and pristine in the wildernesses, and the matter and energy abundant on earth would come to naught. Such a state of affairs describes pre-colonial Africa, to which the colonial powers introduced the wheel and wheeled transport.

"Much of British colonial Africa was transformed during the colonial period," writes Bauer, in *Equality, the Third World, and Economic Delusion*:

> In the Gold coast there were about 3000 children at school in the early 1900s, whereas in the mid-1950s there were over half a million. In the early 1890s there were in the Gold Coast no railways or roads, but only a few jungle paths. Transport of goods was by human porterage or canoe.[23]

Before colonialism, sub-Saharan Africa was a subsistence economy; because of colonialism it became a monetized economy.

Before colonialism, there were only bush back roads through which men trekked with goods on their backs. During colonialism roads were built. In pre-colonial times the absence of public security made investment in Africa too risky. Post-colonialism, investment flowed. With the colonial administrations came scientific agriculture, introduced by the colonists and by "foreign private organizations and persons under the comparative security of colonial rule, and usually in the face of formidable obstacles."[24]

> 'In British West Africa public security and health improved out of all recognition ... peaceful travel became possible; slavery and slave trading and famine were practically eliminated, and the incidence of the worst diseases reduced.' Mortality fell, population increased, communications and 'peaceful contact within Africa and with the outside world' increased in British colonies.[25]

As uneven and problematic as progress often was, "everywhere in Black Africa modern economic life began with the colonial period."[26] "Economic modernity could not have been effected without a mediated imperial structure,"[27] maintains Niall Ferguson. In Africa, colonial governments encountered "conditions unfavorable to material progress,"[28] to wit, civil and tribal war and slavery. By establishing the rule of law, protecting private property and enforcing contractual relations, building infrastructure, and organizing "basic health services," and introducing modern financial and legal institutions—the colonial powers enhanced, rather than hindered, progress. Although—or perhaps because—all these advancements interfered with traditional customs, they also advanced the continent materially.

Clearly, political independence doesn't go hand-in-glove with material progress. But grievance-based explanations have a way of evolving. Before independence, Africa's backwardness was attributed to colonialism. After independence, neocolonialism replaced colonialism as the excuse *du jour* for the failure of African leaders to ameliorate their people's plight. Neocolonialism encompasses any unhappy condition that can no longer be attributed to colonialism. Pizza Hut opening an outlet in Lima can easily be framed as the modern equivalent of Pizarro descending on the Incas, to paraphrase Henri Astier.[29]

On rare occasions the interests of an African politician and his people will converge. On one such occasion, and in desperation, the president of Sierra Leone, Ahmad Tejan Kabbah, where life expectancy is now just thirty-seven years, "asked a visiting British politician, in the presence of journalists, if it might be possible for his country to become part of the British Empire again."[30]

From Bauer to Belich

The dominant historical prism through which the Anglo-Americanization of the world in the nineteenth and twentieth centuries has been described is "imperialism," with its connotations of power and domination and exploitation of the periphery by the center.[31] In *Replenishing the Earth: The settler revolution and the rise of the Anglo-world,* James Belich (of Victoria University, Wellington, New Zealand) offers a countervailing paradigm. The "migration of British [and northern European] people over the globe, including North America," Australia, New Zealand, and South Africa—was not expressly to dominate. "Rather, the aim was to reproduce British-type 'free' societies, usually freer than Britain's own, in what were conveniently regarded as the 'waste' places of the earth."[32]

Belich's achievement is to "uncouple" "settlerism" from "imperialism," and show that the first "was a far more important influence than what is generally understood as imperialism on the whole course of modern history."[33] *Replenishing the Earth,* says its author, posits "a resonant interaction between the American, French, and Industrial Revolutions and an underestimated 'Settler Revolution.' The Settler Revolution, it is argued, was itself a synergy between ideological and (initially non-industrial) technological shifts."[34]

Anglophone elephantiasis, Anglophone divergence; propensity to giganticism: this is the kind of expansive language which the New Zealand scholar uses to describe the Anglophone expansion across continents. Belich's depiction of the Settler Revolution in all its dynamism makes for a pleasant change. From my vantage point, it is perfectly true that, at least in its Anglo form, the process brought about crimes. The horrors of British concentration camps during the Boer War have already been mentioned in this book. And there is little enough to be said in extenuation of Britain's Zulu Wars, which may be summarized in an extract from the once-famous 1930 historiographical parody *1066 And All That*: "War Against Zulus. Cause: the Zulus. Zulus exterminated. Peace with Zulus."[35]

Besides, the difference between Anglo and Dutch attitudes to South African settlement is something Belich fails to emphasize nearly enough. The Dutch genuinely thought of themselves as locals, rather than as Europeans who just happened to have taken up living in South Africa. Still, Belich's enthusiasm for a population movement *from* the West certainly clashes with the contemporary reverence for immigration *into* the West, which is a thematic imperative in the writings of Belich's progressive contemporaries. As I see it, post-colonialism affords the West the opportunity to redraw the frontiers at its own borders—if it has the will to do so.

Slavery: The White Man's Cross

Also attributable to Europeans is the demise of the slave trade in Africa. In *The Slave Trade*, historian Jeremy Black highlights the "leading role Britain played in the abolition of slavery [as]... an example of an ethical foreign policy."[36] Britain agonized over this repugnant institution, failed to reconcile it with the Christian faith, and consequently abolished it. Professor Black condemns the exclusive focus on the Atlantic slave trade to the exclusion of the robust slave trade conducted by Arabs across the Sahara Desert. Or across the Indian Ocean and the Red Sea to markets in the Middle East. This focus, however, "fits with the narrative of Western exploitation."[37]

Bauer bolsters Black's point: "The slave trade between Africa and the Middle East antedated the Atlantic slave trade by centuries, and far outlasted it."[38] "Tens of millions of Africans were carried away—north through the Sahara, and from East Africa, by Arab and Muslim slave traders, well before Europeans took up the trade from West Africa."[39] Arab affinity with slavery, ethnic prejudice and purges lives on in the 2000s, in the treatment of blacks in Darfur. Considering Europeans were not alone in the slave trade, Black also queries "the commonplace identification of slavery with racism," given that, like serfdom, slavery was a device (an inefficient one) "to ensure labor availability and control."[40] At its most savage, child slavery still thrives in Haiti in the form of the "Restavec system." Children are kept in grinding poverty and worked to the bone. In the West this would be considered perverse in the extreme; in Haiti owning a Restavec is a status symbol.

Even less is said in scholarly circles or by media about the vibrant, indigenous slave trade conducted well into the nineteenth century in the interior of West Africa.[41] This savagery owed a lot to the rivalries and relationships between Africans powers.[42] "Both Arabs and Europeans worked in collaboration with native polities that provided the slaves through raids and war carried out against their neighbors."[43]

For the Atlantic slave trade, contemporary Americans and Britons have been expiating at every opportunity. But more than engendering a cult of apology, the Atlantic slave trade has been instrumental in the effort to control and define the past as an "aspect of current politics,"[44] not least in shaping the historical treatment of the Civil War, the South, and the Founding Fathers. Jeremy Black shuns ritual apologies as empty ploys, which "all too often conform to fatuous arguments about 'closure,' resolution, and being unable to move on until we acknowledge the past." In reality, they entail the opposite of all these, and, instead, involve the reiteration of grievance."[45] Grievance is leveled at a collective for infractions it did not commit: Africans who were not enslaved are seen as having an ineffable claim against Europeans who did not enslave them.

The cult of apology that has gripped America and Britain is, nevertheless, uniquely Western. What other people would agonize over events they had no part in, personally, for damages they did not inflict?

At its core, the argument against racism is an argument against collectivism: avoid judging an entire people based on the color of their epidermis. Why then is it acceptable to blame another people based on the lack of pigment in their skin?

Aiding and Abetting Underdevelopment

Angelina Jolie has some nerve. The actress complained in a *Refugees* op-ed (this magazine is a publication of the U.N. High Commissioner for Refugees), that it was "a scandal, really, in such a rich world, that we are not even finding a way to help feed refugee families properly."[46] While the actress crowed, the Bush administration proudly committed seventy cents out of every one hundred dollars earned by Americans to corrupt Third-World coffers. In the approving estimation of *New York Times* columnist Nicholas D. Kristof, Bush spent "three times as much on aid to Africa as the lowest figure during the Clinton years."[47] American conservatives no longer have choice words for foreign aid. It used to be "money down a rathole" (the late Senator Jesse Helms), and amounted to "putting Ghana over Grandma" (Tom DeLay, former Republican leader in the House of Representatives). While not nearly as principled as the late Lord Peter Bauer's opposition to "taxpayer's money compulsorily collected…outside the area of volition and choice"[48]—these quips nevertheless reflect bygone, conservative attitudes toward aid.

Ample Western funding aside, even Kristof, an evangelist for foreign aid, has written of clinics, donated and equipped by the West, standing empty. "Go on to the market," he laments, "and there you may see the clinic's stock of medicines for sale." Stolen! "Bridges built with foreign aid over streams" are so poorly constructed that the result is "erosion on both banks." "In Ethiopia, you greet parents cradling hungry babies and explaining that they have no food because their land is parched and their crops are dying. And two hundred feet away is a lake, but there is no tradition of irrigating land with the lake water, and no bucket; and anyway the men explain that carrying water is women's work."[49]

In the cited essay, "Aid: Can It Work?", a frustrated Kristof has detailed many a failed effort to convince Southern Africans, for example, "to grow sorghum rather than corn, because it is hardier and more nutritious." But because it has been given "out as a relief food to the poor… sorghum [has] become stigmatized as the poor man's food, and no one wants to have anything to do with it." Hand out infant formula to HIV-infected women so that they don't transmit the virus to their babies via breast milk, and the women will dump it before they reach home: "Any woman feeding her baby formula, rather than nursing directly, is presumed to have tested positive for HIV, and no woman wants that stigma. In the heart of poverty-stricken Congo," complains Kristof, "wrenching malnutrition exists side by side with brothels, beer joints, and cigarette stands." The men splurging in these fleshpots cannot be persuaded to put their income toward their flesh-and-blood.

Kristof and his ilk struggle with this reality because they're unprepared to accept that people differ in economic aptitude and in the values they hold. Thus, where there are vast differences, Kristof and company construct vaster injustices.

As argued by Bauer, "You couldn't force a country to grow economically by just injecting money" (in Peter Brimelow's rendition). "There had to be the right incentives and institutions."[50] Injected monies notwithstanding, since decolonization, Africa's share of world exports has declined by two-thirds.[51] Although rich in natural resources, Africa's people remain impoverished. Africans have failed to adopt the institutions of capitalism. Their governments are growing by the day, many industries remain nationalized, taxes are prohibitive, regulation rampant, and price controls a cause of ubiquitous shortages. Private property rights, the cornerstone of prosperity, are precarious, at best. The World Bank concurs: The high costs of trade on the Dark Continent constitute the main barrier to trade liberalization—from transport and transit to customs procedures; the trade-related business climate is abysmal.[52]

As a government-to-government transfer, foreign aid is directly responsible for enriching Africa's political class at the expense of the productive private sector. The wanton purchases Third-World plutocrats are known to make with aid monies are properly described as "the three M's of development aid: monuments [in the dictator's likeness], Mercedes and machine guns."[53] Understand: Governments do not create wealth; they only consume or spread it. A "visionary" bureaucrat is invariably a voracious one; and the grander the government, the poorer and less free the people. Helping to grow governments abroad, as the West does, reduces capital available to their people; an increase in the number of mandarins, managing the foreign aid apparatus, will invariably come at the cost of real, sustainable, consumer-driven jobs in the private economy. As the size of the African governments (and their Zurich bank accounts) increases courtesy of the West's bureaucracy-accreting schemes, the growth of real GDP will decrease. The extent to which government growth as a share of GDP coincides with a decline in GDP growth was quantified by economists James Gwartney, Randall Holcombe, and Robert Lawson, in a paper entitled "The Scope of Government and The Wealth of Nations." To be precise: "A ten percent increase in government expenditure as a share of GDP results in a one percent point reduction in GDP growth."[54] A drop of one percentage point might not sound all that much, but it's a decline that Africa can ill afford.

While the West lavishes welfare liberally on undeveloped countries, it is illiberal in its trade practices toward them. The developed world imposes high tariffs on goods imported from developing countries. Also, it institutes quotas and antidumping penalties to curb the selling of products below market prices. Equally harmful are calls from Western busybodies to impose sanctions on developing countries for not adhering to requisite labor and environmental standards.

The least the West can do for Africa is to avoid foisting democracy on it, or funneling aid to it. The best the West can do for Africa is to liberalize trade with it: to quit the protectionist practices, and the patronizing demands for homogenization of labor, patent and environmental laws.

Other than the conduct of African governments themselves, the most proper object of scrutiny in the question of Africa's underdevelopment is the "expulsion and slaughter of productive minorities."[55] This has been a factor in Zimbabwe's demise and in South Africa's increasing economic insecurity. In both countries, life for the productive European minority is perilous. Although Bono, Brangelina and other benefactors of Africa are not in the habit of expressing compassion for groups that are persecuted for their agency and self-sufficiency, they really ought to try and understand this small thing: strangle the geese producing golden eggs, and economic conditions will worsen for their protégés, the poor.

More than anything, Africans need to develop great institutions—the institutions of private property and the rule of law, freedom of expression and worship. Without those advantages, their plight will only worsen.

CULTURE COUNTS

Let's turn, by comparison, to our own country. Underachievement among Afro-Americans might have been understandable in light of segregation, and slavery before that, but the "racism" and "discrimination" explanations are no longer viable fifty years later. Hispanics have outperformed blacks in underachievement, yet have endured less discrimination—and "no more so than the overachieving Chinese and Japanese immigrants."[56]

With racism, discrimination, and colonialism no longer credible causal factors in divining underdevelopment and delinquency, an "explanatory vacuum" has opened up among academics, and is being filled with reference to culture. In other words, to the "values, attitudes, beliefs, orientations, and underlying assumptions prevalent among people in a society."[57] Yet such a reference often comes at a cost. For example, the black establishment is angered by black scholars like the Manhattan Institute's John McWhorter, who argues that "the problem has a cultural dimension and that academic achievement is simply not emphasized in the black community to the extent that it is among whites and Asians."[58]

The idea that culture is benign and harmonious if not disrupted is a delusion, argues anthropologist Robert B. Edgerton,[59] who also believes that in Africa, "traditional cultural values are at the root of poverty, authoritarianism, and injustice."[60] By taking account of culture, posits David Landes, a Harvard economic historian, and author of *The Wealth and Poverty of Nations*, one could have foreseen the postwar economic success of Japan and Germany. The same is true of South Korea (versus Turkey), and Indonesia (versus Nigeria).[61]

Not for nothing did Alexis de Tocqueville conclude "that what made the American political system work was a culture congenial to democracy."[62] A lesser luminary, Lawrence E. Harrison, has isolated some salient factors that distinguish development-prone from development-resistant cultures.

Progressive cultures emphasize the future; view work as a blessing rather than as a burden; promote individuals based on their merit; value education and frugality, are philanthropic, identify with universal causes, and have higher ethics. In static cultures individuals tend to be fatalistic rather than future-oriented; live for the present or past; work only because they need to do so; diminish or dismiss the value of education, frugality, and philanthropy; are often mired in nepotism and corruption; and promote individuals based on clan and connections, rather than capabilities.[63]

"I am because we are" is how one wag encapsulated the cog-like role of the individual in African culture. I would add that in progressive cultures, the individual, and not the collective, is paramount.

Voodoo for Values

Easily the most controversial thinker on the causes of underdevelopment in Africa is one who has been briefly mentioned earlier in these pages: Cameroonian Daniel Etounga-Manguelle. In 1999, he attended a symposium on "Cultural Values and Human Progress" at Harvard. He had come to bury and not praise the cultures of the Continent. In a paper titled *Does Africa Need a Cultural Adjustment Program?*, Etounga-Manguelle quipped controversially that "The African works to live but does not live to work."[64] Another of his off-the-cuff remarks: "African societies are like a football team in which, as a result of personal rivalries and a lack of team spirit, one player will not pass the ball to another out of fear that the latter might score a goal."[65] Etounga-Manguelle was referring to what he perceives to be the culture of envy—the kind of all-consuming envy that, in the Rwanda of 1994, caused certain Africans (Hutus) to attempt to kill off other, frequently more industrious, better-looking brethren (Tutsis), and that makes it hard for Africa as a whole to rejoice in the success of its exceptional sons and daughters.

A former member of the World Bank's Council of African Advisors, Etounga-Manguelle observes that in Africa, "divination and witchcraft"[66] are integral parts of all aspects of state and civil society among all segments of society. Africans do not believe control over uncertainty is achievable through planning for the future and mastering nature; through reason, the rule of law, or technology. Rather, being by and large fatalistic and superstitious, they all too often resort to magical thinking to cope. The plight of witch children across Africa comports with Etounga-Manguelle's paradigm. These children are blamed for every pestilence to plague the community.[67] Zimbabwean tribal chiefs saddle angry ancestors in need of appeasement for everything from famine to inflation. The solution to the first "supernatural force" is to brutalize the bewitchers. To resolve the second, beer is brewed, drums are beaten and beasts slaughtered.[68]

Africans inhabit hierarchical societies in which "strength prevails over law," and where "the best way to change a social system is to overthrow those who hold power."[69] The paucity of planning and future preparation in African life Etounga-Manguelle puts down to a suspended sense of time. The reverence for the "strongman of the moment" he roots in the sincerely held belief that these men harbor magical powers. Magic wins out over reason; community over individual; communal ownership over private property; force and coercion over rights and responsibilities; wealth distribution over its accumulation.

African totalitarianism was not born with independence, warns Etounga-Manguelle, who counsels the need for a mind-freeing, "cultural adjustment program" for Africa. Such a cultural adjustment program lacks the Compassion Chic that marks the present system for subsidizing dictatorial kleptomaniacs—in Bono and Brangelina it would not inspire the slightest enthusiasm—but Etounga-Manguelle knows whereof he speaks. When he talks of better values and freer minds, he deserves our attention, even if not necessarily our agreement.

Human behavior is, indubitably, mediated by values. Nevertheless, the cultural argument affords a circular, rather than a causal, elegance: people do the things they do because they are who they are and have a history of being that way. But what precisely accounts for the unequal "civilizing potential,"[70] as James Burnham called it, that groups display? Why have some people produced Confucian and Anglo-Protestant ethics—with their mutual emphasis on graft and delayed gratification—while others have midwived Islamic and animistic values, emphasizing conformity, consensus, and control? Why have certain patterns of thought and action come to typify certain people in the first place? Such an investigation, however, is *verboten*—a state-of-affairs Harvard sociologist Orlando Patterson blames on "a prevailing rigid orthodoxy," which is the preferred academic phrase for political correctness:

> Culture is a symbolic system to be interpreted, understood, discussed, delineated, respected, and celebrated as the distinct product of a particular group of people, of equal worth with all other such products. But it should never be used to explain anything about the people who produced it.[71]

Be it Africa or Arabia, liberals labor under the romantic delusion that the effects of millennia of development-resistant, self-defeating, fatalistic, atavistic, superstition-infused, unfathomably cruel cultures can be cured by an infusion of foreign aid, and by the removal of tyrants such as Robert Mugabe and the Palestinian Hamas leader Ismail Haniya. Bad leaders are not what shackle backward peoples. Not exclusively, at least. Africa's plight is most certainly not the West's fault. Rather, Africa is a culmination of the failure of the people to develop the attitudes and institutions[72] favorable to peace and progress.

HOW THE SETTLERS SAVED SOUTH AFRICA

Much as Americans are taught to react to the sins of slavery and Jim Crow, white South Africans treat apartheid as Sisyphus his rock: a burden that defines them. Forgotten in the recriminations over that contemptible caste system is the irony to which leading Africanists have called attention: "[T]he consolidation of a democracy was more likely in the 'settler' societies of Africa, where there was a tradition of electoral competition, than in neopatrimonial regimes like Zaïre or Rwanda where competition was outlawed."

What do you know?

"[T]he existence of a democracy for whites, which for so long was seen as the insuperable obstacle to an inclusive democracy, turned out to be an asset."[73] (To be accurate, South African liberal institutions go back to nineteenth century Cape-Colony liberals, who "strove to free people from human bondage and to give whites and blacks the vote."[74]) Moreover—and as Hermann Giliomee, who might be considered the David Hackett Fischer of South Africa, has observed—"to project the democracy and human rights of the interim constitution of 1993 as the kind of democracy the ANC has always fought for is indeed to produce a giant optical illusion."[75] For the kind of democracy and human rights espoused by the ANC in the 1980s was precisely the fraudulent "democracy" of societies like the USSR and Cuba. "Indeed the Freedom House ratings of 1980 scored Cuba and the USSR lower in human rights than apartheid South Africa!"[76]

For better or for worse, the National Party of the apartheid era was not a Chilean or Argentinean military dictatorship, "but a party re-elected by whites in successive elections."[77] The dominant-party despotic democracy that South Africa is fast becoming is not in this tradition. Still, "Everything that goes wrong with it is considered 'a legacy of apartheid,' writes an exacerbated Jim Peron, an American expatriate, whose idealism drove him to settle in post-apartheid South Africa. "The violence in the rest of Africa is a 'legacy of colonialism.' It's a legacy that has gone on for almost forty years. Every time something goes wrong (and that happens constantly), the same litany of excuses is recited. 'We inherited this problem from the corrupt apartheid regime.'"[78] There's another pesky problem with this particular blame-game: South Africa's flourishing criminal class consists mainly of youngsters who've come of age and blossomed under black rule.

If anything, by staving off communism, the apartheid regime saved black South Africans from an even worse moral and material fate.

Except for Rhodesia before Mugabe, minority-ruled South Africa, with all its depredations, offered Africans more than any other country on the Dark Continent. Patterns of migration have always functioned as clues to social reality.[79] Then as now, "black migration patterns into South Africa far exceeded black migration patterns out of South Africa."[80] Granted, entering African migrants were not "voting with their feet" for apartheid, but they were certainly voting for law and order and a livelihood.

In the "first twenty three years of apartheid, between 1948 and 1981, the South African economy grew at a rate of 4.5 percent."[81] Of course, in the famous words attributed to both Disraeli and Mark Twain, there are lies, damned lies, and statistics. Duly, Marxists put the high growth rate down to exploitation. However, when "exploitation" was replaced with "liberation"—and Africans broke free of the colonial yoke to gain political independence—they promptly established planned economies, in whose shadow nothing could grow, plunging their respective countries into despair and destitution.

To the liberal West, Kenneth Kaunda and Julius Nyerere were the faces of black liberation, but both leaders cut a swathe of destruction through the rural economies of their respective countries, Zambia and Tanzania. One shudders to think what the ANC would have wrought on the sophisticated, industrialized economy of South Africa if given a chance. Had Mandela ascended to power in the 1960s instead of languishing on Robben Island and in Pollsmoor Prison, he would have nationalized the South African economy and banned private enterprise. That's what the ANC's Charter called for in 1955. That's what South Africa's black-ruled neighbors to the north did.

While black Africa and East Europe circled the drain due to communism, South Africa was experiencing an economic explosion, courtesy of the NP's conservative economics,[82] which columnist Andrew Kenny cautiously commends for "guarding some important aspects of private enterprise and protecting some vital areas of democracy,"[83] to say nothing of maintaining the rule of law. An oasis in the African desert, South Africa's economy grew at an annual rate of six percent during the 1960s. *Time* magazine, BPC (before political correctness), crowned H. F. Verwoerd, the architect of this prosperity—and of "separate development"—"one of the ablest leaders Africa has ever produced."[84]

In his submission to the Truth and Reconciliation Commission, F. W. de Klerk, who received a Nobel Peace prize for surrendering South Africa to the ANC, corrected the record: "Apartheid was not only about white privilege but also about development and redistribution of income from whites to blacks. The economy had grown by an average of 3.5 percent per year under apartheid, the black school population grew by 250 percent in the first twenty-five years of apartheid, and the black share of total personal income had nearly doubled from twenty percent in the mid-1970s to thirty seven percent in 1995, while that of whites declined from seventy one to forty nine percent."[85] As bad as the Bantu Education system was, it vastly improved black literacy.[86] Twelve years into the Nationalist government's rule, the rate of literacy among the Bantu of South Africa was already higher than that of any other state in Africa, or that of India.[87]

Indeed, the increase in the African population's learning and longevity under apartheid attests to the constantly improving public health and government services for blacks. From the 8.6 million recorded in the 1946 census, the black population rose to 17.4 million in 1974 and 28.3 million by 1991. From the 1940s to the 1990s, life expectancy for blacks soared from thirty-eight to sixty-one years![88]

Since the dawn of democracy in 1994, life expectancy has plummeted by nine years.[89] Crime has reached crippling levels. As documented in detail earlier in this volume (above all in the chapter called "Crime, The Beloved Country"), crime in the New South Africa is second to none in the world and certainly much higher than in the Old South Africa. By *Time*'s telling,[90] unemployment had jumped from *nineteen percent* in 1994 (before "freedom") to *thirty-one* percent in 2003 (after "freedom"). Less damning data provided by an Economic Advisor to former President Mbeki puts unemployment in 1993 at 31.2 percent, steadily rising until, in 2005, it stood at 38.8 percent. The trend is consistent and persistent.[91] Breyten Breytenbach has been breast-beating over the New South Africa's barbaric criminality, the plague of raping, theft, and fraud, the indecent enrichment of the few, manipulation, redeployment as a form of impunity, public office as an exercise in scavenging, the breakdown of essential services, entrenched and continuing racism, the lack of public morals or even common sense. ... the irrevocable 'progress' of South Africa to a totalitarian party-state.[92]

> Giliomee confirms that both the government and the private sector accelerated wealth distribution from white to black in the 1970s. By 1994, blacks were *consuming* taxes; whites were paying them: Blacks "contributed R23 billion to government revenue, and received R34 billion in cash-and-kind transfers from the government, of which the largest part went to social welfare, housing, health and education." According to the International Monetary Fund, "whites in 1987 paid an average of thirty two percent of their incomes in tax, but received only nine percent in benefits."[93]

DESPERATELY SEEKING BOLLYWOOD'S BRANGELINA

There is a lot to dislike about the self-aggrandizing Brangelina of Benetton and their fashion accessories: *couture*, color-coded kids. But where is Bollywood's match for these giving, gullible, Anglo-American do-gooders? Wherever you look, those perpetually demonized Europeans are untiring in doing the world's good works, and saving the planet and its creatures.

> According to *Forbes Magazine*, the largest charities by revenue in the United States [which, I suspect, means the largest in the world] are the Mayo Clinic, Salvation Army, YMCAs in the United States, United Way, Cleveland Clinic Foundation, American National Red Cross, Catholic Charities USA, NewYork-Presbyterian Hospital, Goodwill Industries International, and The Arc of the United States.[94]

Who were the worthies who founded these magnificent, munificent organizations?

Mayo was founded by William Worrall Mayo (hint: he was not from Bangalore or Beirut). The Salvation Army by William Booth (another WASP). The same goes for the YMCA (George Williams, yet another WASP). Two ministers and a rabbi brought the United Way to fruition. Drs. George Crile, Frank Bunts, and William Lower founded the Cleveland Clinic Foundation in 1921, and Clara Barton the Red Cross. We know who founded Doctors Without Borders or *Médecins Sans Frontières*. The most generous people in the world are Bill and Melinda Gates, founders of the Gates Foundation, the World's largest charitable group.

The same sort of kindly humanitarians are at work at the Chris Hani Baragwanath hospital in Soweto. Soweto is "the black satellite city outside Johannesburg," South Africa. "Saving Soweto"[95] is a superb documentary by the Arab television network Al Jazeera, detailing the heroic work undertaken at the Chris Hani Baragwanath hospital. Back when the present writer's uncle, Professor Charles Isaacson, headed the Department of Pathology there, the place was just plain Baragwanath; nobody thought it essential, in that far-off era, to invoke in the hospital's title an ANC Marxist leader like Chris Hani (who was murdered in

1993). But some things don't change, even if names do. Today, as was the case under apartheid, "Baragwanath" is "the only hospital in South Africa's biggest township." Now as then, the staff members ministering to the multitudes in Soweto are supervised and mentored by selfless Christian and Jewish medical men and women. What would South Africa do without these good people?! Where in the world are their African, Asian and Latin equals? And why is their kind slandered so?

If anything is guaranteed to help freeze a people in time it is a culture of blame. Those who've had their fill of "black pain" will understand why the phrase is held here between the tongs of quotation marks. My family tree was rudely truncated by an event far more fatal than was slavery: the Holocaust. I do not carry this legacy with me. I blame only those, mostly long dead, who planned and executed the Final Solution. Members of my family have never ascribed their misfortunes and misdeeds to that contemporary calamity. They've owned their failings. Like American Japanese, who were interned *en masse* in places like Manzanar or Minidoka during World War II, Jews have gone on to become among the highest earners in the countries to which they migrate.

FREE WILL AND THE WILL OF THE FREE

In *The Constitution of Liberty*, Friedrich Hayek insisted that "The assigning of responsibility is based, not [necessarily] on what we know to be true in a particular case, but on what we believe will be the probable effects of encouraging people to behave rationally and considerately."[96]

Another wise man, libertarian economist Murray Rothbard, counseled that "In dealing with crime ...liberals are concentrating on the wrong root causes. That is, on 'poverty' or 'child abuse' instead of a rotten immoral character and the factors that may give rise to such a character, e.g., lack of respect for private property, unwillingness to work, and emphasis on short-run 'kicks' instead of forethought about the future."[97]

Still another smart man, Thomas Aquinas, "believed we are free to be either virtuous or vicious and are responsible for being one or the other."[98] According to philosopher Anthony Kenny, Aquinas believed "freedom belongs to the will in so far as it is capable of acting on the results of deliberation about alternatives."[99]

Be it in Africa or in America, the cornerstone of a free society rests on the concept of the individual as a responsible, self-determining agent. As long as this concept is under attack, free societies will be imperiled.

However, as essential as it is for the health and wealth of a free society, the idea of individual responsibility is insufficient. The values which people—and peoples—bring to the polity are inestimable, and they have such compounding impacts on social stability from generation to generation that they can all too readily be underestimated. Cultural influences cannot be tweaked out of existence like some unsightly nose-hair. Athena was sprung from her father's head; democracy has grown slowly in the soil below. Athens became Greece became Europe became the West. And there it stopped. Africa has not become America.

CHAPTER 6

Why Do WASP* Societies Wither?

When I am weaker, I ask you for my freedom, because that is your principle; but when I am the stronger, I take away your freedom, because that is my principle.

—Louis Veuillot†

To love the little platoon we belong to is the first principle (the germ as it were) of public affections.

—Edmund Burke, 1790

THE WEST'S INSISTENCE on bringing the Old South Africa to its political knees has had another unforeseeable outcome: an Islam redux. As the influence of Christianity receded after the 1994 transition, that of Islam increased. This is a great shame—and not only because it is to the detriment of America's national interests. Islam is no tonic for a country wracked by unfathomable cruelty and violence. The continent cries out for a spiritual transformation. A belief system according to which the murderous, not the meek, shall inherit the earth—provided they're Muslim—is not what the "Rambo Nation" requires.

---

* WASP: White Anglo-Saxon Protestant

† Nineteenth-century French writer

South Africa was a staunchly traditional Christian country. Stores closed on Sundays, which was a holy day, not a holiday. Television came late to the place but so did pornography and the gay rights movement. "From liberalism to the creation of apartheid, Christianity has been of great importance in shaping many political ideologies,"[1] notes the editor of a volume titled *Christianity in South Africa*. Christian mission schools were the engine of education in Africa,[2] including the education of black, anti-apartheid leaders. Even more than "secular NGOs, government projects and international aid efforts,"[3] Christian evangelism in Africa has helped change hearts.

The Christian faith has shaped the relationship between the European missionaries and the Africans, and it gave contours to the fight both to establish and abolish apartheid.

As for the establishment of apartheid: neo-Calvinist theology lent metaphysical and moral justification to the Grand Design of H. F. Verwoerd, also the architect of apartheid. In the Book of Genesis and in the "happenings at Babel,"[4] Verwoerd and his devout coreligionists believed they had found the firmest foundation for "the idea of the nation as the ordination of God,"[5] in general. And, in particular, for the notion that each nation needed to exist as well as maintain its distinct nature. "The fact that God had given the various nations their separate existences," posited E. P. Groenewald, professor of New Testament Studies, "implied that they should remain separate. Israel itself was the proof of how God had willed national separateness."[6] Scripture itself, argued scholars of Groenewald's ilk, "provided full support for this". For one thing, there was Deuteronomy 32:8:

> When the Most High gave the nations their inheritance
> When he divided the sons of man
> He fixed their bounds according to the number of sons of God…[7]

As for the abolition of apartheid: the struggle to reconcile the idea of separate development with the Christian Gospel moved other Christian intellectuals to oppose apartheid. And in particular, one of Afrikanerdom's foremost anti-apartheid activists was Reverend Beyers Naude, who resigned his position as a Moderator and as minister in the Dutch Reformed Church (NGK),[8] in protest against that body's pro-apartheid stance. There were many others who, like Naude, believed apartheid had defiled their Christian faith. Examples are Dr. Reverend Allan Boesak and Reverend Trevor Huddleston.

The Judeo-Christian teachings underpinned great moral struggles in both South Africa and America, separate development in the former country, slavery and segregation in the latter. There, I said it. Like early Americans, the Puritans of South Africa had a deep affinity for the Mosaic faith and morals. In *The Roots of American Order*, Russell Kirk traced the influence on the New England Puritans of the Hebraic faith and traditions. For sustenance and guidance, the Puritans drew on Exodus—whose theme is the flight from bondage to freedom—as did they on Kings and Romans. Like the New England Puritans, the Dutch Calvinists who settled South Africa were steeped in "John Calvin's Hebrew scholarship."[9] Both in Africa and in America, the Puritans saw in the children of Israel and the story of the Exodus a metaphor for their own quest; their Protestantism they considered as a continuation of God's covenant with the people of the Old Testament.[10] As they interpreted it, the preservation of their respective communities of believers and its cultural characteristics was preordained.[11]

If Deuteronomy furnished the NGK, mainstay of the apartheid state, with the theological justification for "ordained separation," then devout, Jewish, anti-apartheid activists took away something entirely different from this early book—the fifth of thirty nine—in the Hebrew Bible. My own father was a leader in the Promethean struggle to end apartheid. Rabbi Abraham Benzion

Isaacson's fight for justice for South Africa's blacks was inspired by the advanced concept of Jewish social justice showcased in Deuteronomy and in The Prophets. Deuteronomy is replete with instructions to protect the poor, the weak, the defenseless, the widows, the orphans, the aliens. This ethical monotheism, developed centuries before classical Greek philosophy, is echoed throughout the Hebrew Bible, and is expounded upon by the classical prophets, who railed so magnificently against power and cultural corruption.

Roared Isaiah: "There is blood on your hands; wash yourself and be clean. Put away the evil of your deeds, away out of my sight. Cease to do evil and learn to do right, pursue justice and champion the oppressed; give the orphan his rights, plead the widow's cause" (1:11-17). Right or wrong, this was a role Daddy felt compelled to assume. As he explained to the editor of *Cutting Through The Mountain: Interviews With South African Jewish Activists*, his hatred of injustice "was greatly strengthened by the reading of the [Hebrew] prophets. They are the world's teachers":

> I got it from the inner spark of the Torah; from the nineteenth chapter of Leviticus: 'you shall not stand idly by the blood of your neighbor.' ...whatever I did and have done up till now ... was based on ...Jewish teaching. Not Marxism, not Leninism, and not any other 'ism, not liberalism. And not Zionism. But Torah.[12]

In the Hebrew prophets, in particular—from Amos to the second Isaiah—John Adams saw exemplars for the American order, political and private. "A vast majority of Americans at the time of the framing of the constitution"[13] were intimately familiar with the Law and the teachings of the prophets. In Kirk's telling, these laws were "not a set of harsh prohibitions imposed by an arbitrary tribal deity. Instead they are liberating rules that enable people to diminish the tyranny of sin; that teach people how to live with one another and in relation to God, how to restrain violence and fraud, how to know justice and to raise themselves above the level of predatory animals."[14] "The great prophets restrained the kings' ambitions,"[15] and constantly—at great personal risk—rebuked the king and the people for their transgressions.

A FIGHTING FAITH

Since September 11, 2001, a debate has raged in the West as to whether Islamic terrorism is the handiwork of people who've heeded or hijacked Islam. Regular Americans are more or less decided: There are many moderate Muslims, for sure, but a moderate Islam is a chimerical creature akin to the unicorn and the yeti. The term "Islamic fundamentalist" rings, increasingly, like a redundancy. At the very least—and as one wag put it—"if there really is some sort of ongoing war between 'extremists' and 'moderates' for the soul of Islam, it appears to be one of the quietest contests in the history of ideological warfare."[16] Politicians and media pointy heads are another matter entirely. Whenever a Muslim commits odious acts in the name of his faith, these are deemed—post haste and post hoc—a manifestation of the inauthentic Islam. Among the far-left, and some far-gone libertarians, Muslim aggression is viewed as entirely reactive; a function solely of the West's misguided foreign policy, or neo-imperialism. To these factions, an adventurous foreign policy is both a necessary and a sufficient condition for Muslim violence.

Pope Benedict XVI disagreed—that is, he disagreed before he was menaced by Muslims into a *mea culpa*. In a meditation on "faith and reason" at the University of Regensburg in September 2005, the Holy Father worried over the survival of Christendom and the West in the face of Islam, a faith that brooks no reason or reformation and is commanded to will the world to its ways. That

Islam counsels conquest, not coexistence, is ultimately what gave the pope pause. While the Holy See relied, in his eminently reasoned argument, on a medieval text—the debates of the erudite Byzantine emperor Manuel II Paleologus, who reigned in the late fourteenth and early fifteenth centuries, with an educated Persian—the peerless Samuel P. Huntington has drawn on modern history to chronicle "Islam's bloody borders."

"Islam's borders are bloody, and so are its innards," Huntington wrote in his wonderfully learned book, *The Clash of Civilizations and the Remaking of World Order.* "Muslims … have been far more involved in intergroup violence than the people of any other civilization … Muslims and Hindus on the Subcontinent, Russians and Caucasians in the North Caucasus, Armenians and Turks in the Transcaucasus, Arab and Jews in Palestine, Catholics, Muslims, and Orthodox in the Balkans, Russians and Turks from the Balkans to Central Asia, Sinhalese and Tamils in Sri Lanka."[17] Muslim Uighurs and Han Chinese in Xinjiang.

And Arabs against blacks across Africa. The Arabs of Africa seek to dominate or drive to extinction its Africans, be they Muslim, Christian or pagan pastoralists.

While Western governments, abetted by the Fourth Estate (and a fifth column), have framed strife in these regions as sectarian or regional, Huntington did not.

And neither did the NGK, South Africa's dominant church. Well before the West awoke to it, the NGK had been acutely aware of the threat of Islam.[18] Referred to in rarified circles as the "National Party at prayer," for its politicized nature, the NGK belonged squarely to the tradition of a vigorous (if often misguided), fighting Christendom. As its NGK guardians saw it, the Christian faith and its followers were confronted by three mortal dangers: *die swart gevaar* (the black threat), *die rooi gevaar* (the red threat), and the *slamse gevaar* (the Muslim threat).[19] Which is why, in the early part of the twentieth century, NGK and Anglican missionaries had been hard at work converting the natives, "and others, such as the Muslims",[20] to Christianity.

Cross and Crescent Collide on the Dark Continent

Because the Old South Africa was predominantly black, the received wisdom in America about that land was that it constituted an exotic, multicultural society. It was nothing of the sort. Settled and shaped by the Dutch in the mid-1600s, South Africa was Christian, conservative, and, broadly speaking, bi-racial. Blacks had long since been missionized. Islam had not infiltrated the continent's southern tip in any meaningful way; and it was traditionally practiced—to the limited extent that it was practiced at all—by the country's small South Asian and Malay populations.

Currently, the world's commentators are scandalized about "the actions of the Sudan's Islamist government against the Christian minority there."[21] However, from Mogadishu to Marrakesh, Islam's march across Africa has never been especially merciful. "Historically, the other great antagonistic interaction of Arab Islamic civilization has been with pagan, animist, and now increasingly Christian black people to the south," noted Huntington. "In the past this antagonism was epitomized in the image of Arab slave dealers and black slaves. It has been reflected in the on-going civil war in the Sudan between Arabs and black, the fighting in Chad between Libyan-supported insurgents and the government, the tension between orthodox Christians and Muslims in the Horn of Africa, and the political conflicts, recurring riots and communal violence between Muslims and Christians in Nigeria."[22] By Huntington's estimation, "the modernization of Africa and the spread of Christianity [were] likely to enhance the probability of violence along this fault line."[23]

The NGK had prefigured the West in concluding that it was probably safest for all concerned if *dar al-Islam*[‡] was confined to a small spot in South Africa. Together, both the NGK and relevant Anglican Dioceses worked to keep Islam in check.

Obviously, the obligation to convert is a filament of the Christian faith. At the turn of the twentieth century, the NGK General Commission thus appointed a number of church intellectuals to bring the Gospel to the Muslim community. Although the effort was voluntary, and most certainly did not involve the rack and the thumbscrew, Muslim leaders in South Africa viewed Christian conversion as out-and-out aggression.

With conversion as their goal, prodigious studies of the Muslim community were undertaken and published by Christian intellectuals, among them Dr. A.J. Liebenberg's 1926 tome titled *Die Slams*. Another was *The Mission to Moslems in Cape Town,* authored, in 1934, by a Rev. A.R. Hampson. Yet another magisterial survey was *The Cape Malays*; it covered the Cape, the hub of the Muslim community. Among the less-than-subtle titles published during the 1910s was *The Moslem Menace In South Africa*, penned by one Dr. Samuel Zwemer.[24] Rev. Joost de Blank, the Anglican archbishop of Cape Town, opposed apartheid and Islam with equal ardor. In 1958, he expressed the opinion that "Islam was a danger to Christianity."[25] In *Die Kerk and die Islam in Afrika*, another scholar, Ben J. Marais, expatiated: "If Christian communion did not reach the heathen in South Africa then they would fall prey to the communists, nationalists and Islam." In 1964, no less an august authority than the Anglican Episcopate attacked the doctrines of "Muhammadanism."

On the heels of this refutation came a hard-hitting book by two Transvaal missionaries. *The Shape of Power in Africa*, by David Newington and Hubert C. Phillips, characterized Islam as "the secret weapon of Satan," alleging that it entered "through the

---

‡ Areas where Muslims are in the majority.

back-door to world domination," and targeted African Christians for Islamization. The NGK Synod General Commission also authorized and undertook a strategy of "house to house calls,"[26] in the hope that Muslims would respond to the Christian call. To the men who saw themselves as the custodians of the Christian community, the Muslim "menace" was real; outreach, therefore, assumed the utmost urgency.

In at least one instance, during the 1980s, the Directorate of Publication prohibited the distribution of an Islamic text because it was offensive to Christians and other faiths.[27] I have no idea whether "apes and swine," the synonym for Jews among many an Islamic scholar, was one of the phrases referenced, but the dread Afrikaner government's mild response to offensive Muslim speech is nothing if not ironic given that, today, writers, filmmakers, comics, and caricaturists in the West often do what they do under the threat of death. The West has welcomed into its midst large Muslim populations that have a pesky habit of calling for the heads of their hosts when, and if, the latter pictorially depict Muhammad—or describe him less than respectfully in words. At the same time, governments and mainstream media persist in bowing and scraping to the religion of peace and its raging religionists.

During the 1970s, the Iranian Islamic revolution ignited an "Islamic resurgence" across South Africa. Many Christian scholars concluded that "Islam was a rival to the Gospel in Africa." They worried especially over the "the silent swing to Islam" among Africans. In 1986, the "white NGK synod openly called Islam a false religion and a "great danger for Christianity in South Africa and the World in the contemporary period." Their Christian plan of attack? A debate over the merits of energetic versus low-key proselytizing.

It stands to reason that Muslims would be especially active in the anti-apartheid movement, considering the effects of racial classification on that community. Christianity, in a word, was another reason for the Muslim call to political action; South Africa under apartheid was unapologetically Christian. Less reasonable was the manner in which Muslim leaders mischaracterized theological opposition posed by the Churches to the spread of Islam. To deflect from such concerns, South African Muslims screamed, "apartheid." "Islam a Threat to apartheid," blared the headline in a Muslim newsletter.[28] At the time, international faith-based organizations, such as the World Council of Churches, the World Alliance of Reform Churches, and the World Council of Religion and Peace, chose naively to conflate the Anglican and NGK diocese's theological concerns over Azanian Islamization with a vendetta against apartheid's enemies.

Twenty-three years on, "Islam is the largest religion of conversion in South Africa."[29] Not just there, of course. The sound of the muezzin wafts above minarets in Malmö, Sweden—and across the other great cities of Europe. And members of the *crème de la crème* of the American Muslim community routinely masquerade as moderates—pillars of the community—while in private and from their pulpits often advocating violence, advising their followers to work to impose the strict Islamic code of shari'a in the U.S., and swearing allegiances to al-Qaeda's *capo di tutti capi*.[30]

The Hebraic Bond

As mentioned, the Puritans of South Africa were scripturally steeped in the Hebraic faith. In their community they saw an extension of the covenant God formed with the Israelites. To some extent, this accounted for their firm relationship with Israel—forged in the fires of international excoriation and excommunication. Back then, it was South Africa and Israel against the world—and against the forces of nihilistic liberalism intent on snuffing out civilized outposts at the tip of Africa and in the Middle East. In Africa, the United States had the dubious distinction of having joined the "Suicide of the West," often on the side of communists, in supporting assorted "national liberation" movements. Conversely, while it had always condemned apartheid, Israel was friend to South Africa through thick and thin. Perhaps the only friend which the Old, orderly South Africa had.[31]

Against the decree of the United States, Israel's Labor and Likud governments alike chose barter over boycotts. In a 1986 speech in New York, Yitzhak Shamir, at the time Israel's foreign minister, gave expression to the Jeffersonian notion that comity and commerce were far better catalysts for peaceful change than embargos [or democracy delivered with daisy-cutters]. He told his "audience that Israel would not institute sanctions against South Africa."[32] Instead, Jerusalem would leave "entangling alliances" to the great powers and continue its "normal" relations with Pretoria.

Perhaps inevitably, Israel was credibly accused in May of 2010 of offering to provide apartheid-era South Africa with nuclear warheads. The apartheid-era government would never have declassified the relevant documents published by Sasha Polakow-Suransky in *The Unspoken Alliance: Israel's Secret Relationship with Apartheid South Africa*; the ANC did the declassifying. Among the unclassified documents was a letter dated November 22, 1974, and marked "Top Secret," from Israel's then Minister of Defense Shimon Peres to Eschel Rhoodie, Secretary of Information in the Vorster government. (Rhoodie briefly appeared earlier in this book, concerning his "Muldergate" role.) The missive alludes to the two countries' shared determination to resist their enemies and to refuse to submit to the injustices against them. Peres signs off, "With warm personal regards, I am sincerely yours." The sentiment found expression in a comprehensive bilateral agreement signed in 1976 by Prime Minister John Vorster during his visit to Israel. "Essentially, the two nations pledged themselves to each other's survival and freedom from foreign interference."[33]

Always game to discredit the still-extant Jewish state for its real or imagined indiscretions, the "international community" went into a frothing frenzy on receiving confirmation of the "open secret" status of the relationship between Israel and the pariah country said community helped extinguish.

Older Afrikaners and Israelis have not forgotten this epoch in their shared history. Alas, while the Old South Africa reciprocated in kind—during the dismantling of its nuclear arsenal in 1993, under the watch of the International Atomic Energy Agency, South Africa was careful to protect the identity of its Israeli collaborators—the New South Africa is anything but a friend to Israel. Ruled by the ANC, South Africa is now in league with the Arab and Muslim bloc, hostile to Israel and to American interests.

A HOUSE AT PEACE WITH ISLAM

If we go by Roger Scruton's bifurcation between "The West and The Rest,"[34] then the New South Africa, even if brought into being by the West, belongs firmly with the camp called the "Rest."

It is no coincidence that Islamic militants became active in South Africa around 1995, which was shortly after the no-nonsense Afrikaner government ceded power to the anti-law-and-order African government. Nor is it a sheer fluke that more and more blacks in South Africa are converting to Islam. At roughly two percent of the total population, the Muslim community is now a million strong, and enjoys "street cred" with the ANC, because of its members' anti-apartheid activism. "The ANC, for example, became the first political party to elect a Muslim as its Western Cape Provincial leader."[35]

Indeed, agitating for democracy in South Africa has meant rooting for America's enemies, a self-defeating practice which successive American administrations have made into a habit.

America threw money and men to Moloch so that Iraqis could turn out *en masse* for shari'a law. Had George Bush gotten his way, Hosni Mubarak, president of Egypt, would have already been democratically unseated by the banned, Islamist Muslim Brotherhood. The Unites States' Disneyfied view of democracy resulted in another, less-than Magic Kingdom in the Palestinian Authority. There, an overwhelming vote for Hamas catapulted to power an organization whose reason for existing is its neighbor's destruction. On the anniversary of Kosovo's independence, and in the midst of the so-called war on Islamic terrorism, it's worth contemplating the consequences of another of America's interventions, this time on the side of Islam in the Balkans. Consider the following declaration, made by the Bin-Laden-bolstered Alija Izetbegovic, leader of the Bosnian Muslims, on the eve of what was a religious conflict between Orthodox Christians and Muslims:

> The Islamic movement should and must start taking power as soon as it is morally and numerically strong enough not only to overthrow the existing non-Islamic power structure, but also to build a great Islamic federation spreading from Morocco to Indonesia, from Africa to Central Asia.[36]

The Declaration (written in the early 1970s) also states that coexistence between Islam and other political systems (since Islam is both political system and religion) is impossible. For his efforts, Mr. Izetbegovic received support from Iran and Turkey; though he died in 2003, he still commands Muslim respect from Morocco to Malaysia and has a street named for him in Saudi Arabia. Western apologists dismissed their protégé's "Islamic Declaration" as a passing indiscretion.[37] Nevertheless, the outcome of America's indiscretion in the region was to help create a second Muslim bastion in the Balkans, strengthening an already aggressive, intransigent Islamic base in the heart of Europe, one that is there to stay.[38]

So what has the resurgence of Islam and its crusades wrought in South Africa?

PAGAD: A Populist Reign of Terror

When it comes to domestic terrorism, democratic America and South Africa sing from a similar hymnbook. America sits on an Islamic powder keg of Wahhabi-dominated organizations, of which at least one-third supports terrorist groups or employs individuals who are suspected of having terrorist connections.[39] Yet Barack Obama's Homeland Security Department has issued a document counseling vigilance against so-called right-wing nationals (never defined). Practically any patriot who alerts others to the government's "Train of Abuses and Usurpations" makes the grade as a "right-wing national".

The Missouri State police (or more appropriately, the Police State of Missouri) presaged the president. "The Modern Militia Movement" is a report written with "subversives" like this writer in mind. Individuals have the makings of militia members if they are libertarian (check), gold bugs[§] (check), fly unfamiliar flags, or "display paraphernalia associated with the Constitutional, Campaign for Liberty, and Libertarian parties"[40] (a magisterial "Don't Tread On Me" flag snakes across the front page of my website; and a Ron-Paul sticker adorns my GTI motorcar). Allah and al-Qaeda loyalists, or Latino narco-terrorists have not been targeted for extra attention.

Similarly, the ANC-run South African National Intelligence Agency devotes inordinate analytical efforts to tracking ultra-

---

[§] A so-called gold bug is one who supports America's return to the gold standard.

right, Afrikaner nationalists such as the Afrikaner Weerstandsbeweging (AWB) and the Boeremag. Yet, ironically, and amidst anodyne assurances about Islam's compatibility with diversity and democracy, the biggest, organized, armed attack on South African civil society came from the community which the state had ruled out as a possible threat.

Cape Muslims are especially radicalized. According to Anneli Botha, a terrorism analyst with the Jamestown Foundation, Qibla, a movement "that was created in the early 1980s to promote the aims and ideals of the Iranian revolution in South Africa,"[41] has developed a tentacular reach in the Western Cape. The organization expressed the desire to transform South Africa into an Islamic state, under the slogan 'One Solution, Islamic Revolution.'" The "movement" was also behind the People Against Gangsterism and Drugs (PAGAD), a vigilante, paramilitary outfit that began ostensibly to fight crime, but branched into a familiar franchise: terrorism. Extortion, racketeering, and intimidation of witnesses and opponents in the press, politics, and academia—sometimes among Muslim clergy themselves—soon followed. From bashing gays and lesbians,[42] PAGAD proceeded to bombing them, targeting bars such as the "Blah Bar" and "The Bronx" nightclub, frequented by gays and lesbians in Green Point's "Pink Triangle."

Between 1999 and 2000, PAGAD perpetrated eighty bombings against civilians, unheard of in the South Africa in which I lived. First to be pipe-bombed was "Planet Hollywood," an American-themed restaurant in the opulent Victoria and Alfred Waterfront (once my favorite shopping center, situated alongside Cape Town's scenic harbor). Two diners were killed and several others seriously injured, some requiring amputations. Other popular haunts of mine where bombs went off: the Camps Bay St. Elmo's pizzeria (forty-eight wounded), the New York Bagels take-away in Sea Point, and the Constantia Village shopping centre.[43]

The ANC might not know Shiite from Shinola, but its loyalties lie squarely with the Arab and Muslim bloc. In 2006, Mbeki welcomed a visit from the Iranian foreign minister and "expressed support for Iran's campaign for uranium enrichment,"[44] in defiance of the U.S. and the United Nations Security Council. Ronnie Kasrils, the former minister of intelligence, regularly depicts Israel, not the Persian pussycat, as a menace to the Middle East. This, even as Iran's *Majnun*[**]-in-Chief threatens atomic retribution against Israel. Mahmoud Ahmadinejad's Iran is Jihad Central—a gaily-open supporter of terrorism across the Islamic world. It finances Hezbollah in Southern Lebanon and Syria and Hamas in the Palestinian Authority; its reach extends into Iraq, Bosnia and Croatia—and beyond. Kasrils, admittedly, is not working with much (intelligence, that is). He praised Hezbollah's "victories against the Zionist forces," and extended the love to Ismail Haniya, inviting the Hamas leader and prime minister of the Palestinian National Authority to South Africa.

The ANC has accepted millions of dollars in donations from foreign governments and officials including Saudi Arabia, the United Arab Emirates, former Indonesian strongman Suharto and the viciously anti-Semitic erstwhile Malaysian Prime Minister Mahathir Muhammad of Malaysia. Also, it joined in the chorus of those nations calling for the United States and the European Union to lift their sanctions on the Hamas-led Palestinian government.[45] During the period in which PAGAD ran rampant, it planted bombs in Jewish establishments. "The Jewish Book Centre, housed in a private home, was burnt down. A bomb was planted at the Wynberg synagogue."[46] On July 4, 2007, the dwindling Jewish community watched nervously as ANC comrades called on their countrymen to stream into the streets "in solidarity with the Palestinian people."[47]

** Madman in Arabic

Since freedom, South African terrorists have been surfacing like rattlesnakes after winter hibernation. According to James Kirchick, assistant editor of *The New Republic,*

> Pakistani police captured three South Africans who stand accused of plotting to blow up the Johannesburg Stock Exchange and government buildings in Pretoria. Another South African has been arrested in connection to the July 7, 2005, London transit bombings, and earlier this year, the U.S. Treasury named two South African cousins as substantial financial contributors to al-Qaeda.[48]

South Africa's nuclear facility at Pelindaba, west of Pretoria, was attacked. Twice. The individuals who breached the site's outer security perimeter in both incidents remain at large and unknown.[49] Not for nothing does Muslim charity and relief work raise red flags. The Holy Land Foundation, a façade for Hamas, has become a synonym for terrorism. FBI investigations are still unraveling the elaborate maze of shell companies and fronts—religious charities and think tanks included—set up to launder terrorist-bound funds.[50] Late in 2008, two South African Muslims were detained in Uganda on suspicion of terrorism. The duo, Haroon Saley and Mufti Hussain Bhayat, insisted that theirs was a mission of mercy.[51] A year later, Somalia called South Africa: Staff at the State Department had reason to suspect that someone in Cape Town was swimming in some very polluted waters "after a phone call from an al-Qaeda operative [in Somalia] to a number in Cape Town was intercepted—a call in which an attack on U.S. government buildings in South Africa was discussed."[52]

Granted, PAGAD's "covert activities [have come] to a standstill, for the time being, due, in part, to "the arrest and prosecution of its prominent leaders."[53] Given the shoddy police work involved, however, the lull in Islamic unrest is more plausibly attributable to the ANC's "pro-Palestinian stance" and its neutrality in the U.S.'s interminable war against tyrants and terrorists.[54] In essence, South Africa is a house at peace with Islam and its interests.

Iqbal Jhazbhay, South Africa's foremost expert in Islamic and Middle Eastern studies, concurs. The ANC's cozy relationship with Islamic states has served as a magic amulet against further radicalization. The "tacit alliance between mainstream Muslim leaders and the ruling party had successfully managed to sideline more radical voices,"[55] contends Jhazbhay. It's hard to imagine the Afrikaner National Party, which governed South Africa from 1948 until 1994, sprouting "a *de facto* Muslim wing."[56] But the ANC has. It's known as "The Call of Islam."[57] The ANC even sports its own Jew-baiting, mini-Mahathir Mohamad. Like that Malaysian ex-ruler, Fatima Hajaig, South Africa's deputy foreign minister, has claimed that the Jews rule the world by proxy.[58]

In the Palestine Solidarity Committee's (PSC) South African chapter, the local Muslim community has found another political pacifier. In conjunction with the Congress of South African Transport and Allied Workers Union, the PSC has been especially hyperactive in hounding the Jews of South Africa—and the Jew among nations (Israel).[59]

COSATU: Carrying the Torch for "Durban I"[††]

COSATU is a partner in the Tripartite Alliance, together with the South African Communist Party and the once-openly communist African National Congress. The two-million-strong trade-union titan has the signal dishonor of having organized the largest public-sector strike in South Africa's history. When it is not masterminding boycotts on "Snowflake" Flour and Iwisa and

[††] For the meaning of "Durban I," see next heading

Impala maize meal[60] (don't ask why), or mobilizing against the introduction of market principles into the Gulag of ANC government operations, COSATU is leading a fight fronted by one Bongani Masuku against "apartheid Israel."

The apartheid libel is fast replacing the Nazi and fascist ones in the left's name-calling arsenal. Actually, the two metaphors are often combined. In actions and pronouncements about and against Jews, COSATU is matchless. Its anti-Israel offensive gained prominence with the mystifying refusal by unionized Durban dockhands—mystifying because self-defeating—to unload cargo carrying goods from Israel. Praised by the Socialist Resistance network, the COSATU action was coordinated in cahoots with the PSC and Young Communist League, and aimed at "boycotts, divestment and sanctions against apartheid Israel."[61] COSATU spokesman, the aptly named Patrick Craven, announced the union's intention to "boycott all goods to and from Israel until Palestine was free." References were made to the "genocide in Gaza." But it was Masuku who pushed for a more inclusive campaign against the Jewish State by targeting South Africa's 70,000 remaining Jews. "We'll make them leave," he has promised.

On February 6, 2009, three busloads of PSC and COSATU demonstrators disembarked in the Johannesburg suburb of Raedene, in front of the Jewish community centre, and the Sydenham Highlands-North synagogue, to stage an illegal demonstration against "South African Jewry's support for Israel's Gaza operation."[62] This show of force occurred not in front of the Israeli embassy. Rather, it took place in the "epicenter of Jewish communal life in the city"[63]—where Jews live, worship and socialize. While the South African Police Service (SAPS) refused to disperse the illegal demonstration, it did turn away ten other buses! You'd have had to experience the onrush of a riled-up African crowd to comprehend the terror the small community must have endured during the hours of menacing chanting, singing, stomping, and flag-burning (Israel's being the flag thus burned), amplified through loudspeakers. According to eyewitnesses, the rabble's repertoire included "kill the Jews in Arabic."[64] COSATU's Masuku issued a *cri de coeur*, saying that COSATU with its nearly two million members wanted

> to convey a message to the Jews in South Africa that...[our workers] are fully behind the people of Palestine. Any business owned by Israel supporters will be a target of workers in South Africa. ...What Israel is doing to Palestinians is worse than what apartheid did to South Africans.[65]

Not to be outdone, the hyperbolic Kasrils, who materialized among the marchers, declared that Israel's attack on Palestine was the "most shameful genocide the world has seen yet." The kaffiyeh-clad Kasrils had hoisted a banner that read: "The final solution, Gaza 2009," and on which were displayed a Star of David and a swastika.

On the matter of Gaza, South Africa's new elites can learn temperance from the *Al Jazeera* television network, whose correspondent Riz Khan solicited a different perspective from acclaimed Israeli author Amos Oz, a political dove and longtime peace activist. "The blockade on Gaza," Oz told Khan, is "not the *reason* but the *result* of the rocket attacks on Israeli civilians." Oz recoiled at the "Israel is an apartheid state meme."[66] Apartheid was abhorrent, he said, but "describing Israel as the land of apartheid, however, is very one-sided. Israel has its flaws; and the lasting occupation of the West Bank is unjustifiable. Nonetheless, unlike apartheid, it's not based on race. The Israeli oppression and occupation ... is a result of a lasting Palestinian attempt to throw Israel into the ocean."[67]

The COSATU specter is par for the course in the New South Africa. It was rare in the old. Now let us name the dog hiding behind the mask of a conference on racism and slavery.

The "Running of the Jew" at Durban I & II

Google will confirm that the city of Durban is famous, not for its sun and surf, but, rather, for the wildly successful "antiracism" conference held there in 2001 by the United Nations Human Rights Council. So infamous has "Durban I" become, that, although the 2009 sequel was held in Geneva, it is known as "Durban II."

Although South Africa is a veritable crime scene, the culprits of "Durban I" did not return to the scene of the crime. When the time was ripe at the U.N. again for the "Running of the Jew"[68]—to borrow the title from Borat Sagdiyev's favorite annual festival in Kazakhstan—the same enemies of civilization and their patrons at the U.N. convened on the Continent. Unfortunately, unlike the stomping of the Jew in comedian Sacha Baron Cohen's make-believe village of Kuzcek, this U.N. happening was not the stuff of fiction or comedy.

Anyone suggesting that the Durban Series were anti-racist gatherings cannot be serious, and if he is serious, should not be taken seriously. As Alastair Gordon of the Canadian Coalition for Democracies reminded the amnesic, "the last U.N. anti-racism conference held in Durban… degenerated into a hate-fest of anti-Jewish and anti-Israel vitriol, while the most egregious human rights violators escaped criticism."[69] The same card-carrying offenders officiated as goons of honor at the Thugs-Unite reunion in April of 2009. According to the *Toronto Star*, "all of the non-governmental organizations invited to the first conference [had] been invited back to the second, including those that were at the 'forefront of the hatred,' some of which posted pro-Hitler posters at the 2001 gathering."[70]

Befitting the administration of conservative Prime Minister Stephen Harper, Canada withdrew from what a government official described as a "'gong show,' with Libya elected to chair the gathering, Cuba appointed vice-chair and rapporteur," and Iran named to the organizing committee. Befitting George Bush's confederacy of knaves, the American Ambassador to the U.N., Zalmay Khalilzad, requisitioned the State Department to support an appropriation to fund the sequel to the first "jamboree of hatred towards Israel."[71] Obama considered attending, but, wisely, declined. "Durban II" had been defused. South Africa's anti-Jewish record set during "Durban I" had not been dashed.

During "Durban I," my father, Rabbi Isaacson, warned fellow South Africans not to attend "the Racist Conference in Durban." Laying bare his trademark moral consistency in an editorial for *The Jewish Report*,[72] Daddy flayed "those whites who courageously fought the evil of the past," for being "strangely silent in the face of the evils engulfing our country and the continent we live in."

So who are these "feudal lords of the 'developing' world," who gathered under the guise of freedom of speech, and on the dime of the taxpayer? Father effectively etched the identikits of these avatars of racial justice.

> As they arrive in their luxury BMWs plundered from their country's resources, or acquired with monies from foreign aid programs, it will be noticed that hardly any of them permit freedom of speech in their own feudal estates. [These are] the very leaders who have plundered, wasted and stolen the resources meant for their subjects. Somalia, Liberia, Nigeria, Congo, Sierra Leone, Angola, Rwanda, Sudan and the jewel of Africa—Zimbabwe of blessed memory.[73]

These Renaissance Men and Women of Africa were joined by their domesticated European pets—Belgium, France, Germany and others—in equating Zionism with racism. They "roared" about "Israel's violation of human rights," namely, "Israel's refusal to accept the necessity for its citizens to be blown to bits, and Israel's refusal to put down its guns and mobilize an army of stone throwers to throw stones back at the persecuted Arabs, thereby not committing the crime of using excessive force."[74]

Slavery was also on the agenda at the first Zionism-equals-racism event. "But did they discuss the origins of slavery and the role played by the Arab slave traders? Did they discuss the current slave trade horrendously perpetrated by the Muslim north of Sudan against the Christian south, or did freedom of speech stop at Arab atrocities?"[75]

No, the Durban despots did not take time from their high-roller habits to belabor Islamic horrors. But Daddy did. He wrote of "the Syrian massacres of thousands of its own citizens while suppressing a Muslim rebellion launched from the town of Hama in February 1982." He reminded a world, "which has no respect for democracy but shows understanding for terror," about "King Hussein's annihilation of the PLO in 1970"; about "Hosni Mubarak's ongoing massacre of Islamic fundamentalists of the Muslim Brotherhood in Egypt"; and of "the ongoing murder of thousands of Islamic fundamentalists in Algeria by that country's military, even though the former won a democratically contested election."[76]

Ostensibly, the racist conference goers targeted Israel "to cover up their misdemeanors." On a deeper level, father surmised that "The European nations, many of which collaborated with the Nazis, chimed along with Africa and Arabia because the Jew has done the unthinkable, he has denied the right of the world to exterminate him."

Approximately 500,000 Jews were forced to flee their homes in Iraq, Egypt, Yemen, and Morocco, in 1948, as a reprisal for the declaration of the State of Israel. Did the refugees and survivors of Christian and Islamic persecution sit on their behinds, wallowing in their own misery, allowing themselves to be used as pawns by unscrupulous politicians? No, they got off their backsides and built from a howling wilderness a flourishing oasis—institutions of education, science and technology among the best in the world. What is more, they defended what they built successfully—too successfully for the world.

Israel represents the national, cultural, spiritual and political revival of the Jewish people. The Jews had become a sickly, disembodied, and diasporic people. In returning to the cradle of the Hebrew civilization, they regrouped as a nation, revived a desolate land and a long-dead biblical language, and have attempted—with varying degrees of success—to breathe life into the region. In much the same way was Afrikaner nationhood forged on the land of Southern Africa. As the Jew belonged in Israel, the Afrikaner believed that he belonged in Africa as much as any Bushman or Hottentot.[77]

In speaking of Israel, that small spot of sanity in a sea of savagery, Daddy might as well have been describing the Puritans of Africa, the Afrikaners.

With one exception.

THE PATHOS AND PARADOX OF THE PURITAN

Unlike the Israelis who've endured as a nation-state, Afrikaners have not. They burned bright for a relatively short while, and then, despite superior military prowess, Afrikaners simply surrendered without defeat.[78] Ferocious though it was, the South African Defence Force (SADF) ceded to the African demotic and its representatives. "You, me and our men can take this country in an afternoon,"[79] said former Chief of the SADF General Contand Viljoen, famously, to the reigning Chief, General George

Meiring. He uttered this comment as President de Klerk prepared to cave into ANC demands, forgoing all checks and balances for South Africa's Boer, British and Zulu minorities. Yet, the very same Afrikaner people, in the same spirit, went on to peacefully dismantle the six nuclear devices they had built at Pelindaba.

Why, then, did the Afrikaner give up his birthright for a mess of pottage?

Reconciling Pietism with Power

Some clues as to why WASP societies tend to wither from within are offered up by W. A. de Klerk (no relation to the president). In *The Puritans In Africa*, de Klerk devotes his authorial energies to fleshing out the archetypal Afrikaner with an almost forensic objectivity. The tragedy of the Afrikaner and the American—a function of a shared Calvinist-Puritan ancestry—is the struggle to reconcile Pietism with power:

"The basic dilemma of Western man is how to reconcile power with justice. ... Those within the Calvinist-Puritan ethic, who secretly yearn for power, find it impossible to do so openly and unashamedly."[80] "Naked power... is not possible for Western Christian man, especially of Calvinist-Puritan leanings." For Puritan man, the quest for power—a quest very much alive—cannot be "an open bid for supremacy," but, rather, has to be "power acceptable in Christian terms"; it must be power driven by a devotion to a "great ideal." In the case of the Afrikaner, power—arguably necessary for national survival—thus "became couched in terms of a socio-political ideal"; "in terms of what is, in a sense, basic to man's spiritual life, that is to say, freedom." But because this great ideal is invariably "a self-created idea ... it becomes an abstraction of freedom. What it wills is a programmatic re-structuring of the world in terms of abstraction."[81]

The Afrikaner's "great ideal"—"survival, identity, fulfillment and happiness"[82]—was ineluctably tied to enduring as a biblically sanctified nation. If such endurance was to be accomplished, the exercise of power was essential. Apartheid was the political superstructure within which the *Volk* sought safety for what they saw as their divinely ordained sovereignty. Separate development itself was cast as a "sound and noble structure, accommodating a great variety of peoples, providing everybody with the necessary living space, containing every possible amenity for the various groups, offering everyone goods according to their needs, while demanding contributions from everyone according to their abilities."[83]

But the "exceedingly tough" Puritan mind was crippled by a correspondingly "tender conscience." The "great ideal" had turned the Boers into something they detested. The people who had fought imperial Britain in Africa's first anti-colonial war were now lords and masters of their own satrapies: the African Bantustans. Soon, the biblically blessed country became an Ishmael, an outcast. The charges of racism were especially difficult to withstand and rationalize. Petty perhaps, but no less intolerable for these South African Spartans was their banishment from sparring in international sports. Patriots that they are, Afrikaners resented being expected to feel ashamed of their country. Puritans that they were, the resentment soon turned inward. As an abstraction, the grand ideal of separate, but equal, development failed to reconcile power with justice. True to type, the Puritans of Africa relinquished the former to achieve the latter.

Such, then, was the Puritan impact upon the Afrikaner mind. Upon the American mind, Puritanism left a very different mark. While the Afrikaner's "great ideal" turned him into an outcast, America's messianic calling made it a crusader for democracy.

The U.S.'s exceptionalism gave imprimatur to its expansionism. Yes, John Quincy Adams counseled that America not "go abroad in search of monsters to destroy." He also urged that America remain "the well-wisher of the freedom and independence of all," but "the champion and vindicator only of her own." However, in defiance of the sixth president, the United States became "an empire of liberty." Or so the third president, Thomas Jefferson, called this contradiction in terms, for empire is unfriendly to freedom, both at home and abroad. America's seemingly intractable warring and nation-building are inimical to national survival. Thus has the United States been hoisted on its own petard, its "great ideal" harboring the seeds of its own destruction.

Of the many important observations Huntington made, one stands out: "Multiculturalism at home threatens the United States and the West; universalism abroad threatens the West and the world."[84] More might have been said by Huntington about the fact that persisting in policies that are impossible to achieve both bankrupts and corrupts those who try it. The American Puritanical toughness has manifested itself primarily in never-ending expeditions overseas. Its corresponding—and paradoxical—Puritanical "tenderness" has culminated in a national death-wish: mandating multiculturalism and mass immigration at home, while pursuing a monoculturalist Manifest Destiny abroad. These are two sides of the same coin.

Huntington characterized America as an unrepresentative democracy in which a patriotic people is routinely flouted by the ruling elites, especially "on domestic and foreign policy issues affecting national identity."[85] The dwindling historical majority often exhibits the healthy patriotism (even petty provincialism, at times) associated with robust particularism. This majority finds itself pitted against a governing, deracinated "custodian class"[86] of bureaucrats, educators and intellectuals who, in addition to ensuring that the income curve is rearranged, also make sure that "homophobes," "sexists" and "xenophobes" are kept in check. The social scientist is integral in helping to execute and enforce the "public philosophy" of pluralism, which has mired Americans in misery.

Nowhere is the pathos—or is it bathos?—of Puritan America more evident than in the findings of Harvard political scientist Robert Putnam. Putnam recently discovered that diversity is not a strength, but a weakness; and that the greater the diversity in a community, the greater the distrust. Across the diverse neighborhoods canvassed by Putnam, thousands of Americans hunkered down, literally[87]. Those whom he surveyed were not intolerant, bigoted, or even hostile; they were merely miserable. Much to his surprise, Putnam was forced to conclude that state-engineered mass immigration and its attendant diversity cause mass depression, the kind that stems from loss, resignation, and hopelessness.

Needless to say that as an immigrant, I second Putnam's findings, but not his cruel, contradictory recommendations. It will surprise some to learn that I experienced the greatest multicultural shock to my system in Canada and the US, rather than in South Africa. The very first time I had been unable to communicate with a neighbor was not in faraway South Africa, from which I emigrated, or Israel (I grew up there), but in Canada, where I lived among Iranian, Korean, and Iraqi immigrants. (They seemed perfectly charming, but I had no way of telling for sure.) Since immigration into South Africa was relatively low, I simply did not know many immigrants. Africans, Afrikaners, and English: those were the only people that had been competing over that much-contested corner of the continent for an eternity. My own family had arrived in South Africa at the turn of the last century—Jewish traders (and a couple of rabbis) who fled the massacres and Marxism of Russia. As a consequence, while South Africa was a politically fractious society, it had a hegemonic culture.

What is, then, the solution to America's ethnically engineered neighborhoods where—among the historic population especially—activism alternates with escapism, unhappiness with *ennui*? Putnam pelts us with utilitarian platitudes. Evidently, the ethnic engineering that historic populations have suffered at the hands of soviet-style planners dwarfs compared to the long term benefits of mass, Third-World immigration. The many thousands of miserable individuals Putnam interviewed must soldier on, their pursuit of happiness sacrificed for the collective gains of cheap Tyson chicken and colorful cuisine.

Unhappily, when an academic discovers what ordinary mortals have known for eons, it's called social science. Let us at the very least agree that when a social scientist does what Putnam has done, and reaffirms the glories of forced integration and a loss of national identity in clear defiance of his own research—then the result is not science at all, but rather, social planning.

Protestant Death Wish vs. Jewish Defiance

The Hebrews, with whom American and Afrikaner settlers identified so strongly, are unburdened by Pietism. Despite their political liberalism, the Jews of Israel are disinclined to turn the other cheek and apologize for their existence. The Israel in which I grew up believed almost unanimously that its cause was just and that an unjust world was conspiring against it. Besides which, Jews have had centuries of practice as a despised minority, and see nothing new or nerve-wracking about existing in a state of antagonism with the world. "Like Shintoists in Japan, Jews as a rule are not afflicted by the politics of guilt, a sentiment that seems to arise in decaying Protestant societies," observers Professor Paul E. Gottfried. Gottfried is Jewish—and easily the most erudite, most underrated American scholar of Europe's (not to mention his own country's) political right.

"Jews," he avers, "do, however, appeal to Christian guilt when they are living as a minority in Western societies. They may even take advantage, in the way Nietzsche once described, of the special inclination of Christians toward social guilt. But this is mostly tactical, in the same way that patriarchal Hindus in the U.S. support the Democratic Party, as the more leftist and therefore less nativist of the two parties in an alien society. I'd even concede," Gottfried told me, "that many Jewish educators and journalists may by now half believe the leftist bilge they inflict on non-Jews, but the ideas that they preach are totally extraneous to their Jewish identity. Rahm Israel Emanuel, White House Chief of Staff to President Barack Obama, is the classic case of this Jewish adjustment to a double standard. Although a right-winger on Israeli politics and a self-identified Jewish nationalist,[‡‡] Emanuel is quite happy serving an American leftist regime presided over by Reverend Jeremiah Wright's chief parishioner. All in all, in Israel most Jews act differently from the guilt-ridden former Calvinists of South Africa because their cultural worldview is entirely different. There is no reason why Israelis would act like the Afrikaners unless they absorbed their liberal Protestant poisons, which is unlikely to happen."

Where this "deformed Protestant culture" persists, so do the politics of guilt. In the seminal *Multiculturalism and the Politics of Guilt*, Gottfried plumbed other peculiar manifestations of the "Protestant deformation," which have become fixtures in American and South African societies, not least of which is the "spiraling process of confessing to and compensating for historical burdens." This ritual of public expiation allows the keen flagellant "to feel righteous individually while being part of a historically wicked society. And as a country redeemed from its own racist, sexist, homophobic past, the repentant Protestant is allowed to go forth and bring enlightenment to others." Energetically, in the

[‡‡] I know Emanuel's father was a member of the Irgun; I do not know whether Emanuel shares his father's sympathies.

case of the American Protestant crusader, in his "never ending global missions."[88]

The Afrikaners illustrate perfectly what has happened to the Protestant-Calvinist world; it has sunk into a paralyzing paroxysm of guilt, for which there seems to be no cure. Consider General Meiring's response to General Viljoen's call to take back their beloved country before the ANC overtook it: "Yes, that is so, but what do we do the morning after the coup?"[89] "Celebrate" is how a member of the African National Congress would have answered Viljoen. But then the ANC is unencumbered by the Afrikaner's thanatotic urges. Free of the perpetually repentant Protestant death wish, the secular, libertine ANC—whose ideological roots are in socialism, communism, and tribalism—wields brute political force with perfect ease.

AFRICA CRIES OUT FOR CHRISTIANITY

"As an atheist, I truly believe Africa needs God,"[90] ventured Matthew Parris of the London *Times*, a sentiment I share despite my own impiety. Eager to strike a pose against the evils of ethnocentrism, Western academics tend to hold all cultures in equal esteem. But, as Parris points out perspicaciously, and as I have done elsewhere in this book, "tribal belief … suppresses individuality. People think collectively; first in terms of the community, extended family and tribe. This rural-traditional mindset feeds into the 'big man' and gangster politics of the African city: the exaggerated respect for a swaggering leader, and the (literal) inability to understand the whole idea of loyal opposition."[91] On the other hand, "Christianity, post-Reformation and post-Luther, with its teaching of a direct, personal, two-way link between the individual and God, unmediated by the collective, and insubordinate to any other human being, smashes straight through the philosophical/spiritual framework … just described. It offers something to hold on to [for] those anxious to cast off a crushing tribal groupthink. That is why and how it liberates."[92]

Granted, in Islam, young Africans seek and find "a way out of gangsterism and drugs... a refuge from the early sex, AIDS, alcoholism, and domestic violence rampant in many poor black communities in places like Soweto."[93] Faced with a choice—and for the sake of peace—parents would, indubitably, prefer that their troubled youngsters find Jesus or Jehovah, not Allah. While ascetic Islam may offer personal discipline, as Huntington put it plainly, "Muslims have problems living peaceably with their neighbors."[94]

Most pointedly, from the 2009 American Religious Identification Survey comes the news that Northeastern America, where Protestantism was first planted by the pilgrims, is now "the new stronghold of the religiously unidentified."[95] New England has joined the march toward "a post-modern, post-Christian, post-Western" United States,[96] in which "the percentage of self-identified Christians has fallen ten points in the past two decades." It could be said that Americans have just elected their first post-Christian president.

Before Barack Hussein Obama got religion on the presidency, he spent decades imbibing Afrocentric Black Liberation Theology from the pulpit of Trinity United Church of Christ. Jesus said, "I am the way and the truth and the life. No one comes to the Father except through me." Obama said, "There are many paths to the same place." While Obama has claimed that America is not a Christian nation, Huntington countered that America has a secular government, but it is a predominantly Christian nation, founded and peopled by Christians.[97]

Whether the Obama or Huntington tack is taken as Bible from Sinai in modern-day America, Parris is incontrovertibly right in his pronouncements about Africa: "Removing Christian evangelism from the African equation" does not bode well for the bloodied continent.

Granted, a de-Christianized America would be unlikely, as yet, to fall prey to "a malign fusion of Nike, the witch doctor, the mobile phone and the machete."[98] A de-Christianized America, however, would not be America.

CHAPTER 7

The Anglo-American-Australian Axis of Evil

Men may have order without liberty, but they cannot have liberty without order.

—Samuel P. Huntington

The tyranny of a multitude is a multiplied tyranny.

—Edmund Burke

ALL TOO OFTEN, American foreign policy has been informed less by what Samuel P. Huntington termed civilizational consciousness,[1] than by the idea of the propositional nation. America, to her governing neoconservative and left-liberal elites, is not a nation but a notion,[2] a community of disparate peoples coalescing around an abstract, highly manipulable, state-sanctioned ideology. Democracy, for one.

Yet to Russell Kirk, the father of American conservatism, and an old-school conservative—as well as, arguably, to the founders of the nation themselves—society was a community of souls, joining the dead, the living, and those yet unborn. It cohered through what Aristotle called friendship and what Christians call love of neighbor,[3] facilitated by a shared language, literature, history, habits and heroes. These factors, taken together, constitute the glue that binds the nation. By contrast, the rather flimsy whimsy that is the American "creedal nation" is, ostensibly, united in "a common commitment to a set of ideas and ideals."[4] If anything, when it is expressed by the historical majority, the natural affinity for one's tribe—a connection to kith, kin and culture—is deemed inauthentic, xenophobic, and even racist, unless asserted by non-Occidentals.

The disregard a country's policy makers evince for the fellow-feelings stirred among countrymen by a common faith and customs—secular and sacred—is invariably reflected in its foreign policy. America's foreign policy looks at populations as interchangeable as long as they are "socialized in the same way," and "molded by a suitable public administration and a steady diet of human-rights talk."[5] The generic American government's foreign policy reflects America's denationalized elites, who are committed to "transnational and sub-national identities"[6] both at home and abroad.

According to her ruling sophisticates, America's mission is to "democratize mankind." To fulfill this mission, and to do justice to American exceptionalism, Americans are "indoctrinated in a fabricated creed that teaches they are being untrue to themselves and faithless to their fathers unless they go abroad in search of monsters to destroy."[7] One such "monster" targeted for rapid reform was South Africa.

BETRAYED

Cold War confrontation prompted the United States to acknowledge South Africa as a surrogate for American interests on the Dark Continent. In defense of these interests in the region and against the communization of their neighborhood, South African soldiers fought Russia's Cuban and Angolan proxies with the same fortitude that the country's founders displayed when battling the Zulus in the Battle of Blood River. Yes, South Africa had faithfully fulfilled its role as a Cold Warrior. It fought alongside other advanced Western nations, led by the United States, and "engaged in a pervasive ideological, political, economic, and, at times, military conflict with [other groups] of somewhat poorer, communist societies led by the Soviet Union."[8] A surplus of courage, however, was no panacea for a deficit in democracy.

Thus, although South Africa was regarded as "an important Western geostrategic bulwark"[9] against Soviet encroachment in the region, the American reservoir of good will toward South Africa was quick to run dry. It's not that the US did not have democratically flawed allies; it did and does. But such imperfections are usually the prerogative of non-Western nations.

For South Africa this meant fighting communism's agents while being handicapped by sanctions. "The United States had imposed an arms embargo on Pretoria in 1964 and had joined the international consensus in refusing to recognize the 'independence' of four of South Africa's black homelands between 1976 and 1984."[10] While during the 1970s and the 1980s all American administrations condemned apartheid, they had generally opposed broad economic sanctions, arguing reasonably that these would hurt the very population they were intended to help.[11] With the Carter administration (1977-81) came an even "tougher line toward Pretoria." Jimmy Carter viewed black African nationalism as perfectly "compatible with US interests."

In fairness, the left turn in American foreign policy came well before Carter. When, exactly, it started is a matter for dispute. Did it begin with John F. Kennedy, or was America's support for Soviet satellites such as the ANC a hangover from Yalta; a long-standing official policy of support for the Soviet alliance, and the subsequent ceding of most of Central and Eastern Europe to Stalin? Whichever was the case, the shift in American foreign policy ironically saw the US adopt and deploy slogans popularized by the Soviet Union in support of African liberation and against the "imperial, colonial" West. There was a "pullback of military forces around the communist periphery"[12] and the "frequent support of the Third World in disputes with Western nations"[13] around the world. Thus, left-wing revolutionaries were propped up, instead of a Western ally like Salazar in Portugal; Mugabe was favored over Ian Smith, as was Nasser above Britain and France; Batista was ousted to make way for Castro.

If Edmund Burke had lived to witness such myopia, it would not have surprised him, though it would have saddened him. For as one very recent commentator has put it, Burke—quite contrary to Voltaire and Rousseau—"opposed all schemes of fundamentalist reconstruction and the formulation of policy on the basis of purely abstract reasoning." Voltaire and Rousseau's "theoretical reification, as we might term it today, aroused in Burke a deep distrust. This suspicion was the core of his opposition to the Revolution in France, as he preferred to call the French Revolution. Burke's prescience in respect of this political earthquake seems uncanny."[14] In *Reflections on the French Revolution*, Burke, who was "a great publicist of the American Revolution," warned of the "predominantly French dangers to the European civilization." What were these dangers? There were, among other things, "[V]ainglorious projects comprising vast, sentimental abstractions, abandoning sane and temperate political reason and historically rooted ... practicalities."[15]

So to Ronald Reagan. Reagan at least favored "constructive engagement" with South Africa, together with a tough resistance to communist advances in the Third World. But political pressure, not least from the Republican majority, mounted for an increasingly punitive stance toward Pretoria. This entailed an "elaborate sanctions structure,"[16] disinvestment, and a prohibition on sharing intelligence with the South Africans. In 1986, the Soviet Union, which had until the 1980s supported a revolutionary takeover of white-ruled South Africa by its ANC protégés, suddenly changed its tune and denounced the idea.

Once again, the US and the USSR were on the same side—that of "a negotiated settlement between Pretoria and its opponents."[17]

For advocating "constructive engagement," members of his Republican party issued a coruscating attack on Reagan. Senator Lowell P. Weicker Jr., in particular, stated: "For this moment, at least, the President has become an irrelevancy to the ideals, heartfelt and spoken, of America."[18] Republicans had slipped between the sheets with the fashionable left.

Christopher Hitchens, a retread Trotskyite recently turned neoconservative, wrongly equated Reagan's "constructive engagement" with a support for apartheid.[19] Proponents of ordered liberty, in the spirit of Reagan and Margaret Thatcher's gradualism, found expression in the ideas that, whereas "wholesale change is catastrophic" to stability, men had "the right ... to live in a civil society based on the rule of law."[20] For sustainable change to take place, change must be gradual and "rooted in the institutions of society."[21] In tracing the contours of such Burkean thinking, Kirk referred to "that aspect ... which is prepared to tolerate an old evil lest the cure prove worse than the disease."[22]

To Kirk's contention that "true freedom can be found only within the framework of a social order,"[23] I'd wager that in my former homeland, this bulwark against barbarism is near collapse. In my new homeland, the framework that sustains the country's ordered liberty is being eroded. Decades back, no less a classical liberal thinker than Ludwig von Mises warned that liberty in the United States could not—and would not—endure unless the founding nation retained its historic national identity and cultural hegemony.[24] An ahistoric, rootless America, reduced to rivalries between identity groups, is an America in which liberty has been lost.

SIDELINED

"Apartheid showed a gross disrespect for human rights and international law, but it was never lawless,"[25] as the new democracy is. In fact, "the state showed a strong tradition of legalism. Afrikaner rule was characterized by an obsession with imposing restrictions through proper legislation and with due process in executing these laws."[26] In his wisdom, Reagan foresaw the chaos and carnage of an abrupt transition of power. So did the South Africans Fredrick van Zyl Slabbert, RIP (he died in May 2010), and Dr. Mangosuthu Buthelezi. The first was leader of the opposition Progressive Federal Party, who, alongside the late, intrepid Helen Suzman, became the PFP's chief critic of Nationalist policy. The second was Chief Minister of the KwaZulu homeland and leader of the Zulu people and their Inkatha Freedom Party (IFP). Buthelezi still is "the only black leader with any mass following who could act as a counter to the ANC."[27] These men were not "lunch-pail liberals" from the West, but indigenous, classical liberal Africans—one white, one black—who understood and loved the county of their ancestors and wished to safeguard it for their posterity.

Both Buthelezi and Slabbert had applied their astringent minds to power-sharing constitutional dispensations. Both leaders were bright enough to recognize democracy for the disaster it would bring to a country as divided as theirs; they understood that "a mass-based black party that received enough votes could avoid having to enter into a coalition and could sweep aside the minority vote."[28] Thus, Buthelezi espoused a multi-racial, decentralized federation, in which "elites of the various groups" would "agree to share executive power and abide by a system of mutual vetoes and spheres of communal autonomy."[29] Paramount to Buthelezi was "the preservation of the rights of cultural groups and the protection of minorities."[30] Slabbert studied a "new system that entrenched individual rights, encouraged power-sharing through a grand coalition of black and white parties, and gave a veto right to minorities in crucial issues."[31] Although he eventually threw his intellectual heft behind simple majority rule, in better days, Slabbert had spoken with circumspection about "unrestrained majoritarianism," expressing the eminently educated opinion that, were majority rule to be made an inevitable corollary of South Africa's political system, the outcomes would be severely undemocratic.[32] It's worth considering that even Zimbabwe for its first seven, fat years of independence, allowed "white members of parliament, [to be] elected on a special roll to represent white interests."[33]

Less-Than-Sexy Statistics

In surveys administered between 1986 and 1989, two-thirds of South Africa's whites indicated they preferred some form of power-sharing accommodation of blacks.[34] The total "white control" option was rejected outright by the whites surveyed even though they acknowledged "quite candidly that they would expect to experience positive 'conditions and quality of life' under a white-controlled government and negative conditions and quality of life under a black-controlled government."[35] Certainly Afrikaners ceded control despite their negative expectations of black rule. "More than eighty per cent believed that the physical safety of whites would be threatened. Less than ten per cent believed that life would continue as before."[36]

Americans eager to press flesh with Mandela will find this difficult to imagine, but whites were not wild about the idea of Mandela running the country. By comparison—and during the same time-frame—pollsters recorded a high approval level for Buthelezi, who fought for a federated republic with a constitution that dispersed rather than concentrated power. It helped, no doubt, that Buthelezi's affinity for free-market economics and

Adam Smith saw him pepper eloquent speeches with terms such as "enlightened self-interest,"[37] anathema in ANC circles. Duly, fully thirty-nine percent of English whites wanted Buthelezi in power; only three percent trusted Mandela.[38] The ANC, with its communist roots and insistence on simple majority rule, did not inspire confidence among the same demographic, which demanded a system with a balance between the new black majority and the other racial minorities"[39] Whites asked only that "the new, multi-racial order guarantee security, predictable politicians, competent civil servants, a strong economy and secure property rights."[40] They got zip.

Far more revealing were the attitudes of ordinary black South Africans, also left out of the charmed circle that chartered the constitutional future of South Africa. "Only thirty-five per cent of Soweto blacks in 1978 favored a government 'in which blacks as the majority rule the whites,' compared to fifty-seven per cent of that sample preferring 'equal numbers of blacks and whites in [the] Cabinet.'" And, "Only twenty-five per cent of urban black respondents approved of a black majority government."[41]

In all, the sampled data contrast with the simplistic assumptions prevalent within the Anglo-American and European orbits of white ruling elites that refused to let go of privilege and dominance. Perhaps most blacks, no less than most whites, realized that being disenfranchised in a functioning state was preferable to being masters in a failed one.

In the all-white referendum of 1992, in which South African whites were asked to endorse the reform process (*we* overwhelmingly did), the Gorbachev-like reformer President de Klerk campaigned on the slogan, "Oppose majority rule." This was an allusion to de Klerk's promise (*he* broke it) to push for power-sharing. Unhappily, the president forfeited the promise of equal treatment and opportunities for white South Africans within a democratic South Africa. When he acceded to unadulterated majoritarianism, moreover, he acted without a mandate[42]: turning the screws on his constituents, and failing to fight for and secure a government in which black and white interests would be balanced.[43]

RACIAL VOTING COMING TO A POLLING STATION NEAR YOU

That South Africa is riven by race is indisputable. Each election is "a racial census as far as whites and blacks are concerned."[44] In the much-ballyhooed, historic election of 1994, "only two to three per cent of whites voted for historically black parties and perhaps five per cent of blacks voted for historically white parties. The ANC relied for ninety-four per cent of its vote on black support. The historically white parties had been barred from campaigning in the black townships."[45] That all the elections since 1994 have had the blessing of every liberal alive doesn't change the fact that they were determined by "a muscular mobilization of a race-based community, coercive control of territory and appeals by powerful charismatic leaders."[46] In their vain attempt to forestall what Alexis de Tocqueville deemed a despotic democracy, and in search of a mean between simple democracy and a representative system in which fewer issues are left to the adjudication of a national majority, Buthelezi and Slabbert had indeed been in good company.

"Elections to be meaningful presuppose a certain level of political organization. ... The primary problem is not liberty but the creation of a legitimate public order. Authority has to exist before it can be limited, and it is authority that is in scarce supply in the modernizing countries,"[47] warned the aforementioned Samuel Huntington in *Political Order In Changing Societies*. "The rule of the people, *demos*, and the people's ethnicity, *ethnos*"[48] invariably clash, argued Michael Mann, "one of the leading historical sociologists of our time." In *The Dark Side of Democracy:*

Explaining Ethnic Cleansing (2004), Mann contends that in the earlier, more formative stages of their development, democracies are prone to carrying out murderous ethnic cleansing, which in extreme forms can become genocidal. "The growth of popular sovereignty, the institutionalization of universal citizenship, [and] the creation of mass society" have often seen "ethnic groups laying claim to the same territory resort to the use of force, and, when frustrated, to murderous ethnic cleansing and even genocide."[49] Examples of this phenomenon in modernity: the ethnic expulsions and massacres in the democratized former Yugoslavia and Rwanda during the 1990s, the genocide of the Armenians in the Ottoman Empire under the Young Turks (particularly in 1915-1916), and the mechanized mass murder of the Jews in Nazi Germany.[50] While the infant South-African democracy fits snugly within his thesis, democracy devotees have accused Mann of twisting like a *Cirque du Soleil* contortionist to stretch the definition of democracy in making his case.

Where Mann is at pains to prove the murderous nature of young democracies, the arguments against democracy for South Africa, which have been propounded by Duke University scholar Donald L. Horowitz, have considerable force. Finely attuned to "important currents in South African thought,"[51] Horowitz offered up an excruciatingly detailed analysis of South Africa's constitutional options. In *A Democratic South Africa?: Constitutional Engineering in a Divided Society* (1991), Horowitz concluded that democracy is, in general, unusual in Africa, and, in particular, rare in ethnically and racially divided societies, where majorities and minorities are rigidly predetermined.[52] Alas, prone to seeing faces in the clouds, South Africa's Anglo-American cheerleaders were impervious to such sobering pronouncements. It remained for students of democracy such as Horowitz to hope only that "the probability … recede that one person, one vote, one value, and one state will degenerate into only one legal party and one last election."[53]

Not nearly as hopeful as Horowitz was that "noted student of nationalism,"[54] Elie Kedourie. "If majority and minority are perpetual, then government ceases to have a mediatory or remedial function, and becomes an instrument of perpetual oppression of the minority by the majority," concluded Kedourie. It was after a visit to South Africa that he wrote the following, in the November 1987 issue of the *South Africa International*:

> ... The worst effects of the tyranny of the majority are seen when parliamentary government on the *unalloyed Westminster* model is introduced into countries divided by religion or language or race. Such for example was the case of Iraq ... where an extremely heterogeneous society came to be endowed with constitutions which made no provision for diversity, and where the result was tyranny of one groups over the other groups in the society.[55] [My italics]

A prerequisite for a classical liberal democracy is that majority and minority status should be interchangeable and fluid; that a ruling majority party should be as likely to become a minority party as the obverse. By contrast, in South Africa, the majority and the minorities are permanent, not temporary. Indeed, every democratic theorist worth his salt—Robert Dahl and Elaine Spitz come to mind—has urged that the principle of majority rule be severely curtailed "whenever people of different languages, races, religions, or national origins with no firm habits of political co-operation and mutual trust are to unite in a single polity."[56]

"Democracy: The God That Failed"

Over the span of decades, bolstered by intellectuals who are not necessarily intelligent, America's political class has been tinkering with the country's historical majority-minority composition. The consequence of the mass importation of poor, Third World immigrants is that minorities intractably hostile to the host culture are on their way to consolidating a permanent majority. The Democratic Party is this nascent majority's political organ, offering a platform of preferential policies for a voting bloc whose "interests are viewed through the prism of racial affiliations."[57] As sure as night follows day, the American democracy will then come to resemble that of South Africa, where racial voting is the rule. Those who think a bill of rights (South Africa has one too), proportional representation and periodic elections[58] will obviate this peril might want to think again.

As for democracy, there are those who contend that it has no intrinsic value—good or bad—and is only "as good or as bad as the principles of the people who operate it."[59] According to this notion, crisply enunciated by writer Lawrence Auster, not all cultures are amenable to the principles of individual rights and limited government which undergird a liberal constitutional democracy.

Others, most notably political philosopher Hans-Hermann Hoppe, disavow democratic government altogether, implicating it in the decay ("decivilization") engulfing Western welfare states. The process of civilization is something that Hoppe associates with "individual savings, investment, the accumulation of consumer and capital goods,"[60] and the display of foresight and future-orientation. A publicly owned government is inimical to these processes, says Hoppe, for the following reasons: "A presidential government caretaker is not held liable for debts incurred during his tenure of office. … his debts are considered 'public' to be paid by future (equally non-liable) governments. If one is not held liable for one's debts, however, the debt load will rise, and present government consumption will be expanded at the expense of future government consumption. In order to repay a rising public debt, the level of future taxes (or monetary inflation) imposed on a future public will have to increase."[61]

With the expectation of a higher future tax burden, "the nongovernment public" also becomes possessed by the incubi of present consumption and short-term investment, throwing to the wind saving and long-term investment. Most pointedly, the main function of democratic government, performed through incessant legislation, is wealth and income redistribution.[62] As H. L. Mencken put it, "Every election is a sort of advance auction sale of stolen goods. If a politician found he had cannibals among his constituents, he would promise them missionaries for dinner." Since reelection rests on politicians informing voracious voters of what is on the menu next time around, the advocacy and adoption of redistributive policies is a prerequisite for retaining leadership positions. It is thus of little or no concern to these campaigners that redistribution will reduce future productivity. And indeed, observes Hoppe, "All redistribution, regardless of the criterion on which it is based, involves 'taking' from the original owners and/or producers ... and 'giving' to nonowners and non-producers." The unintended consequences of this process are that "the incentive to be an original owner or producer is reduced, and the incentive to be a non-owner and non-producer is raised."[63] To sum up: subsidize individuals because they are poor, and you'll get more poverty; support them because they are unemployed, and more unemployment will ensue; siphon taxes to succor single mothers, and single motherhood, and illegitimacy and divorce will proliferate; prop up the old by taking from the young, and the institution of the family—the intergenerational bonds between parents, grandparents, and children—will be systematically weakened.

In short, the erosion of civilization itself.

Both the economy and the traditional family in *fin de siècle* America are in tatters. That America, the greatest democracy in the world, is a debtor nation—a broke and bankrupt consumer economy in the grip of deep moral torpor—appears to second Hoppe's diagnosis and prognosis.

Property Rights vs. Political Rights

A sizeable majority of people inhabiting contemporary social democracies "receives in disbursements more than they pay in taxes."[64] The minority funding the orgy "pays in taxes more than it receives back in disbursements."[65] With nations neatly bifurcated into taxpayers and tax consumers, the predictions made by America's seventh Vice-President, John C. Calhoun—in his *Disquisition on Government,*[66] about the consequences of taxation in a democracy—have come full circle.

Calhoun has been vindicated. In the United States, the ratio of voters to taxpayers is approximately two to one; in South Africa it is a stupefying eleven to one.[67] Not being democrats, America's founders foresaw today's pillage politics—and they understood that, unchecked, overbearing majorities could be more malignant than monarchs. The notion, moreover, that only the propertied ought to have the vote was quite acceptable to the Founders. All too well did they know that, granted a vote, the unpropertied masses would help themselves to the belongings of the propertied. Classical liberals of their times saw men as endowed with *natural*—but not necessarily *political*—rights. Thus the constitution under which the Cape Colony had been governed in the mid-1800s limited the franchise by property, not race. It made "no mention of color" and required no literacy test, but stipulated that "the franchise was limited to those who dwelt in immovable structures worth at least £25."[68]

Benjamin Constant (1767-1830), the author of the towering treatise *Principles of Politics*, defined liberty as the people's right to "enjoy a boundless freedom in the use of their property and the exercise of their labor, as long as in disposing of their property or exercising their labor they do not harm others who have the same rights."[69] "Only property can render men capable of exercising political rights," contended Constant. "Only owners can be citizens." Today, everyone has the franchise, but only some fork over for the privilege. Accustomed as we are to such an unfair state of affairs, Constant's demands sound quaint.

People still fuss about apartheid having denied the majority its democratic rights. But it did more than disenfranchise the majority; it denied the majority's economic freedoms. Citizenship rights, after all, are not natural rights. It is natural rights that the law ought to always and everywhere respect and uphold. In its police state methods—indefinite detention without trial, declarations of a state of emergency—apartheid destroyed the individual defenses of equality before the law, the presumption of innocence, *habeas corpus* and various other very basic freedoms. That the apartheid regime contravened natural justice by depriving Africans of rights to property and due process is indisputable as it is despicable. Nevertheless, denying people political privileges does not amount to depriving them of natural justice.

Democracy and Prosperity

The deification of democracy has given us an unrestricted majority in South Africa, which has, in turn, done little to improve the lot of the officially oppressed. Contrary to the belief held among left-liberals, observes Giliomee, free markets and democratic politics do not necessarily reinforce each other to produce high growth, political liberty and the easing of ethnic tensions. "This model works for developed countries, but ... breaks down in those developing countries where ethnic and class cleavages coincide." In such societies, as scholars such as Amy Chua and Samuel Huntington have shown, "a free market democracy has tended to produce a worsening of racial or ethnic tensions, violence, pervasive instability—together with a downturn of growth—and an erosion or collapse of democracy."[70]

Democracy is neither necessary nor sufficient for political stability or economic growth. "Singapore is not a liberal democracy, but it is rich. India is the world's most populous democracy but it is poor," notes Richard A. Shweder, an isolationist cultural anthropologist.[71] Iraq is a democracy, sort of, but was more prosperous and less chaotic when it was a rogue state. (It's a little late, though, to dust Saddam off, give him a sponge bath, and beg him to restore law and order to Iraq.)

Post World-War-Two South Africa was blessed with abundant natural resources (still is), a competent civil service (which is no more), a gold-backed currency (gone), and a sophisticated banking and financial system (going). But for the international fits of pique in the form of boycotts and embargoes, South Africa would have, in all likelihood, experienced steady and stable economic growth and produced a sizable black middle-class vested in political stability.

The Franchise: A Foolish Fetish on a Good Day

Be it in the Bantustans or in the greater South Africa, voting, of course, should never be conflated with freedom. Even fans of democracy confess that "the franchise is a necessary—if insufficient—condition for democracy in conditions of mass society." The point is worth pressing. While it seems obvious that the minority in a democracy is openly thwarted, the question is, do the elected representatives at least carry out the will of the majority? The answer is, "No." It is not the national majority, but rather its ostensible representatives who triumph in this or the other election. The People's representatives have *carte blanche* to do exactly as they please. As Benjamin Barber has written:

> It is hard to find in all the daily activities of bureaucratic administration, judicial legislation, executive leadership, and paltry policy-making anything that resembles citizen engagement in the creation of civic communities and in the forging of public ends. Politics has become what politicians do; what citizens do (when they do anything) is to vote for politicians.

Randy E. Barnett further homes in on why the informed voter has little incentive to exercise his "democratic right":

> If we vote for a candidate and she wins, we have consented to the laws she votes for, but we have also consented to the laws she has voted against.
> If we vote against the candidate and she wins, we have consented to the laws she votes for or against.
> And if we do not vote at all, we have consented to the outcome of the process whatever it may be.

This "rigged contest" Barnett describes as, "'Heads' you consent, 'tails' you consent, 'didn't flip the coin,' guess what? You consent as well.'"[72]

The American founders restricted the federal government to a handful of enumerated powers. Decentralization, devolution of authority, and the restrictions on government imposed by a Bill of Rights were to ensure that few issues were left to the adjudication of a national majority. If anything, freedom will have arrived when elections don't matter; when one can sleep through an election, because, Democrat or Republican, ANC or SACP (South African Communist Party)—in a free society none of these entities would be able to unjustly tamper with what rightfully belongs to the individual citizen.

Readers will often admonish me for dismissing those purple Iraqi digits. I tell them I've lived under a relatively peaceful authoritarian dispensation and was fortunate to escape a violent democracy. I tell them that voting is synonymous with freedom only if strict limits are placed on elected officials' powers, and only if the individual's right to live unmolested is respected. Without those preconditions, voting is worse than meaningless. And if my own testimony isn't good enough for such readers, they need look no further than the aforementioned Horowitz, who observed that universal suffrage in South Africa did not necessarily have to imply majority rule.

ACORN* WITH MACHETES

Majority rule, especially as it applies in Middle Eastern and African countries, doesn't always reward the right rulers. Introduced into modernizing societies, moreover, "elections serve only to enhance the power of disruptive and often reactionary social forces and to tear down the structure of public authority."[73] Representing that authentic indigenous authority which had been so thoroughly undermined in South Africa was Buthelezi, a Zulu prince and devout Christian who eschewed populism. Representing a non-indigenous tradition introduced into Africa was the ANC, which is of the West (although Marxism-Leninism was perfected in the center of Eurasia). It is abundantly clear why Buthelezi, who campaigned against the concentration of rule in a dominant-party state—the endgame of the ANC, abetted by its Anglo-American buddies—was tarred as the *Tokoloshe*† by the same axis. Mandela's mafia—the ANC and its partners, the South African Communist Party and the Congress of South African Trade Unions (whose communism was unswerving too)—stood for "the radical Africanist model"[74] that had decimated

* The largest radical group in America

† Evil spirit in Zulu mythology

postcolonial Africa. This troika was entrusted by the United States to bring ordinary democracy—the kind that works best in small, homogeneous, Western societies, and is imperiled even in those—to South Africa.

In the church of American politics, the ANC could do no wrong. Duly, in 1990, President Bush Senior expressed his preference to de Klerk for black South Africa having "equality of outcomes" instead of "equality of opportunity."[75] Naturally "equality of outcomes" was a result that the ANC could be trusted to deliver. The same tack was taken by Herman Cohen, US Under-Secretary of State for Africa: "Minorities ... cannot expect a veto," he inveighed. "All sides [have] to recognize the right of the majority to govern." And, "no side could insist on 'overly complex arrangements intended to guarantee a share of power to particular groups, which will frustrate effective governance."[76]

The ANC wanted "a liberal democracy on the British model in a unitary state, without checks, such as a second house, to safeguard minority rights."[77] It said a categorical "No" to minority veto power, power-sharing, or any meaningful devolution of power to the regions. Its wish was the command of power-brokers in Britain and America. Raw democracy for South Africa was certainly the hobbyhorse of the British left, members of the Communist Party in that country, the Anglican Church under Archbishop Trevor Huddleston, and the noisy Fourth Estate, this last being led by the likes of hard-leftist Anthony Sampson. They were joined by American diplomats and community organizers, who too returned a resounding "Yes" to ANC demands.

Extra, and significant, support from the ANC came from antipodean meddlers, such as the lecherous and buffoonish drunkard Bob Hawke, Prime Minister of Australia from 1983 to 1991. Hawke played a crucial role in organizing the global campaign of disinvestment, which South Africa's erstwhile Finance Minister Barend du Plessis described as "the dagger that finally immobilised apartheid." In 1990 Mandela, newly released from jail, assured Hawke on an Australian visit: "I want you to know, Bob, that I am here today, at this time, because of you."[78] Mandela, of all people, is hardly likely to have been mistaken about this matter. (When acting *ultra vires* on sub-Saharan African issues, Hawke was simply following the tradition founded by Mugabe's sanctimonious enabler Malcolm Fraser, who immediately preceded Hawke in the Prime Ministerial office. "Really motivated by a liberal philosophy," is how Mugabe endorsed Fraser.[79‡])

The ANC's conga-line of Western apologists did not consider that in the South African version of the "winner takes all" Westminster system, "the winners will always be winners and the losers will always be losers," with "no real prospect of a change-over of ruling party."[80] In short, the losers would become mere spectators in the political bleachers.

For its backing, America was recently thanked profusely by Moeletsi Mbeki, brother of Thabo Mbeki. Moeletsi delivered an address at the Woodrow Wilson Center in Washington, D.C., in June 2009, where he expressed gratitude for America's steadfast support during "The Struggle." Although he forgot to thank the most militant ANCniks—academia, the Council on African Affairs, the Pan-African movement, and the African-American community—Mbeki Jr. singled out "the Congressional Black Caucus, TransAfrica, Trade Unions and the Churches." And, of course, "citizens like the Kennedy brothers." The manner in which the late Senator Ted Kennedy short-circuited President Reagan's conservative, cautious policies *vis-à-vis* South Africa rates a

‡ During recent years Fraser has attempted to defend his actions in print, notably in "Why I backed Mugabe," *The Australian*, April 17, 2008. A typical extract from this attempt at self-exculpation runs: "No white face has been capable of changing Mugabe for many years, if ever. Why the quality of his Government changed so dramatically after the death of Sally Mugabe [the dictator's first wife] is an open question."

mention. In 1985, Kennedy traveled to South Africa with a press posse, under the pretense of pulling open and holding back a curtain to reveal the horrors of apartheid. Leslie Dach, a former aide to Kennedy, sings posthumous praise to the senator with an account of the trip. Unfortunately, Dach's story is more spin than substance. For energetically executing their duties to protect a foreign dignitary, whose brothers had been assassinated, from volatile crowds, he accused "the dictatorship and the police"[81] of sabotaging the Kennedy trip. Shopworn stories and shibboleths aside, Kennedy got to posture at every spot he selected, including in front of Pollsmoor Prison where Mandela was incarcerated. On returning to the United States, and over Reagan's objections, Kennedy forced through a bill to choke off investment to South Africa. This was the one occasion in the twentieth century when the Senate overrode a presidential veto.

Naturally, Reagan did not make Moeletsi's fairy-godmother list. That president had bucked received wisdom, first by condemning the ANC's ardent sponsors as the "Evil Empire," and then by opting for a policy of "constructive engagement" with the minority government of South Africa. Reagan's deviationism notwithstanding, "The great majority of South Africans see the United States as a friend who was supportive during their hour of need,"[82] stressed Mbeki.

And so they should. Toiling in non-governmental and governmental structures, Americans worked assiduously to provide the ANC with instruction, from anything as organizing mass marches to seeding the racial spoils system of affirmative action. In his tome, *Partner to History: The US Role in South Africa's Transition to Democracy* (2002), Princeton Nathan Lyman, the American Ambassador to South Africa from 1992 to 1995, records the active role Americans performed in the transition to democracy, especially in "dissuading spoilers"—the author's pejorative, it would appear, for perfectly legitimate partners to the negotiations. One such partner was Buthelezi; another was military hero and former chief of the Defense Force, Constand Viljoen.

Avoid "wrecking the process"[83]: this ultimatum was the message transmitted to the Afrikaner general and the African gentleman, loud and clear. The United States, with Lyman in the lead, failed to lean on the ANC to accommodate a federal structure. It promised merely to hold a future South African government to its "pre-election commitments, including shared power and the protection of minorities."[84] Until then, the skeptical Buthelezi was instructed to trust the ANC to relinquish the requisite power.[85] Enraged, Buthelezi threatened to take his case to the American people and "spotlight" the knavish confederacy between their government and the ANC.[86] (Republicans were generally with Buthelezi, Democrats with the ANC.) Being the man de Klerk was not, Buthelezi rejected the pressure and overtures from the West. "I am utterly sick of being told how wrong I am by a world out there," he wrote to Lyman. The dispensation being hatched was "an instrument for the annihilation of KwaZulu."[87]

Viljoen, who represented the hardliner Afrikaners and the security forces, believed de Klerk had abdicated his responsibilities to this electorate. He planned on leading a coalition that would have deposed the freelancing de Klerk and negotiated for an Afrikaner ethnic state. Likewise, Buthelezi, whose championship of self-determination had been denied, was fed up to the back teeth with being sidelined. He and his Zulu *impis*[§] were every bit as fractious as Viljoen; every bit as willing to fight for their rightful corner of the African Eden. For setting his sights on sovereignty, the Zulu royal and his following (close on twenty percent of the population) were condemned as reactionaries by the West.

[§] Zulu warriors

Hardly a dog of a commentator missed the opportunity to lift his leg in protest against Buthelezi, for making common cause with Afrikaner decentralists and against the ANC. "Wreckers" is how the gray eminence of American newspapers—*The New York Times,* also known as "Pravda on the Hudson"—dubbed the two leaders and the millions whom they represented. The two, alleged the *Times* in a 1994 editorial, were locked in an "unscrupulous alliance to disrupt the first elections in South Africa in which all races will have a vote."[88] Following the might-makes-right maxim—and committing a *non sequitur* in the process—*Times* editorialists demanded that the leaders of these African and Afrikaner ethnic minorities relinquish demands for sovereign status because their political power was at best "anemic." Meanwhile the *Times* dismissed Buthelezi as a puppet in Pretoria's blackface minstrelsy.

This was drivel. Buthelezi, a crafty leader who had rejected "the ignoble independence accorded to other homelands"[89] within apartheid's framework, was never a collaborator. Understand: For two centuries Africans and Afrikaners had been clashing and alternately collaborating on the continent. Shaka (1787-1828), Dingane (1795-1840), Mpande (1798-1872), Cetshwayo (1826-1884)—Buthelezi was heir to these Zulu kings who had been wheeling, dealing and warring with Boers well before the inception of *The New York Times.*

Masters of mass mobilization, the ANC used the political tinderbox ignited in the ramp-up to the first democratic elections to great effect in discrediting the security forces, and claiming that the apartheid government was fomenting the intra-ethnic violence between Inkatha (Zulu) and the ANC (Xhosa). But while the ANC accused the security forces of arming Inkatha, the latter faction blamed the security forces for allying themselves with the ANC, especially when Zulu hostels and squatter camps were raided in response to ANC pressure.[90] For the government, the ongoing ethnic conflict was a lose-lose proposition. But not for the savvy

ANC. Mandela harnessed the situation by accusing de Klerk of "either complicity or of not caring enough about black deaths"[91] to stop black-on-black violence. The foreign press helped fuse fact with fancy by transmitting this claim, later to be dismissed by the Truth and Reconciliation Commission. (That body eventually determined that there was "little evidence of a centrally directed, coherent and formally instituted third force."[92]) Nevertheless, a constellation of unfavorable circumstances was aligned against Buthelezi, who capitulated in the end.

Buthelezi is still the intellectual *bête noire* of the ANC—and one of the few leaders in South Africa to mine the Western canon widely and wisely for what it teaches about liberty. To describe "the inexorable centralization of power"[93] which is under way in South Africa, he cited with characteristic passion and poignancy, in July 2009, a poem ("The Second Coming") that W. B. Yeats wrote in January 1919:

> Things fall apart; the centre cannot hold;
> Mere anarchy is loosed upon the world,
> The blood-dimmed tide is loosed, and everywhere
> The ceremony of innocence is drowned …

The United States is a country where the constitution was supposed to thwart the tyranny of the majority. This averting was meant to occur by means of a federal structure, in which powers are divided and dispersed between—and within—a central government and the constituent states.[94] Yet an ossified American officialdom sided with the ANC against its partners to peace. And against James Madison, the Father of the American Constitution. Madison was no democrat; he denounced popular rule as "incompatible with personal security or the rights of property."[95] Democracy, maintained Madison, must be confined to a small spot like the ancient Athenian polis.

THE NOTIONAL AFRO-SAXON NATION

Perhaps it was the ingrained American notion of a propositional nation that accounts for America's aggressive insistence on minute-made democracy for South Africa. Alternatively, perhaps the blame lies with America's "indifference to political development," an indifference which derives from a gap in its own "historical experience," and which "has made it peculiarly blind to the problems of creating effective authority in modernizing countries." "America," after all, "was born with a government, with political institutions and practices imported from seventeenth-century England. Hence Americans never had to worry about creating a government."[96] Like exotic political marsupials, they have developed in isolation and, thus, in a self-referential and self-reverential vacuum.

Bred-in-the-bone Afrikaner patriot Dan Roodt, who has been cited in earlier chapters, argues convincingly that "American and ANC views on Africa have actually converged."[97] The compact and comity between the ANC and the US, as Roodt sees it, go well beyond the assistance which the latter gave to "radical pan-Africanist movements like the ANC, MPLA and ZANU-PF."[98]

South Africa under the Afrikaners was a European-style nation-state; under the ANC it has adopted "American radicalism which aims at abolishing the nation state and replacing it with a kind of global corporatism and welfarism." Like successive American governments, the "progressive," lax-on-law-and-order ANC government is indifferent to immigration enforcement. There is no pressure on the South African border, simply because, to all intents and purposes, the Rainbow Nation—enthralled by American-style multiculturalism—has abolished its borders in pursuit of an African union (and Renaissance). "Progressive" doesn't mean actual progress. By contrast, under the tough-on-law-and-order Afrikaner government, illegal immigrants from the killing fields to the north dared not brave the Boer border guards and their equally ferocious, indigenous assistants: four-legged, wild beasts (lions and the like). If an illegal immigrant did actually make it into the Old South Africa, he was turned back at the gate.

Like endless immigration, the global super-state in the form of the North-American, African and European Unions is equally all-American, and enjoys cross-party consensus in the US. No entity jeered louder than the Bush State Department and National Security Council when the Euroskeptic, nationalistic, French and Dutch people voted a respective "*non*" and "*nee*" to the European Union's illiberal Constitution. The ancient political communities of Europe have the contempt of America's *illuminati*.

Roodt maintains: "We [South Africans] already live in an American-style utopia, a welfare state where millions of people are kept barely alive, but rich enough to afford a Coke, a cell phone and the occasional Mac and fries." For my money, what Roodt describes is no utopia—or even dystopia—but, rather, an "Idiocracy" similar to the one depicted on celluloid in Mike Judge's futuristic film by that name.

Whatever were the reasons for throwing South Africa into the proverbial briar patch—be it the American *idée fixe* of the propositional nation, or the infatuation among America's liberal political class with the black liberation movement—the United States was and remains unburdened by doubt. It was, and still is, convinced of the propriety and the obligation of compelling South Africa's permanent minority "to legislate itself into a position of political subordination."[99]

CONCLUSION

Saving South Africans S.O.S.

If I am not for myself, then who will be for me? And if I am only for myself, then what am I? And if not now, when?

—Rabbi Hillel the Elder

TAKE AWAY 3,037 for the number of South African farmers murdered, and you are left with approximately 40,000 commercial farmers who remain on the land of their ancestors. This is about half the number of refugees the US takes in each year. To date, "there has been a trickle of South Africans applying for asylum in the United States on the grounds of racial persecution. Almost all have been deported."[1]

To Canada—not to the US—is owed the distinction of granting refugee status to the first white South African victim of hate crimes. Thirty-one-year old Brandon Huntley of Cape Town had survived several run-of-the-mill assaults which saw him savagely stabbed and sworn at by his African assailants for being a "white dog" and a "settler."[2] The cruel and craven ANC protested Canada's show of mercy. The idea that Africans would "persecute" Huntley was racist in itself, South Africa's ruling Solons announced. As this book went to press, a Canadian Federal Court, having been petitioned by Canada's Minister of Citizenship and Immigration, ruled to set aside the Refugee Board's finding for Huntley. A good section of the Honorable Mr. Justice Russell's ruling, handed down on November 24, 2010, is devoted to assessing a raft of "alleged chilling and coercive attempts by the South African authorities to assert political and diplomatic pressure to subvert the rule of law in Canada." Justice Russell stated at once that "the government of South Africa did not like the [Refugee Board's] Decision and asked the government of Canada to have it appealed to the Federal Court," and that, around the same time, the Minister opted to commence judicial review proceedings over which he, Justice Russell, presided. Even so, the Judge found no connection between the ANC's strong-arming tactics and the Canadian government's decision to succumb.

No longer eligible for American or Canadian amnesty, however remote, is sixty-six-year old Stephanus (Doppie) Cilliers, a lawyer and sheep farmer from Bronkhorstspruit, about thirty-five miles east of Pretoria. Cilliers was slain early in 2009. He had been hog-tied and tortured before being strangled and shot.[3] When Cilliers Junior discovered his father in the blood smeared hallway of his home, he "ran up and down like a madman,"[4] inconsolable.

David Greig, aged sixty-five, of Hartzenbergfontein, in Gauteng, is beyond rescue too. Greig was killed, also during 2009, in his kitchen, exactly where his mother was shot dead in 1996 by a gang of twelve. Viciously assaulted and stabbed, David's wife, Jeanette, survived the attack. She lives with permanent hearing loss, the trauma, and a hole in her heart for her husband.

"I will give you AIDS," promised Helene Potgieter's assailants. At four o'clock in the morning, four armed men broke down the fortified security doors behind which she and her husband slept. The two farmers escaped with their lives (for the time being), when farm hands arrived to milk the cows.

Dr. Meyerm, a veterinarian in his late thirties, was not as fortunate. He was shot dead, execution-style, in front of his wife Marelise and baby son Wouter, after being kidnapped along with their neighbors from the family farm in the Selati wildlife reserve.[5]

In January 2009, Saar Holtzhauzen, an elderly widow and a farmer, was found throat slit on her much-coveted Macadamia farm near Nelspruit, close to the Mozambican border. Macadamia nuts are one of the costliest (and most coveted) yields, supplying a lucrative export market.

So far, seals clubbed to death on ice floes have garnered more attention in the US than farming South Africa.

Farmers, in particular, qualify as refugees. We defer to the United Nations High Commissioner for Refugees for a definition of a refugee as "a person who [has] a well-founded fear of being persecuted for reasons of race, religion, nationality, membership of a particular social group, or political opinion."

Not only has the South African government refused to protect farmers, but also, as I've already pointed out, it plans on dismantling the only defense at their disposal: the Commando System. America should take the Boers in, given its energetic role in the Faustian pact that has facilitated the depravity that mars the New South Africa. A humane society—as America purports to be—has an obligation, at the very least, to help South Africa's endangered minority help itself.

The obstacles to the importation of the farmers of South Africa are considerable, if not insurmountable. It should be news to no one that American refugee policies do not favor the Boer. Instead, they privilege the likes of the photogenic "Lost Boys of Sudan," to give but one, representative, example.

Thousands of young men from war-torn Sudan, many of whom served in the Sudan People's Liberation Army, were brought to the US by courtesy of left-liberal dreamers within and without the United States government. Overwhelmingly, the "Lost Boys" rejected the American dream, and most of them became mired in alcohol, petty and violent crime, including murder and even fratricide. Unlike the assimilation of these disturbed young men into America, the integration of English-speaking, law-abiding Calvinists—possessors of a fierce work ethic—is not predicated on the naïve belief that if the nurture aspect of the environment were rearranged, nature would automatically realign favorably.

In America, moreover, sharp cultural cleavages pit the "moral majority" against the elites in politics, academia, journalism, Hollywood and the arts. A left-leaning establishment that squints at small-town white Protestants from behind all-too-familiar parapets is unlikely to look favorably upon another country's Calvinists.

Unless, of course, appeals are made to self-interest and the workings of Adam Smith's "Invisible Hand." "By pursuing his own interest," wrote Smith in *The Wealth of Nations*, "[man] frequently promotes that of the society more effectually than when he really intends to promote it. I have never known much good done by those who affected to trade for the public good." Invoking America's urgent economic needs may just sway her immigration policy- and opinion-makers to consider South Africa's food producers as possible future players in America's economic recovery—and, thus, indispensible to their own well-being. To make the case, a brief excursion into the United States' endemic economic woes is called for here.

FROM FELLINI-STYLE CONSUMPTION TO PURITAN-WORTHY PRODUCTION

Decades of credit-fueled, consumption-based living have pulverized our economy, the defining current characteristic of which is now debt—micro and macro; public and private. "By 2007, Americans' personal debt had surged to 133 percent of national income."[6] Personal consumption has hovered since the 1980s at seventy percent of GDP. Our improvident State's debts, liabilities, and unfunded promises exceed the collective net worth of its wastrel citizens. Here is a measure of the degree to which the governments under which Americans groan have run the country into the ground: By the time the ANC's picayune spending, by comparison, reaches forty percent of GDP in 2013, America's duopoly will have incurred a debt in excess of the country's national income.

Non-stop consumption—enabled by government monetary and regulatory policies—has coincided with a transition from a manufacturing-based economy to a service-based one; and from an export- to an import-oriented economy. For some unfathomable reason, this reality has excited febrile libertarian imaginations such as that of Virginia Postrel, author of *The Future and its Enemies*. Postrel lauded the general shift in the American economy from knowledge-related to retail jobs. She even faulted the Bureau of Labor Statistics for not recognizing the rise of spa-related personal services as the powerhouse growth industries they are.

Financier Peter Schiff is not as excited by the prospects for the economy of manicure and massage therapy. The time is ripe for the country to "rebuild its manufacturing base, shore up its crumbling infrastructure, and support those few industries where it remains a world leader,"[7] Schiff has urged. In short, stop the buy, buy, buy Brownian motion, and begin making things again.

"As the service economy recedes," writes Schiff, other sectors will experience resurgence—agriculture, in particular:

> Right now we import a surprising amount of food we eat from other countries, and also export soybean, wheat, and other foodstuffs. As imports become prohibitively expensive, the United States will have no choice but to grow and raise more of its own food. At the same time, as the dollar falls and we struggle to redress the *trade imbalance*, exports of all descriptions will become vitally important. This should spell

> opportunity in the agricultural arena for years to come.[8] [Emphasis added]

In this context, the trade deficit *is* significant, inasmuch as it reflects not an increase in wealth but an increase in indebtedness. The gap between U.S. exports and U.S. imports is frequently dismissed by libertarian economists as an insignificant economic indicator. It shouldn't be. When it comes to the glories of an aggregate, negative balance of trade, allow me to preempt the typical libertarian post-graduate cleverness. In one respect libertarians are right: there is nothing wrong with my running a trade deficit with Costco (the equivalent of the South African Pick 'n Pay), the GTI dealer, or with my hair stylist, as I do—just so long as I pay for my purchases. The data demonstrate that Americans, in general, don't. All in all, "U.S. households, corporations and various levels of government" owe fifty three trillion dollars![9] Unless one is coming from the Keynesian perspective, this is an economically combustive combination. The consumption being lauded by libertarians is debt-driven consumption.

Far from comprising discrete parts, the economy is ineluctably interconnected. Between 2000 and 2006, the trade deficit widened from less than $400 billion to nearly $800 billion."[10] At $42.3 billion in May of 2010, the monthly trade deficits are at their highest since 2008. Libertarians ought to recognize that this trade deficit *belongs* to a nation enmeshed in debt. From the fact that America purportedly ran trade surpluses during the Great Depression it does not follow that the nation's current trade deficit is inconsequential as economic indices go. It could just as well mean that the economic fundamentals today are worse than they were during the Great Depression, since this country has never before been so deeply in hock as it currently is.

Contra the Keynesians who control the economy, real wealth is created not by printing paper money, and galvanizing the globe's governments to buy this government's bonds, but by the production and consumption of products. An abundance of goods, not money income, is what makes for an increase in wealth. A natural shift must, therefore, take place in the US from an economy founded on consumption and credit to one rooted in savings, investment and production.

Unfortunately, the government is doing everything in its power to retard this necessary, natural correction. Legislative intervention is delaying the liquidation of bad debt and worthless, illiquid assets at prices set by the market, not manufactured by government; a credit-card bill of rights has further entrenched and enabled the dysfunctional debtor mindset; Federal Reserve Bank supremo Ben Bernanke has yet to raise interest rates as he should; and Fed-funneled liquidity is preventing prices from free-falling—as they should do—to reflect reality and permit people to purchase the same amount of goods with less available funds. Americans have not begun saving in earnest. America is still a broke and bankrupt consumer economy, enervated by a tentacular bureaucracy.

How can South Africa's farmers help in America's economic recovery?

There are no better farmers than the hardy Boers, currently operating in the "most violent environment in the world outside of a war zone."[11]

> South Africa's commercial farmers are among the best in the world, if not the best. They have to contend with a plethora of problems—the vagaries of the weather, constant drought, rising taxes on everything from the rain on their trees to municipal levies (for which they receive nothing), and excessively high toll road costs. South Africa's land tenure laws make it difficult to dismiss workers, let alone remove these workers from their properties, and they are besieged by land invasions

> and squatters. They are the victims of crop and stock theft, more murders per capita of their group than any other community on earth. They are burnt out, their fences are destroyed, and they are intimidated to the point where many have abandoned their farms.[12]

Despite a life of graft and grief, most persist and persevere. These are just the kind of men and women whom America, once a frontier nation, needs on its road to "financial sobriety."

EMIGRATION

Back on *terra firma,* South Africans face serious obstacles in immigrating to the US. Americans should be disabused of the fiction that the United States' deliberative body would willingly welcome law-abiding, middle-class, white South Africans.

Here is a personal instance of what happens in fact. The year was 2002, the month, February. My family and I were waiting at the American Immigration and Naturalization Service headquarters in Montreal to complete the final leg of our immigration odyssey. We were, as far as I could hear, the only English-speaking family present. It was hard not to notice this, though because I did notice it, the PC Patrol will undoubtedly hit the roof. We were migrating to the United States of America, but the room was a linguistic Tower of Babel, minus the English language. Moreover, unless American companies really had started recruiting wizened old people and small children who all spoke Urdu, most of the immigrants assembled with us must have been the extended families of current citizens. My spouse's "outstanding researcher" designation was very clearly the exception, and not the rule, in our intake.

Indeed, since the 1965 Amendments to the Immigration and Nationality Act took effect—with no real debate or voter participation—immigration to the US has been predicated on a multicultural, egalitarian quota system. The result of this system in practice has been an emphasis on mass importation of people from the Third World. Family reunification supersedes America's economic or cultural interests.

At the time, Congress was more circumspect about the pitfalls of radically transforming America, through state-engineered immigration policies, than it is today. Members of the Senate openly conceded in their debates that America had a distinct and undeniable identity, which previous immigration—being mostly from the traditional northern and western European sources—had not altered. The representatives promised (falsely) that the radical new amendments would generally preserve the country's historical and cultural complexion.

So eager was one senator to pass the Act—which was to herald the age of mass, indiscriminate immigration—that he vowed: "our cities will not be flooded with millions of immigrants annually...under the proposed bill, the present level of immigration [will remain] substantially the same," and "the ethnic mix of this country will not be upset."[13] These pre-PC assurances came not from a "nativist" or a member of the Know-Nothing Party,* but from no other than then-Immigration Subcommittee Chairman Edward Kennedy. This was all before it became taboo to discuss openly, as the late senator did on that occasion, the reshaping of America by means of central planning. (Such discussion is now regularly squelched with accusations of racism or via totemic, robotic incantations of "We are a multicultural nation of immigrants.") In 1965, when Edward Kennedy was promoting his "vision" for America, he candidly acknowledged that (for better or for worse) the country had not always been a mess of multicultural pottage, and that an adventurous

---

*Also called the American Party. Founded in 1849, its members strongly opposed immigrants.

immigration policy had the potential to render the place unrecognizable.

The 1965 Act has produced a torrential influx of immigrants. Every qualified immigrant holds an entry ticket for his extended family. Stephen Steinlight of the Center for Immigration Studies—in "High Noon to Midnight: Does Current Immigration Policy Doom American Jewry"[14]—courageously (for it runs counter to the views of most of our fellow American Jews) highlights the bizarre situation where entire villages from rural Mexico and the West Bank in Israel have U.S. citizenship. Why do they have it? Because one member qualifies for it, and then brings in the entire town.

The Center for Immigration Studies concurs: "The ending of the national origins quotas opened the doors to mass entry of people from Asia and Latin America (regions where people are far more likely to want to emigrate), and the law's emphasis on family reunification ensured that those through the door first would be able to bring in their relatives, freezing out potential immigrants from Europe and from other developing nations."[15] The realities of chain migration explain why "eighty five percent of the 11.8 million legal immigrants arriving in the US between 1971 and 1990 were from the Third World," and why "in 1986 less than 4 percent of the over 600,000 legal immigrants were admitted on the basis of skills."[16] Decades down the line, Anglo and Afrikaner candidates will find themselves crowded out from the "overall quota" as immigration candidates.

Another peculiarity of American immigration public policy is that it carefully weeds out people who show what the recently deceased journalist Mary McGrory called "Early American probity." Or, to use a statistical term, it selects for low moral character.

Most individuals who come to the United States legally—especially middle-class professionals—have an aversion to breaking the law. Call it one of those inexplicable bourgeoisie peculiarities or tics, if you like. But still this aversion exists. Yet the conditions attached to the most frequently granted professional work visa make remaining in the country *without* breaking the law nearly impossible. After all, on losing a position with the sponsoring company, the visa holder must depart *within ten days*. Rather than subject his dependents to such insecurity and upheaval, a responsible, caring, family man—the kind of man who is now hoping to flee from South Africa—would opt to escape to Australia, New Zealand or Canada.

"Current US immigration policy in effect enforces the law only against those who obey it,"[17] is how Peter Brimelow, author of the devastating survey *Alien Nation*, captures the law's impetus. Conversely, the upshot of a persistent, conscious refusal of successive American administrations to enforce immigration law is to reward unacceptable risk-taking and law-breaking. Put it this way: whatever deep-seated personality defect obeying the law might portend, America's law-makers guard against it scrupulously.

In its immigration policies, the US has hitherto shown consideration for Spanish-speaking scofflaws (also the fastest-growing segment in American society) by sidestepping its own statutes, and pushing perennial amnesty programs. And it continues to pander, slavishly, to crasser corporate interests. These interests enjoy the spoils of an immigration-visa racket that encourages the dispossession of the American worker, who, in turn, is forced to subsidize the costs of imported labor. Costs are socialized, profits remain private. Is there no place, within this scheme, for the highly productive, educated (and endangered) South Africans, who, unlike the aforementioned privileged groups, will not impose a net burden on the nation?

Ultimately, American identity politics are a highly organized affair. Immigrants who don't belong to the official ranks of the "excluded" and the "oppressed," and who don't have legions of advocates on their side, will have a tough time garnering sympathy from the immigration establishment. As that maverick columnist Joe Sobran said, "It takes a lot of clout to be a victim."[18]

SECESSION

The Afrikaner nation, like the American one, was born of secession from the British Crown. The Great Trek of 1835 and the early 1840s was an act of secession rather than a revolt.[19] For the endangered Afrikaner, if present policies continue, the future options appear to range from ethnocide to genocide to subjugation. So the possibility of an unconditional, peaceful, "political divorce" (*sans* alimony) for him seems as good as any.

Secession is the political complement of the individual right of free association. At its core are individual rights[20]; the soul of secession is individual liberty—the right to disassociate at will, or not to be forced into associations against one's will. Therefore, should a group wish to secede, it can't resort to mob or democratic tactics and compel naysayers to join. It should simply refuse to associate.

The political thought, if you can call it thought, that prevails among the Western welfare states is aimed at legitimizing the modern, centralized nation-state. Secession therefore threatens all central governments. It represents a movement away from the consolidation of authority, toward the dispersal of that same authority.

This fact might explain why a peaceful—and thus eminently civilized—political parting of the ways has been cast as "atavistic"[21] by public intellectuals in the service of the state. In fiction, the Orwellian Ministry of Truth is a reified entity. In reality, there isn't one concrete ministry that decides how a nation thinks. Rather, there are many such entities. They've evolved over time, and they issue countless subliminal edicts that lodge, like shrapnel, in a nation's collective conscience.

In American political culture, the Many Ministries of Truth—media, academia, pedagogues and politicians—have successfully equated the right of secession, for the purposes of discrediting that right, with a support for slavery, Jim Crow, and racism.

State sovereignty and individual sovereignty (both of which are supposed to be provided by the American Constitution) have further been eroded, thanks to the collusion among the members of the unholy federal trinity: the judicial, legislative, and executive branches of government. In South Africa the situation is like that of America, only worse. Ambient, institutionalized lawlessness makes a mockery of a constitution which already grants the state overweening powers to act as socialist leveler.

Forrest McDonald, who has been dubbed "our greatest living Constitutional scholar," lamented that "what we invented, and others imitate, no longer exists on its native shores."[22] "An essential Americanism," secession is an ingenious American contribution to political philosophy. Both Tocqueville and Lord Acton agreed that the United States was founded as a pact among sovereign states, with which the ultimate power lay, and that "the right to self-government rests on the right to withdraw consent from an oppressive government."[23]

Jefferson, especially, viewed extreme decentralization as the bulwark of the liberty and rights of man. The Jeffersonian doctrine of interposition and nullification allowed states to beat back the (figurative) federal occupier by voiding unconstitutional federal laws. "Jefferson," explains historian Thomas E. Woods, Jr., "considered states' rights a much more important and effective safeguard of people's liberties than the 'checks and balances' among the three branches of the federal government."[24] "For his own generation, and several following," historian Clyde N. Wilson emphasizes, "it was understood that the state sovereignty of the Kentucky resolutions [these were documents written by Jefferson and James Madison in 1798] was Jefferson's primary platform as an American leader."[25]

Sadly, the United States has degenerated from a decentralized republic into a highly consolidated one, to which secession is no longer foundational.

Still, the potency of these principles "can be employed to protect liberty elsewhere in the world."[26] "We see, all over the Western world, a ferment of people against consolidation, in favor of regionalism, devolution, secession, break-up of unnatural states, and the return to historic identities in preference to universal bureaucracies,"[27] writes Wilson.

Contrary to popular misconception, it is not ethnicity that is a catalyst for this driving force. Rather, "Secession or escalating ethnic conflict occurs ... because of the absence of democracy or the failure of a particular democratic system."[28] This absence, and this failure, secession can obviate.

"By its very nature," argues legal theorist James Ostrowski, "the utility of majority rule *increases* as the political unit is divided into smaller and more homogenous units. Far from being hostile to majority rule, secession allows multiple satisfied majorities to be created out of large political units which can only satisfy one majority block at a time. The only difference, of course, is that the old majority is no longer able to impose its will on the old minority."[29]

On the liberating, anti-democratic dynamics of secession, political philosopher Hans-Hermann Hoppe has this to say:

> [I]t eliminates with one stroke the oppressive and exploitative relations between various ethnic, cultural, religious or linguistic communities. By virtue of the simple fact that secession involves the breaking away of a smaller from a larger number of people, it is a vote against the principle of democracy (majority rule) in favor of private (decentralized)—rather than majoritarian—property and ownership.[30]

Hoppe is buoyed by the economic prospects in seceding territories. He holds that while political integration—territorial expansion of government power—may or may not further economic development, "political disintegration is always compatible with economic integration (free trade)."[31] However, to overcome resistance to freedom, a propagandized public would have to be persuaded that an amicable political divorce is perfectly compatible with economic cooperation and prosperity.

Ultimately, secession aims at removing the monopoly power behind a single state, and unleashing competition in government. "By increasing the number of competing governments and territories and the opportunities for inter-territorial migration, a secessionist government is under increased pressure to adopt more liberal domestic policies, i.e., a larger private sector, and lower taxes and regulations."[32]

It goes without saying that seceding territories can just as well violate individual rights as centralized states can. Yet there is a crucial difference between the two kinds of territory, and that difference is this: there is no monopoly power behind a seceding state's action. If a state wants to outlaw alcohol, and you have no wish to become a teetotaler, then you can move to a state that doesn't outlaw alcohol. (That's one way for state legislators to ensure that their states will be about as densely populated as the moon.) If a state wishes to establish a religion, and its own constitution doesn't prohibit this, one can move to a state with a different constitution, where you can practice your religion freely.

The secessionist impulse reveals a great deal about the power differential between the parties involved. "By and large," observes Ostrowski, "the parties that urge various legal, political, and moral arguments for the right of secession, do so because they are less powerful than the majority block. If they were more powerful they would simply secede and be done with it!"[33] By logical extension, "a seceding group is generally the weaker and economically exploited junior partner in a nation-state."[34]

The plight of the distinct Afrikaner nation, and the push among a portion of its people to secede: such phenomena prove that these "citizens believe they are being harmed by being subjects of the large nation."[35] As things stand, Afrikaners cannot hope to achieve self-determination, much less to endure, within the framework of the existing South African state.

The ANC, notes Giliomee, "celebrates culture as long as it is a matter between the citizen and the state."[36] South Africa's dominant party is, however, "dead set against any sub-national identities based on culture or ethnicity as a second tier of loyalty."[37]

The ANC has registered its objection to Zulu traditionalism. It has also stipulated that Afrikaans no longer be accepted as the sole medium of instruction in major Afrikaans schools and universities by forcing these historically Afrikaans institutions into embracing a dual medium system of instruction with English.[38]

ANC spokespersons routinely demand a homogenized nation. They cloak this nation-building project in the raiment of the fight against racism and divisions. But in Giliomee's assessment (he's a liberal), the ANC's project is of a Jacobin, not a pluralist, sort—the goal being to submerge the Afrikaner culture, assert "black numerical superiority," and oversee the rise of a common culture with English as its *lingua franca*.[39]

The outcome: Afrikaner history is slowly being expunged from official annals, and a segment of the community is being hunted down and extinguished.

The United States has outlawed secession.

Why not let South Africa allow it?

THE MOST PRECIOUS THING ON EARTH

The hallmark of a civilized society is the sanctity it accords human life. You needn't be religious to live by this maxim. You must, however, be observant of the most precious thing on earth: the life of an innocent human being. Government's only legitimate function is to protect these innocents—one by precious one.

In the *Second Treatise on Civil Government*, John Locke articulated this solemn duty: "No one ought to harm another in his life, health, liberty, or possessions." Following Locke, Jefferson recognized the right of all men to take the acquisitive actions necessary to sustain and satisfy life. Government's role was to secure these inalienable, natural rights.

Sir Isaiah Berlin, the great British political philosopher, pointed out more than half a century ago that liberties can be either positive or negative. Positive liberties are liberties to act, which, as Berlin observed, can all too quickly turn into abuses of power. Negative liberties involve freedom from being coerced: the freedom, in short, to be left alone. South Africa's Constitution is mostly a charter of positive liberties. The idea is that while making some supply others with work, water, wearables; sustenance, schooling and medicine might compromise the sovereignty of the individual, it nevertheless will increase overall liberty in a society. Liberty is treated as an aggregate social project. Thus, where negative, "leave-me-alone" rights do appear, they are almost always circumscribed and predicated upon the "need to redress the results of past racially discriminatory laws and practices," to quote verbatim from the constitution. Nevertheless, even this document, dreadfully flawed though it is, entrusts the state to protect the individual on the road to serfdom. In this duty, its most fundamental obligation, the African National Congress has failed miserably.

Should Boers and Brits emigrate or secede, the ANC will, no doubt, fume about the loss of power over the goose that lays the golden egg. However, if the ANC's oleaginous officials will not protect the men and women who feed their country, let them all eat cake.

WITH GRATITUDE

To the publisher of this volume to whom added appreciation is due.

To Thomas Szasz, Thomas DiLorenzo, Paul Gottfried, Barbara Grant, and Erik Rush—firm friends all.

To my proof-reader and copy-editor R. J. Stove: The manuscript was polished for publication by the epistolary Wizard of Oz.

To James Ostrowski and Nebojsa Malic for useful comments.

To researcher Rhona Karbusicky, who provided unstinting assistance.

To a nineteen-year-old homeschooled, consummate professional named Aaron Sleadd.

To my dear daughter, who helped me through a punishing publication process.

To my sweet mother, Ann-Wendy Cumes, and my beloved father, Rabbi Abraham Benzion Isaacson, for their backing.

And to my husband, Sean Russell Mercer, who kept me going.

~ Ilana Mercer

NOTES

INTRODUCTION: RAMBO NATION

[1] Donald L. Horowitz, *A Democratic South Africa?: Constitutional Engineering in a Divided Society* (Berkeley: California,1991), p. 99
[2] "Between staying and going," *The Economist,* September 25, 2008
[3] Ilana Mercer, "Self-defense: A universal right," *WorldNetDaily.com*, June 25, 2004.
http://www.wnd.com/news/article.asp?ARTICLE_ID=39139 (accessed October 20, 2009).
[4] Carvin Goldstone, "Who do criminals target in SA?", *IOL,* August 4, 2007.
[5] Robert Guest, "The World's Most Extreme Affirmative Action Program," *Opinion Journal*, December 26, 2004.
[6] *Ibid.*
[7] Peter Hitchens, "He has four wives and he faced 783 counts of corruption," *Daily Mail,* March 31, 2009.
[8] "Zuma: South Africa's comeback kid," *BBC News,* December 28, 2007.
[9] "Wounded Nation," *The Herald* [Glasgow], February 9, 2008.
[10] Andrew Kenny, "The Future Looks Black," *The Spectator*, April 9, 2005.
[11] David Harrison, *The White Tribe of Africa* (Berkeley and Los Angeles, 1981).
[12] Hermann Giliomee, "Liberal and Populist Democracy in South Africa: Challenges, New Threats to Liberalism," p. 18, Presidential Address, Delivered in Johannesburg on February 15, 1996. p. 30.
[13] W. A. de Klerk, *The Puritans in Africa* (London, 1975), p. 35.
[14] Tim Taylor, "Unpalatable but true: cannibalism was routine," *Daily Telegraph* [London], October 20, 2003.
[15] Robert Mayhew (ed.), *Ayn Rand Answers: The Best of Her Q&A* (New York, 2005)
[16] Lawrence E. Harrison and Samuel P. Huntington, *Culture Matters: How Values Shape Human Progress* (New York, 2000), p. 74.

CHAPTER 1: CRIME, THE BELOVED COUNTRY

[1] Sheree Bega, "We just don't feel safe anymore," *The Star,* May 10, 2008

[2] Amir Mizroch, "Cries from the Beloved Country, Part II," *Forecast Highs*, February 8, 2008

[3] Moira Schneider, "SA Jews worried," *SomethingJewish*, March 19, 2008 http://www.somethingjewish.co.uk/articles/2680_sa_jews_worried.htm (accessed June 2008).

[4]"UCT prof dies of injuries," *News24.com*, February 5, 2005 http://www.news24.com/News24/South_Africa/News/0,,2-7-1442_1658014,00.html (accessed June 2008).

[5] Brian D. Hahn, Associate Professor, Department of Mathematics & Applied Mathematics, University of Cape Town, http://www.mth.uct.ac.za/~hahn/ (accessed June 2008).

[6]Breyten Breytenbach, "Mandela's Smile: Notes on South Africa's failed revolution," *Harper's Magazine*, December 2008.

[7] Rob McCafferty, "Murder in South Africa: a comparison of past and present, first edition," *United Christian Action,* June 2003.

[8] Hermann Giliomee, *The Afrikaners: Biography of a People* (Charlottesville, Virginia, 2003), pp. 623-624.

[9] NationMaster, *Murders per capita per country* http://www.nationmaster.com/graph/cri_mur_percap-crime-murders-per-capita (accessed June 2008).

[10]The Disaster Center, "District of Columbia Crime Rates 1960–2006" http://www.disastercenter.com/crime/dccrime.htm (accessed June 2008).

[11] NationMaster, *Rapes Per Capita By Country* http://www.nationmaster.com/graph/cri_rap_percap-crime-rapes-per-capita (accessed June 2008).

[12] Gordon Barclay and Cynthia Tavares, *International Comparisons of Criminal Justice Statistics 2001,* October 24, 2003 http://www.homeoffice.gov.uk/rds/pdfs2/hosb1203.pdf (accessed June 2008).

[13] Barnaby Phillips, "Baby rapes shock South Africa," *BBC News*, December 1, 2001.

[14] "South Africa's rape shock," *BBC News*, January 19, 1999 (accessed

June 2008).

[15] Bureau of Justice Statistics, "Homicide trends in the United States," http://www.ojp.usdoj.gov/bjs/homicide/homtrnd.htm (accessed July 2008).

[16] Infoplease, United States, Population by State, http://www.infoplease.com/ipa/A0004986.html (accessed July 2008).

[17] Demographics Studies, "United States Crime Rates 1960-2006," www.DemographicsNow.com (accessed July 2008).

[18] Gordon Barclay and Cynthia Tavares, *op. cit.*

[19] John Simpson, "Battle over Jo'burg crime," *BBC News*, December 12, 2006

[20] *Ibid.*

[21] Rob McCafferty, *op. cit.*

[22] Jon Williams, "Is the BBC Racist?", *BBC News,* February 20, 2007.

[23] Thabo Mbeki, "Propaganda and reality: The truth as the first casualty of war," *ANC Today*, Volume 7, No. 6, February 16-22, 2007.

[24] Institute of Security Studies, *National Victims of Crime Survey,* Chapter 4, July 2004.

[25] Martin Meredith, *The State of Africa: A History of Fifty Years of Independence* (Sydney, 2006), p. 658.

[26] Hermann Giliomee, *op. cit.*, p. 511.

[27] Rob McCafferty, *op. cit.*

[28] IOL.co.za, "DA sceptical about latest crime statistics," June 30, 2008 http://www.int.iol.co.za/index.php?art_id=nw20080630153311404C859917 (accessed June 2008).

[29] South African Police Service, "Crime Situation in South Africa," June 2007, http://www.saps.gov.za/statistics/reports/crimestats/2007/_pdf/crime_situation1.pdf (accessed May, 2008).

[30] "South Africa," *CIA World Factbook* https://www.cia.gov/library/publications/the-world-factbook/geos/sf.html# (accessed June 2008).

[31] Approximated by the author from the reported two percent decrease in murder rate since 2006, thus 0.973x17034=16574.

[32] "United States", *CIA World Factbook*, https://www.cia.gov/library/publications/the-world-

factbook/geos/us.html (accessed June 2008).
[33] Joseph Lelyveld, *Move Your Shadow: South Africa Black and White* (Johannesburg & London, 1986), p. 207.
[34]*Ibid.*, p. 82
[35] Hermann Giliomee, *op. cit.,* pp. 623-624.
[36] Carvin Goldstone, *op. cit.*
http://www.int.iol.co.za/index.php?set_id=1&click_id=13&art_id=vn20070804085801910C187216 (accessed June 2008).
[37] Andrew Kenny, "Why is our country so violent?", *The Citizen,* December 18, 2006.
[38] Joseph Lelyveld, *op. cit.,* p. 55
[39] Fredrik van Zyl Slabbert, *The Last White Parliament* (New York, 1987), p. 151
[40] Hermann Giliomee, *op. cit.*, pp. 506-507.
[41] Derek Catsam, "The Langa Massacre and State Violence in South Africa," SERSAS Meeting, Contemporary History Institute, Spring 2000, April 14-15, 2000.
http://www.ecu.edu/african/sersas/Catsam400.htm
[42] Peter Clottey, "Mixed Reaction from Dissolution of South Africa's Anti-Corruption Unit," *VOA*, February 13, 2008
http://www.voanews.com/english/archive/2008-02/2008-02-13-voa3.cfm?CFID=13646652&CFTOKEN=49317316 (accessed June 2008).
[43] Hermann Giliomee, *op. cit.,* p. 586.
[44] Keith B. Richburg, *Out of America: A Black Man Confronts Africa* (New York, 1997).
[45] *Ibid.*, p. 198.
[46] Simon Robinson, "The Second Revolution," *Time Europe,* April 11, 2004
http://www.time.com/time/magazine/article/0,9171,610026,00.html (accessed June 2008).
[47] Scott Baldauf, "In South Africa, home sweet fortress," *The Christian Science Monitor,* December 6, 2006
http://www.csmonitor.com/2006/1206/p20s01-lihc.html (accessed February 2007).
[48] "Public-private partnerships have worked wonders in fighting crime," *The Economist,* April 8, 2006.

[49] Nondumiso Mbuyazi, "Petrol attendants stabbed, shot as price skyrockets," *Cape Argus*, June 29, 2008.
[50] Jon Williams, *op. cit.*
[51] Martin Meredith, *op. cit.*, p. 649.
[52] "Public-private partnerships have worked wonders in fighting crime," *The Economist,* April 8, 2006 (accessed July 2008).
[53] YouTube, Farm Murders, "*Carte Blanche*," 2007 http://www.youtube.com/watch?v=3S71PbichSw (accessed August, 2008).
[54] Mohammed Allie, "SA's controversial police chief," *BBC News,* January 11, 2008
[55] Linda M. Richler, "Baby Rape in South Africa," *Child Abuse Review*, Vol. 12, 2003, pp 392-400, at p. 395.
[56] NationMaster.com, Crime Statistics, "Rapes (most recent) by country" http://www.nationmaster.com/graph/cri_rap-crime-rapes (accessed June 2008).
[57] Linda M. Richler, *op. cit.*
[58] *Ibid.*
[59] Barry Bearak, "South African Ministers Resign, Then Return," *The New York Times,* September 23, 2008 (http://www.nytimes.com/2008/09/24/world/africa/24safrica.html?em) (accessed September 23, 2008).
[60] AVERT, HIV & AIDS in South Africa, http://www.avert.org/aidssouthafrica.htm (accessed June 2008).
[61] Dave Kopel, Paul Gallant and Joanne Eisen, "South African Stupidity: Disarming the citizenry is not the answer," *National Review,* October 11, 2000 http://www.nationalreview.com/kopel/kopel101100.shtml (accessed June 2008).
[62] "Public-private partnerships have worked wonders in fighting crime," *The Economist,* April 8, 2006 (accessed July 2008).
[63] Martin Meredith, *op. cit.*, p. 667.
[64] *Ibid.*
[65] Lawrence E. Harrison and Samuel P. Huntington, *Culture Matters: How Values Shape Human Progress* (New York, 2000), p. 299.
[66] Breyten Breytenbach, *op. cit.*, p. 39.
[67] Gill Gifford, "Brave Courtney cherishes first steps," *IOL*, July 1, 2009 http://www.int.iol.co.za/index.php?set_id=1&click_id=139&art_id

=vn20090701051428859C938531 (accessed July 1, 2009).
[68] Anton du Plessis, "When Can I Fire? Use of lethal force to defend property," Institute for Security Studies, *SA Crime Quarterly*, June 8, 2004
[69] Nicolize van der Walt, "'It's self-defence, not racism," *Beeld*, *News24.com*, May 21, 2008 http://www.news24.com/News24/South_Africa/News/0,9909,2-7-1442_2326050,00.html (accessed July 2008).
[70] "Man charged after intruder dies," *News24.com,* January 23, 2006 http://www.news24.com/News24/South_Africa/News/0,,2-7-1442_1867951,00.html (accessed July 2008).
[71] Llewellyn Prince, "Elderly couple hit back," *News24.com,* May 25, 2007.
[72] "Police muzzle 90% of new gun license applications," *Cape Argus,* June 23, 2004. http://www.capeargus.co.za/index.php?fSectionId=49&fArticleId=2124634 (accessed July 2008).
[73] B. Nortje, "Firearm registry chaos," *News24.com*, April 29, 2008 http://www.news24.com/News24/MyNews24/Your_story/0,,2-2127-2128_2313826,00.html (accessed July 2008).
[74] Dave Kopel, Paul Gallant and Joanne Eisen, *op. cit.*
[75] "Police muzzle 90% of new gun license applications," *Cape Argus*, June 23, 2004.
[76] *Ibid.*
[77] "Castle Doctrine in the U.S.," *Wikipedia* http://en.wikipedia.org/wiki/Castle_Doctrine#State-by-state_positions_on_Castle_Doctrine (accessed July 2008).
[78] Heather Mac Donald, "Crime and the Illegal Alien: The Fallout from Crippled Immigration Enforcement," *CIS,* June 2004.
[79] Johan Burger & Henry Boshoff, "An Overview of Crime in South Africa," Institute For Security Studies, 2008
[80] "Freedom and security of the person," *Constitution of South Africa* http://en.wikipedia.org/wiki/Constitution_of_South_Africa_Chapter_2:_Bill_of_Rights#Freedom_and_security_of_the_person (accessed July 2008).
[81] The United States Of America Vs. New Black Panther Party For Self-Defense, Civil Action No.: 09-0065, July 25, 2008

[82] Bureau of Justice Statistics, "Homicide Offending Rates per 100,000 Population by Race," 2005. http://www.ojp.usdoj.gov/bjs/homicide/tables/oracetab.htm
[83] Bureau of Justice Statistics, "Percent of All Homicides by Racial Composition of Victims and Offenders," 2005 http://www.ojp.usdoj.gov/bjs/homicide/tables/ovracetab.htm (accessed July 2008).
[84] Bureau of Justice Statistics, "Homicide Offending Rates per 100,000 Population by Race," 2005 http://www.ojp.usdoj.gov/bjs/homicide/tables/oracetab.htm (accessed July 2008).
[85] U.S. Census Bureau, "2000 Census of Population and Housing," 2000 http://www.census.gov/prod/cen2000/dp1/2kh00.pdf (accessed July 2008).
[86] Bureau of Justice Statistics, "Homicide Offenders by Race," 2005 http://www.ojp.usdoj.gov/bjs/homicide/tables/oracetab.htm (accessed July 2008).
[87] Bureau of Justice Statistics, "Prisoners on death row by race," 2006 http://www.ojp.usdoj.gov/bjs/glance/tables/drracetab.htm (accessed July 2008).
[88] Blacks on death row (1352) divided by total black population (34658190) multiplied by 100000. The same was done for whites on death rows. The ratios derived were divided: 3.9/0.9=4.6
[89] Ilana Mercer, "Mob Gives Imus the Ol' Heave-Ho," *WorldNetDaily.com*, April 13, 2007.
[90] Christopher Plante, "The Untold Knoxville Murders," *Human Events*, May 21, 2007
[91] Joseph Farah, "Hate crime' victims: Young, poor, white," *WorldNetDaily.com,* February 22, 2006.
[92] *Ibid.*
[93] Caroline Wolf Harlow, Ph.D., "Hate Crime Reported by Victims and Police," Bureau of Justice Statistics, November 2005 http://www.ojp.usdoj.gov/bjs/pub/pdf/hcrvp.pdf (accessed February, 2009).
[94] *Ibid.*, p. 3.
[95] *Ibid.*, p. 7.
[96] *Ibid.*, p. 8.

[97] *Ibid.*, p. 8.
[98] Bureau of Justice Statistics, Criminal Victimization in the United States, "Victims and Offenders," 2005 http://www.ojp.usdoj.gov/bjs/pub/pdf/cvus0502.pdf (accessed July 2008).
[99] Human Rights Watch, "No Escape: Male Rape in US Prisons," http://www.hrw.org/reports/2001/prison/report4.html (accessed July 2008).
[100] Human Rights Watch, "No Escape: Male Rape in U.S. Prisons," http://www.hrw.org/reports/2001/prison/report4.html (accessed July 2008).
[101] Toby Lichtig, "Ruined," *The Times Literary Supplement*, May 7, 2010, p. 18
[102] Mathews S., Abrahams N., Martin L.J., Vetten L., van der Merwe L. and Jewkes R., "A national study of female homicide in South Africa," South African Medical Research Council, 2005 http://www.csvr.org.za/docs/gender/sixhours.pdf (accessed July 2008).
[103] Department of Correctional Services, "Inmate Gender and Racial Composition as on the last day of 2008/06" http://www.dcs.gov.za/WebStatistics/ (accessed July 2008).
[104] *Ibid.*
[105] Wikipedia, "White South African Demographics" http://en.wikipedia.org/wiki/Whites_in_South_Africa
[106] South African Migration Project, "Where have all the whites gone," Queen's University, October 2006 http://www.queensu.ca/samp/migrationnews/article.php?Mig_News_ID=3997&Mig_News_Issue=22&Mig_News_Cat=8 (accessed November 2008).
[107] Barry Bearak, "Post-Apartheid South Africa Enters Anxious Era," *The New York Times,* October 6, 2008.
[108] Medical Research Council/UNISA, "The Ninth Annual Report of the National Injury Mortality Surveillance System (NIMSS)," November 5, 2008 http://www.mrc.ac.za/crime/nimms_rpt_Nov08.pdf. (accessed November 18, 2008).
[109] John Kane-Berman, "Fight against crime is a race against race hatred," *South Africa Institute of Race Relations*, March 20, 2008.

[110] *Ibid.* http://www.sairr.org.za/press-office/institute-opinion/fight-against-crime-is-a-race-against-race-hatred.html/?searchterm=racial%20crime (accessed July 2008).

[111] Carvin Goldstone, *op. cit.*

[112] "National Victims of Crime Survey," *Institute for Security Studies,* July 2004 http://www.issafrica.org/pubs/Monographs/No101/Chap4.htm (accessed July 2008).

[113] *Ibid.*

[114] "Public-private partnerships have worked wonders in fighting crime," *The Economist,* April 8, 2006.

[115] Department of Correctional Services, "Inmate Gender and Racial Composition as on the last day of 2008/06" http://www.dcs.gov.za/WebStatistics/ (accessed July 2008).

[116] Tim Wise, "The Color of Deception," *www.zmag.org*, November 19, 2004 (accessed July 2008).

[117] Denise Noe, "The Wichita Horror," *truTV Crime Library*, http://www.trutv.com/library/crime/notorious_murders/classics/carr_brothers/index.html (accessed July 2008).

[118] Nicholas Stix, "Assailant Gets 422 Years for Attack on Raceless Victim," *VDARE.com*, July 27, 2008 http://blog.vdare.com/archives/2008/07/27/assailant-gets-422-years-for-attack-on-raceless-victim/ (accessed July 2008).

[119] Rodney Warwick, "Is SA crime a 'race war'?", *Cape Argus*, April 5, 2008 http://www.capeargus.co.za/index.php?fArticleId=4338427 (accessed July 2008).

[120] Rory Carroll, "South Africans told to stop 'whingeing' [sic] about crime," *The Guardian*, June 21, 2006 http://www.guardian.co.uk/world/2006/jun/21/southafrica.rorycarroll (accessed July 2008).

[121] Rodney Warwick, *op. cit.*

[122] *Ibid.*

[123] Hermann Giliomee, *op. cit.,* p. 586.

[124] Keith B. Richburg, *op. cit.*

CHAPTER 2: THE KULAKS OF SOUTH AFRICA VS. THE XHOSA NOSTRA

[1] "A Bloody Harvest," *Carte Blanche*, June 29, 2003 http://beta.mnet.co.za/carteblanche/Article.aspx?Id=2268 (accessed November 29, 2009).
[2] Shannon Sherry, "Farm Murders: Fertile soil for friction," *Financial Mail,* February 1, 2008.
[3] Aidan Hartley, "South Africa World Cup 2010...and the shooting's already started," *Daily Mail,* September, 10, 2009 http://www.dailymail.co.uk/home/moslive/article-1192088/South-Africa-World-Cup-2010--shootings-started.html#ixzz0kxwkbmYL (accessed April, 2010)
[4] Mail Foreign Service and Jane Flanagan, "Nazi salutes and swastikas as hundreds gather for funeral of murdered white supremacist Eugene Terreblanche," *Daily Mail,* April 10, 2010.
[5] Adriana Stuijt, http://censorbugbear-reports.blogspot.com/
[6] Rachel Zupek, "World's Most Dangerous Jobs," *CareerBuilder.com,* December 17, 2007.
[7] NewsHourOnline, "South Africa's Land Programs," April 14, 2004 http://www.pbs.org/newshour/bb/africa/land/gp_safrica.html (accessed April, 2010).
[8] "Statement by the South African Institute of Race Relations on the ramifications of the killing of Eugène Terre'Blanche - 6th April 2010," http://www.sairr.org.za/sairr-today/sairr-today-press-release-statement-by-the-south-african-institute-of-race-relations-on-the-ramifications-of-the-killing-of-eugene-terreblanche-6th-april-2010/ (accessed April, 2010).
[9] *The Economist*, "The Price of Freedom," June 3, 2010, p. 7
[10] "A Bloody Harvest," *op. cit.*
[11] "Sky News report on racist farm murders in South Africa," YouTube, July 19, 2006 http://www.youtube.com/watch?v=v2E9oz4dfLs&mode=related&search (accessed November 29, 2009)
[12] *Carte Blanche*, *op. cit.*
[13] *Ibid.*

[14] Shannon Sherry, *op. cit.*
[15] Aidan Hartley, *op. cit.*
[16] *Ibid.*
[17] Philip du Toit, *The Great South African Land Scandal* (Centurion, South Africa, 2004), p. 263
[18] *Ibid.*, p. 252
[19] Farmer's Weekly, A community shaped by murder, July 30, 2010
[20] Cedric Mboyisa, "'Kill whites' Facebook page not ours—PAC," *The Citizen,* February 25, 2010
[21] *Ibid.*
[22] Cedric Mboyisa, "Savagery posted on Facebook," *The Citizen,* March 21, 2010
[23] Hilda Fourie, "Murdered girl's hands cut off," *Beeld*, March 12, 2010
[24] AWB (The Afrikaner Resistance Movement), "Information," http://www.awb.co.za/inligting_e.htm (accessed April 5, 2010)
[25] Peroshni Govender, "South Africa's ANC defends 'Kill the Boer' song," Reuters, March 30, 2010
[26] *Ibid.*
[27] Wikipedia, "Peter Mokaba" (accessed March 30, 2010).
[28] Dan Roodt, *The Scourge of the ANC: Two Essays*, PRAAG (Cape Town, 2004), pp. 95-96.
[29] Barbara Levick, "Tacitus: Annals: translated by A. J. Woodman," *The Times Literary Supplement*, February 11, 2005, p. 28.
[30] Jenni O'Grady And Natasha Marrian, "Zuma: 'It's only the Afrikaners who are truly South African,'" *Mail & Guardian* , April 3, 2009.
[31] W. A. de Klerk, *op. cit.*, p. 41.
[32] Hermann Giliomee, *op. cit.*, p. 22.
[33] Donald R. Morris, *The Washing Of The Spears: The Rise And Fall Of The Zulu Nation* (Cambridge, Massachusetts, 1998), p. 127
[34] *Ibid.*
[35] *Ibid.*, p. 138
[36] David Harrison, *The White Tribe of Africa: South Africa in Perspective* (London, 1981), p. 15.
[37] J. A. Spender, *The Life of the Right Hon Sir Henry Campbell-Bannerman*, 2 vols. (London, 1923), p. 351.
[38] David Harrison, *op. cit.,* p. 48.

[39] *Ibid.*, pp. 52, 55.
[40] Hermann Giliomee, *op. cit.,* p. 376.
[41] *Ibid.*, p. xvii.
[42] David Harrison, *op. cit.,* p. 151.
[43] Hermann Giliomee, *op. cit.,* p. 520.
[44] Anon, "The Great White Laager," *Time,* August 26, 1966.
[45] Alexander Hepple, *Verwoerd* (Harmondsworth, Middlesex, England, 1967), p. 203.
[46] Christoph Marx (trans. S. Gordon-Schröder), Oxwagon Sentinel: Radical Afrikaner Nationalism and the History of the Ossewabrandwag (Pretoria, 2008), p. 325.
[47] Martin Meredith, *Nelson Mandela: A Biography* (New York City, 1998), p. 323.
[48] Hermann Giliomee, *op. cit.,* pp. 576-578.
[49] Anon., "Truth Commission Looks At First 'Necklace' Murder," South African Press Association, February 4, 1997.
[50] Martin Meredith, p. 375.
[51] Hermann Giliomee, p. 632.
[52] *Ibid.*
[53] Hermann Giliomee, "Democratization in South Africa," *Political Science Quarterly* (Volume 110, Number 1, 1995), p. 93.
[54] Library of Congress Report, "The 1994 Elections", http://countrystudies.us/south-africa/77.htm
[55] Hermann Giliomee, "Democratization in South Africa," p. 103.
[56] Carlos García-Rivero, "Race, Class, and Underlying Trends in Party Support in South Africa," *Party Politics,* Vol. 12, No. 1 (2006), pp. 57-75.
[57] Joseph Lelyveld, *Move Your Shadow: South Africa, Black And White* (Johannesburg, 1986), p. 54
[58] *Ibid.*, p. 120
[59] Sophie Quinn-Judge, "Lawless Zones," *The Times Literary Supplement*, February 26, 2010.
[60] Hermann Giliomee, "Liberal and Populist Democracy in South Africa: Challenges, New Threats to Liberalism," *The South African Institute of Race Relations*, address delivered February 15, 1996, p. 4
[61] Hermann Giliomee, *The Afrikaners,* p. 613.
[62] Ilana Mercer, "Nation, State & Mass Immigration," *WND.COM*, April

7, 2006
[63] *Ibid.*
[64] Donald R. Morris, *op cit.,* p 247
[65] *Ibid.*, p. 250.
[66] W. A. de Klerk, *op cit.,* p. 246
[67] *Ibid.*, p. 236.
[68] *Ibid.*, p. 230.
[69] *Ibid.*, p. 248.
[70] Joseph Lelyveld, *op cit.*, p. 64.
[71] W. A. de Klerk, *op cit.*, p. 248.
[72] Hermann Giliomee, *The Afrikaners*, p. 497.
[73] *Ibid.*, p. 208.
[74] *Ibid.*, p. 211.
[75] *Ibid.*, p. 208
[76] Arthur Conan Doyle, *The Great Boer War*, Chapter I (London, 1902).
[77] *The Economist*, *op. cit.*, p. 9.
[78] Simon Barber, "Land 'expropriation' in context," *SouthAfrica.info*, May 5, 2006.
[79] South African Institute For Race Relations, "Institute calls for Expropriation Bill to be withdrawn," May 15, 2008 http://www.sairr.org.za/press-office/archive/institute-calls-for-expropriation-bill-to-be-withdrawn-15th-may-2008.html/?searchterm=land%20reform (accessed April 2010).
[80] *Ibid.*
[81] South African Institute For Race Relations, "Warning bells for South Africa," March 18, 2010 (http://www.sairr.org.za/sairr-today/sairr-today-warning-bells-for-south-africa-18th-march-2010) (accessed May 2010).
[82] South African Institute For Race Relations, "Warning bells for South Africa," March 18, 2010 (http://www.sairr.org.za/sairr-today/sairr-today-warning-bells-for-south-africa-18th-march-2010) (accessed May 2010).
[83] *Ibid.*
[84] *The Economist*, op cit., p. 9
[85] South Africa: Land Claims Court, "Mahlangu v. De Jager" (LCC1/96) [1996] ZALCC 1 (25 April 1996)
[86] South Africa: Land Claims Court, "Macleantown Residents

Association Re: Certain Erven and Commonage in Macleantown (LCC12/1996) [1996] ZALCC 3 (4 July 1996)

[87] In the Land Claims Court of South Africa, In the matter between the Popela Community, Department of Land Affairs, and Goedgelegen Tropical Fruits (Pty) Ltd, June 3, 2005

[88] Mazizini Community v. Emfuleni Resorts (Pty) Ltd and Others (LCC 23/07) [2010] ZALCC 3 (12 March 2010).

[89] Philip du Toit, *op cit.*, p. 82.

[90] Aidan Hartley, *op cit.*

[91] *Sunday Times*, "Jacob Zuma warns ANC to halt racial anger," *Sunday Times*, April 11, 2010. http://www.timesonline.co.uk/tol/news/world/africa/article7094305.ece (accessed March, 2010)

[92] Aidan Hartley, *op. cit.*

[93] du Toit, *op cit.,* p. 114.

[94] *The Economist*, op cit., p. 7.

[95] Samuel P. Huntington, *Who Are We? The Challenges to America's National* Identity (New York City, 2004), p. 174.

[96] Hermann Giliomee, "Liberal and Populist Democracy in South Africa," p. 32

[97] Dan Roodt, "Cleaving the Boks in two could aid nation-building," *SuperSport.com*, October 28, 2007, (accessed July 22, 2009) http://www.supersport.com/forum/forum_posts.asp?TID=437

[98] Donald R. Morris, *op cit.* pp. 21-22.

[99] *Ibid.*, p. 26.

[100] *Ibid.*, p.96.

[101] *Ibid.*, p.56.

[102] *Ibid.*, p. 37.

[103] *Ibid.*, p. 60.

[104] *Ibid.*, p. 57.

[105] *Ibid.*

[106] *Ibid.* p. 76.

[107] *Ibid.*, pp. 197-198.

[108] du Toit, *op cit.* p. 87.

[109] *Ibid.*, p. 25.

[110] Walter Block and Guillermo Yeatts, "The Economics and Ethics of Land Reform: A Critique of the Pontifical Council for Justice and

Peace's 'Toward a Better Distribution of Land: The Challenge of Agrarian Reform,'" *Journal of Natural Resources and Environmental Law*, Vol. 15, No. 1, 2000, p. 5.
[111] Donald R. Morris, *op cit.* p. 122
[112] *Ibid.*, pp. 170-171
[113] *Ibid.*
[114] *Ibid.*, p. 44
[115] Dr. Clarissa Fourie, "Land And The Cadastre In South Africa: Its History And Present Government Policy," Paper presented as a Guest Lecture at the International Institute of Aerospace Survey and Earth Sciences (ITC), Enschede, The Netherlands, November 1, 2000.
[116] Walter Block and Guillermo Yeatts., *op cit.,* p. 39.
[117] *The Natives' Land Act*, No. 27, 1913, vol. 10, pp. 135-68.
[118] Donald R. Morris, *op cit.* p. 171.
[119] Eric Beauchemin, "Land ownership in South Africa," 07-03-2008, Radio Netherland Worldwide.
[120] Walter Block and Guillermo Yeatts., *op cit.,* p. 42.
[121] du Toit, *op cit.,* p. 103.

CHAPTER 3: DISPOSSESSION IS NINE-TENTHS OF THE LAW

[1] Simon Robinson, "The Second Revolution," *Time Europe,* April 11, 2004.
[2], "De Beers to sell 26 percent of SA unit," *BBC News,* April 5, 2006.
[3] Government of South Africa, "Broad Based Black Economic Empowerment Act, 2003," Government Gazette, January 9, 2004, http://www.labour.gov.za/download/9478/Act%20-%20Broad-Based%20Black%20Economic%20Empowerment%20-%202003.pdf (accessed August 18, 2008), p. 12.
[4] Simon Robinson, *op. cit.*
[5] Tom Masland, "A Good Life For a Few; Critics say economic empowerment policies have created a black elite but done little to help the masses," *Newsweek,* January 24, 2005.
[6] Max Hastings, "Africa: Thy Name is Death & Disease," *The Daily Mail,* August 13, 2002.

[7] Robert Guest, *op. cit.*
[8] *Ibid.*
[9] "De Beers to sell 26 percent of SA unit," *BBC News*, April 5, 2006 (accessed August 22, 2008).
[10] Government of South Africa, *op. cit.*
[11] *Ibid.*
[12] Donwald Pressly, "Pressure builds for BEE enforcement," *Business Report,* August 19, 2007 (accessed August 18, 2008).
[13] Department of Trade and Industry, "Financial Sector Charter of Black Economic Empowerment," February 9, 2007 http://www.info.gov.za/view/DownloadFileAction?id=72724 (accessed August 20, 2008).
[14] Richard Pipes, *Property and Freedom: The Story of How Through The Centuries Private Ownership has Promoted Liberty and the Rule of Law* (New York, 2000), p. 267.
[15] "The long journey of a young democracy," *The Economist,* March 3, 2007, p. 32-34
[16] Robert Guest, *op. cit.*
[17] Dan Roodt, "Affirmative action is ruthless looting," *The Times* (South Africa), September 7, 2008.
[18] Department of Trade and Industry, *op. cit.,* p. 14
[19] *Ibid.*, p. 111.
[20] "Prevention of Illegal Eviction From and Unlawful Occupation of Land Act," June 5, 1998.
[21] *Ibid.*
[22] *Ibid.*
[23] *Ibid.*
[24] Cobus Claassen, "Couple attacked 2x in 4 days," *Beeld* (South Africa), January 3, 2008.
[25] Carvin Goldstone, "SA's protectors can't protect themselves," *The Star*, December 20, 2008.
[26] Stephen Bevan, "Power line theft leaves South Africa in dark," *Daily Telegraph*, Jun 24, 2007.
[27] *Ibid.*
[28] Barry Bearak, "Post-Apartheid South Africa Enters Anxious Era," *The New York Times*, October 6, 2008.
[29] "Eskom's darkest hour Date," *Carte Blanche*, January 27, 2008

http://www.mnet.co.za/Mnet/Shows/carteblanche/story.asp?Id=3444 (accessed October 20, 2008).
[30] Andrew Kenny, "Eskom are now desperate," *The Citizen* (South Africa), March 25, 2008.
[31] YouTube, "Poor Whites - South Africa" http://www.youtube.com/watch?v=pFj0HdW2iDs (accessed August 27, 2008)
[32] David Harrison, *op. cit.*, p. 66.
[33] Peter Biles , "South Africa's hidden white poverty," *BBC News*, July 29, 2008.
[34] YouTube, "Poor Whites - South Africa" http://www.youtube.com/watch?v=pFj0HdW2iDs (accessed August 27, 2008)
[35] Bill of Rights, "Limitation of Rights," South African Constitution, http://www.info.gov.za/documents/constitution/1996/96cons2.htm#36 (accessed August 18, 2008).
[36] Margaret A. Burnham, "Constitution-Making in South Africa", *Boston Review*, December 1997-January 1998.
[37] Hermann Giliomee, *The Afrikaners,* p. 639.
[38] Kanya Adam, "The Politics of Redress: South African Style Affirmative Action," *The Journal of Modern Africa Studies*, 35, 2 (1997), pp. 231-249.
[39] *Ibid.*, p. 233.
[40] Dan Roodt, *op. cit.*
[41] Mathatha Tsedu, "Why Can't Africans Measure Up to the Job of Leadership?", *Sunday Times* (South Africa), July 13, 2003
[42] Dan Roodt, *op. cit.*
[43] Tom Masland, *op. cit.*
[44] Marian L. Tupy, "Mbeki's Legacy," Cato Institute, September 22, 2008 http://www.cato.org/pub_display.php?pub_id=9656 (accessed September 24, 2008) .
[45] Kanya Adam, *op. cit.,* p. 245
[46] *Ibid.*, p. 239
[47] Dan Roodt, *Scourge*, p. 110
[48] Sonia Sotomayor, "I am a product of affirmative action," YouTube, early 1990s (accessed July 13, 2009), http://www.youtube.com/watch?v=RrSXeLiT_0w&eurl=http%3A%

2F%2Fbarelyablog.com%2F%3Fp%3D9782&feature=player_embedded

[49] Patrick J. Buchanan, "Miss Affirmative Action, 2009," *WorldNetDaily.com*, June 12, 2009 http://www.wnd.com/index.php?pageId=100835 (accessed July 13, 2009)

[50] *Ibid.*

[51] Richard Pipes, *op. cit.* p. 268.

[52] *Ibid.*

[53] Frederick R. Lynch, *Invisible Victims: White Males and the Crisis of Affirmative Action* (Westport, Connecticut, 1991), p. 141.

[54] *Ibid.*, p. 178.

[55] *Ibid.*, p. 150.

[56] *Ibid.*, p. 148.

[57] James Webb, "Diversity and the Myth of White Privilege," *The Wall Street Journal*, July 22, 2010

[58] *Ibid.*

[59] *Ibid.*

[60] Frederick R. Lynch, *op. cit.*, p. 148.

[61] *Ibid.*, p. 148

[62] Patrick J. Buchanan, "Bias and Bigotry in Academia," WorldNetDaily, July 19, 2010.

[63] *Ibid.*

[64] Patrick J. Buchanan, *State of Emergency: The Third World Invasion and the Conquest of America* (New York, 2006), p. 42.

[65] Thomas Jefferson, *Notes on Virginia*, Q.VIII, 1782. ME 2:118

[66] *Ibid.*

[67]John F. Kennedy Presidential Library & Museum, White House Diary, "Dinner honoring Nobel Prize winners of the Western Hemisphere," April 29, 1962.

[68] Thomas E. Woods Jr., *33 Questions about American History You're Not Supposed to Ask* (New York, 2007), p. 15.

[69] Ann Coulter, "They Gave Your Mortgage To A Less Qualified Minority," *anncoulter.org*, September 24, 2008.

[70] Steve Sailer, "Karl Rove—Architect Of The Minority Mortgage Meltdown," *VDARE.com*, September 28, 2008.

[71] Thomas E. Woods Jr., *op. cit.,* p. 150

[72] CNN, "US Foreclosures By State," February 18, 2009.
[73] Thomas E. Woods Jr., *op. cit.,* p. 144.
[74] *Ibid.*, p. 150.
[75] "President Bush Signs American Dream Downpayment Act of 2003," December 2003 http://www.americandreamdownpaymentassistance.com/whsp12162003.cfm (accessed Jan 25, 2009).
[76] Zachary Karabell, "End of the 'Ownership Society," *Newsweek,* October 20, 2008.
[77] Thomas Sowell, *Affirmative Action Around the World: An Empirical Study* (New Haven & London, 2004), p. 175.
[78] P.T. Bauer, *Equality, the Third World, and Economic Delusion* (Cambridge, Massachusetts, 1981), p. 11.
[79] Richard A. Epstein, *Forbidden Grounds: The Case Against Employment Discrimination Laws* (Cambridge, Massachusetts & London, England, 1995), p. 503
[80] Frederick R. Lynch, *op. cit.,* p 12.
[81] *Ibid.*, p. xiv.
[82] *Ibid.*, p. 29.
[83] *Ibid.*, p.12.
[84] Ilana Mercer, "UCLA Bureaucrats Subvert Anti-Quota Law. But Where Is GOP?", *VDARE.com,* September 18, 2008.
[85] Heather Mac Donald, "Elites to Anti-Affirmative-Action Voters: Drop Dead," *City Journal*, Winter 2007.
[86] Timothy Groseclose, "Report on Suspected Malfeasance in UCLA Admissions and the Accompanying Follow Up" http://www.ocregister.com/newsimages/news/2008/08/CUARSGrosecloseResignationReport.pdf, August 28, 2008.
[87] Heather Mac Donald, *op. cit.*
[88] *Ibid.*
[89] Frederick R. Lynch, *op. cit.,* p. 144
[90] *Ibid.*, p. 146
[91] Justin Raimondo, "Nationalists Without a Nation," Taki's Magazine, May 28, 2009
[92] Frederick R. Lynch, *op. cit*, p. 147
[93] Thomas E. Woods Jr., *op. cit.,* p. 146
[94] *Ibid.*

[95] *Ibid.*
[96] *Ibid.*
[97] Simon Robinson, *op. cit.*
[98] George Bornstein, "A New Tyranny?", *The Times Literary Supplement*, January 16, 2009.
[99] *Ibid.*
[100] Richard A. Epstein, *op. cit*, p. 16.
[101] *Ibid.*, p. 137.
[102] Felix Morley, *Freedom and Federalism* (Indianapolis, 1981), p. 86.
[103] Richard Pipes, *op. cit.,* p. 267.
[104] Ronald Bailey, "Grande Conservative Blogress Diva Ann Althouse Among the True Believers —What Really Happened?", *Reason,* December 29, 2006.
[105] Richard Pipes, *op. cit.,* p. 266.
[106] Thomas Sowell, *op. cit.,* p. 115.
[107] Title VII of the Civil Rights Act of 1964, "Unlawful Employment Practices," SEC. 2000e-2. [Section 703], (j)
[108] Richard Pipes, *op. cit.,* p. 267.
[109] *Ibid.*
[110] Richard A. Epstein, *op. cit.,* p. xiii.
[111] *Ibid.*, xiv.
[112] P.T. Bauer, *op. cit.,* p. 11.
[113] *Ibid.*, p. 133.
[114] James Madison, *The Federalist Papers*, No. 10, p. 46.
[115] *Ibid.*, p. 52.
[116] Frederick R. Lynch, *op. cit.,* p. 152
[117] Steven Farron, "Prejudice is Free, But Discrimination Has Costs," *Journal of Libertarian Studies*, Summer 2000, p. 194.
[118] *Ibid.*, p. 189.
[119] *Ibid.*, p. 216.
[120] *Ibid.*, p. 230.
[121] *Ibid.*, p. 199.
[122] Corinne Sauer and Robert M. Sauer, *Judaism, Markets, and Capitalism: Separating Myth from Reality* (Acton Institute, Grand Rapids, Michigan, 2007)
[123] *Ibid.*, p. 179.
[124] Steven Farron, *op. cit,* p. 181

[125] Robert P. Murphy, *The Politically Incorrect Guide to Capitalism* (Washington, D.C., 2007), p. 29.
[126] P.T. Bauer, *Dissent on Development: Studies and Debates in Development Economics* (London, 1971), p. 158.

CHAPTER 4: MANDELA, MBEKI, AND MUGABE SITTING IN A BAOBAB TREE K-I-S-S-I-N-G

[1] George H. Wittman, "African Suicide," *The American Spectator*, April 16, 2008
[2] The Bureau of Democracy, Human Rights, and Labor, "Country Reports on Human Rights Practices (Zimbabwe)," March 6, 2007.http://www.state.gov/g/drl/rls/hrrpt/2006/78765.htm (accessed October 20, 2009).
[3] Brett D. Schaefer, "The Crisis in Zimbabwe: How the U.S. Should Respond," The Heritage Foundation, March 23, 2007.
[4] Martin Meredith, *The State of Africa* (New York, 2006), p. 681
[5] *Ibid.*, p. 634.
[6] Martin Fletcher, "Nothing to lose: how Mugabe's banker turned Z$1,000,000,000,000 into Z$1," *The Times*, February 3, 2009.
[7] Martin Meredith, *op. cit.,* p. 619.
[8] *Ibid.*
[9] Alan Cowell, "Ian Smith, Defiant Symbol of White Rule in Africa, Is Dead at 88," *The New York Times,* November 21, 2007.
[10] *Ibid.*
[11] J. E. Davies, "Constructive Engagement? Chester Crocker and American Policy in South Africa, Namibia and Angola 1981-88 (Athens, Ohio, 2007).
[12] Niall Ferguson, "Trials of Heinz," *The Times Literary Supplement,* May 30, 2008.
[13] *Ibid.*
[14] Keith B. Richburg, *op. cit.,* p. 212
[15] *Ibid.*
[16] *Ibid.*
[17] *Ibid.*
[18] *Ibid.*

[19] *Ibid.*
[20] *BBC News*, "Zimbabwe targets foreign business," September 26, 2007.
[21] *Ibid.*
[22] Movement for Democratic Change, http://www.mdc.co.zw/ (accessed October 20, 2009).
[23] J.C, "Laughing at Lenin," *The Times Literary Supplement*, June 6, 2008.
[24] Catherine Philp, "Zimbabwe faces starvation as mobs rampage through farms," *Times Online*, April 9, 2008.
[25] *Ibid.*
[26] Martin Meredith, *op. cit.*, p. 687
[27] Keith B. Richburg, "Zimbabwe shows Africa is still in the despots' grip," *The Observer*, June 22, 2008.
[28] Martin Meredith, *op. cit.*, p. 686.
[29] *Ibid.*
[30] *Ibid.*
[31] *Ibid.*
[32] "Zimbabwe squatters' leader says land grabs to continue," *CNN,* April 14, 2000
[33] Martin Meredith, *op. cit.*, p. 637.
[34] *BBC News*, "Scores of Zimbabwe farms 'seized'," February 23, 2009
[35] Max Hastings, *op. cit.*
[36] *Ibid.*
[37] "The Zimbabwe impasse," *The Washington Times*, April 16, 2008.
[38] Dan Roodt, *Scourge.*
[39] Anon., "The luvvies' big night out," The *Daily Mail,* June 27, 2008.
[40] *Ibid.*
[41] Hermann Giliomee, *The Afrikaners, op. cit.,* p. 630.
[42] *Ibid.*
[43] "Nelson Mandela Sings about Killing Whites," YouTube, July 21, 2006 http://www.youtube.com/watch?v=fcOXqFQw2hc (accessed October 20, 2009).
[44]Anon., "Medal of Honor for a Terrorist," *The Pittsburgh Tribune-Review*, July 27, 2003 http://www.pittsburghlive.com/x/pittsburghtrib/s_146312.html (accessed October 20, 2009).
[45] Dan Roodt, *op. cit.*

[46] "Medal of Honor for a Terrorist."
[47] Hermann Giliomee, *op cit.,* p. 533.
[48] John B. Battersby, "Mandela Release In 4 Weeks Seen," *The New York Times,* August 21, 1988.
[49] *National Post* , "Mandela's mixed legacy," January 20, 2009
[50] "Tokyo Sexwale," "Controversies," *Wikipedia,* http://en.wikipedia.org/wiki/Tokyo_Sexwale (accessed October 20, 2009).
[51] Hermann Giliomee, *op. cit.,* p. 630.
[52] *Ibid.*
[53] "Mandela defends Lesotho intervention," *BBC News,* September 24, 1998.
[54] Dan Roodt, *op. cit.,* p. 15
[55] Paul Seabright, "It's Chicago's Fault," *The Times Literary Supplement,* April 11, 2008.
[56] Steven Farron, *op. cit.*
[57] David Harrison, *op. cit.,* p. 78,
[58] *Ibid.*
[59] *Ibid.*
[60] "South Africa Tries Affirmative Action," *CNN*, October 8, 1998 http://www.cnn.com/WORLD/africa/9810/08/safrica.affirmative.action/ (accessed October 20, 2009).
[61] Dan Roodt, *op. cit.*
[62] *Ibid.*
[63] Robert H. Phinny and Dan Burton, "South Africa Doesn't Need Communists," The International Herald Tribune, November 19, 1991.
[64] James Kirchick, "South Africa's Betrayal," *The Opinion Journal*, August 8, 2007.
[65] Dan Roodt, *op. cit.*
[66] Hermann Giliomee, *op. cit.*, p. 630.
[67] Breyten Breytenbach, *op. cit.*
[68] South African Migration Project, "Where have all the whites gone," October 2006 http://www.queensu.ca/samp/migrationnews/article.php?Mig_News_ID=3997&Mig_News_Issue=22&Mig_News_Cat=8. (accessed October 13, 2008).
[69] Human Sciences Research Council, "Skills migration and the brain

drain in South Africa," February 25, 2004.
[70] *The Economist,* "Between staying and going," September 25, 2008.
[71] Bronwynne Esbach, " Who's packing for Perth?," *Sunday Argus,* August 5, 2007 .
[72] John Carlin, "A saint's patience is tried, and found wanting," *New Statesman*, January 1, 1999.
[73] Andrew Kenny, "The Future Looks Black," *The Spectator,* April 9, 2005.
[74] *Ibid.*
[75] John Pilger, "The silent war on Africa," *Mail & Guardian Online*, July 7, 2008.
[76] *Ibid.*
[77] David Blair, "Zimbabwe's white farmers in new land grabs," *The Daily Telegraph*, April 9, 2008.
[78] "Country profile: South Africa," *BBC News*, February 29, 2008.
[79] Andrew Kenny, *op. cit.*

CHAPTER 5: THE ROOT-CAUSES RACKET

[1] Anderson Cooper 360 Degrees, "Angelina Jolie: Her Mission and Motherhood," *CNN*, June 20, 2006.
[2] Simon Robinson, "The Second Revolution," *Time Europe,* April 11, 2004.
[3] Dan Roodt, "Adapt and Die - South Africa's New Motto," *Praag*, November 2004
[4] James Burnham, *Suicide of the West* (New York, 1964), p. 16.
[5] Kenneth Minogue, "Us and Them," *The Times Literary Supplement*, February 19, 2010, p. 28
[6] Keith Windschuttle, "In Defense of Colonialism,*" American Outlook*, Summer 2002
[7] Kenneth M. Newton, "Second Sight: Is Edward Said right about *Daniel Deronda?" The Times Literary Supplement*, May 9, 2008.
[8] Lawrence E. Harrison and Samuel P. Huntington, *Culture Matters: How Values Shape Human Progress* (New York, 2000), p. 65.
[9] *Ibid.*, pp. xvii, xix.
[10] *Ibid.*, p. xx

[11] P. T. Bauer, *Equality, the Third World, and Economic Delusion* (Cambridge, Massachusetts, 1981), p. 12.
[12] David Dollar and Aart Kraay, "Growth Is Good For The Poor," *Journal of Economic Growth*, March 2002.
[13] Lawrence E. Harrison and Samuel P. Huntington, *op. cit.*, p. xx
[14] *Ibid.*, p. xiv.
[15] *Ibid.*, p. xx.
[16] Kenneth M. Newton, *op. cit*
[17] *Ibid.*
[18] P. T. Bauer, *op. cit.*, p.4.
[19] Donald R. Morris, *op cit.*, p. 175
[20] Lawrence E. Harrison and Samuel P. Huntington, *op. cit.,* p. 132.
[21]*Ibid.*, p. 72.
[22] *Ibid.*, p. 68.
[23] P. T. Bauer, *op. cit.,* p. 165.
[24] *Ibid.*, p. 167.
[25] *Ibid.*, p. 165.
[26] *Ibid.*, p. 166.
[27] Dennis O'Keeffe, *Edmund Burke* (New York, London, 2010) p. 29
[28] P.T. Bauer, *Dissent on Development* (London, 1971), p. 149.
[29] Ilana Mercer, "Don't Silence Ward Churchill, Sack Him," *Antiwar.com*, April 20, 2005
[30] Max Hastings, "Africa: Thy Name is Death and Disease," *The Daily Mail*, August 13, 2002.
[31] Bernard Porter, "Giant Vegetables," *The Times Literary Supplement*, September 25, 2009, pp. 8-9
[32] *Ibid.*
[33] *Ibid.*
[34] James Belich, *Replenishing the Earth: The Settler Revolution and the Rise of the Angloworld* (Oxford, 2009), p. 9
[35] Walter C. Sellar and R. J. Yeatman, *1066 And All That* (London, 1930), p. 105.
[36] Jeremy Black, *The Slave Trade* (London, 2006), p. 9.
[37] *Ibid.*
[38] P.T. Bauer, *Dissent on Development*, p. 72.
[39]Azar Gat, "Is genocide a modern phenomenon?", *The Times Literary Supplement,* March 23, 2007

[40] Jeremy Black, *op. cit.,* p. 139.
[41] *Ibid.*, p. 140.
[42] *Ibid.*
[43] Azar Gat, *op. cit.*
[44] Jeremy Black, *op. cit.,* p. 133.
[45] *Ibid.*, p. 136.
[46] Michelle Malkin, "A Refugee Reality Check For Angelina Jolie," *VDARE.com*, October 17, 2006.
[47] Nicholas D. Kristof, "Aid: Can It Work?" *New York Review of Books*, October 5, 2006.
[48] P.T. Bauer, *Dissent on Development*, p. 126.
[49] *Ibid.*
[50] Peter Brimelow, "In Memoriam: Peter, Lord Bauer," *VDARE.com*, May 03, 2002.
[51] The World Bank, "Why Trade Costs Matter to Africa," June 17, 2008 http://econ.worldbank.org/WBSITE/EXTERNAL/EXTDEC/EXTRESEARCH/0,,contentMDK:21808702~pagePK:64165401~piPK:64165026~theSitePK:469382,00.html (accessed Nov 27, 2008).
[52] *Ibid.*
[53] Peter Bauer is thought to have said this during a lecture.
[54] Gwartney, J., Holcombe, R. and Lawson, R. "The Scope of Government and the Wealth of Nations" (1998), *The CATO Journal* vol. 18 (2); pp 163-190.
[55] P. T. Bauer, *Equality, the Third World, and Economic Delusion*, p. 79.
[56] Lawrence E. Harrison and Samuel P. Huntington, *op. cit.,* p. xxi
[57] *Ibid.*, p. xv.
[58] Thomas E. Woods Jr., *33 Questions about American History You're Not Supposed to Ask* (New York, 2007), p. 148.
[59] Lawrence E. Harrison and Samuel P. Huntington, *op. cit.,* p. xxv.
[60] *Ibid.*, p. xxvii.
[61] *Ibid.*, p. 3.
[62] *Ibid.*, p. xxi.
[63] *Ibid.*, p. 299.
[64] *Ibid.*, p. 72.
[65] *Ibid.*, p. 75.
[66] *Ibid.*, p. 67.
[67] Faith Karimi, "Abuse of child 'witches' on rise, aid group says," *CNN*,

May 18, 2009
[68] Robyn Dixon, "Zimbabweans say angry ancestors are behind road accidents," *The Los Angeles Times*, May 23, 2009
[69] *Ibid.*, p. 68.
[70] James Burnham, *op. cit.*, p.86.
[71] *Ibid.*, p. 202.
[72] P.T. Bauer, *Dissent on Development*, p. 132.
[73] Hermann Giliomee, "Liberal and Populist Democracy in South Africa: Challenges, New Threats to Liberalism," *The South African Institute of Race Relations*, addressed delivered February 15, 1996, p. 4
[74] *Ibid.*, 14
[75] *Ibid.*, p. 9
[76] *Ibid.*, p. 9
[77] *Ibid.*, p. 12
[78] Jim Peron, "Die, the Beloved Country (South Africa)", April 18, 2000 http://www.gwb.com.au/2000/pc/race9.htm (accessed October 19, 2008).
[79] Kenneth Minogue, *op. cit.*, p. 28
[80] Hermann Giliomee, *The Afrikaners,* p. 174.
[81] *Ibid.*
[82] *Ibid.* p. 539.
[83]Andrew Kenny, "How Apartheid Saved South Africa," *The Spectator*, November 27, 1999.
[84] Hermann Giliomee, *op. cit.*, p. 539.
[85] *Ibid.*, p. 650.
[86] *Ibid.*, p. 539.
[87] W. A. de Klerk,.*op. cit.,* p. 251
[88] Hermann Giliomee, *op. cit.*, p. 596.
[89] Dollie Brathwaite, "Elderly citizen's perception of their health and care provided in a rural South African community," March-April, 2002, *Journal of The Association of Black Nursing Faculty* http://findarticles.com/p/articles/mi_m0MJT/is_2_13/ai_93610977?tag=untagged (accessed December 8, 2008).
[90] Simon Robinson, *op. cit.*
[91] Dr. Haroon Bhorat, *Unemployment in South Africa: Descriptors & Determinants*, University of Cape Town and Economic, Advisor to the President, p. 5

http://siteresources.worldbank.org/INTEMPSHAGRO/Resources/Bhorat_Unemployment_SouthAfrica.pdf (accessed December 27, 2008).
[92] Breyten Breytenbach, *op. cit.*
[93] Hermann Giliomee, *op. cit.*, pp. 600-601.
[94] William P. Barrett, "The 200 Largest U.S. Charities," *Forbes Magazine*, November 22, 2006.
[95] "Saving Soweto," *Al Jazeera*, January 2009 http://english.aljazeera.net/programmes/general/2009/01/200919143440701450.html (accessed January 2009).
[96] Friedrich A. Hayek, *The Constitution of Liberty* (Chicago, 1960), p. 77.
[97] Murray N. Rothbard, "Hutus vs. Tutsis," *LewRockwell.com*, June 1994 http://www.lewrockwell.com/rothbard/rothbard74.html (accessed November 3, 2008).
[98] Anthony Kenny, "Just So," *The Times Literary Supplement*, October 17, 2008.
[99] *Ibid.*

CHAPTER 6: WHY DO WASP SOCIETIES WITHER?

[1] Richard Elphick and Rodney Davenport, *Christianity in South Africa: A Political, Social, and Cultural History* (Berkeley: University of California Press, 1997).
[2] Wikipedia, "Education in South Africa" http://en.wikipedia.org/wiki/Education_in_South_Africa#Pre-colonial_education (accessed January 2009).
[3] Matthew Parris, "As an atheist, I truly believe Africa needs God," *Times Online*, December 27, 2008.
[4] W. A. de Klerk, *op. cit.*, p. 260.
[5] *Ibid.*, p. 259
[6] *Ibid.*, p. 221.
[7] *Ibid.*
[8] *Ibid.*, p. 259.
[9] Russell Kirk, *The Roots Of American Order* (Washington D.C., 1991), pp. 11-49.
[10] Hermann Giliomee, *op. cit.*, p. 42.
[11] *Ibid*, p. 42.

[12] Emmanuel Suttner, *Cutting Through The Mountain: Interviews With South African Jewish Activists* (Parktown, South Africa, 1997), pp. 568-569.
[13]Kirk, *op. cit.*, pp. 11-49.
[14] *Ibid.*
[15] *Ibid.*
[16] Ilana Mercer, "For The Love Of Islam," *WorldNetDaily.com*, November 4, 2005
http://www.wnd.com/news/article.asp?ARTICLE_ID=47222
(accessed May 13, 2009).
[17] Samuel P. Huntington, *The Clash of Civilizations and the Remaking of World Order* (New York, 1997), pp. 256-259
[18] Muhammed Haron, *The Dynamics of Christian-Muslim Relations in South Africa (circa 1960-2000)*, paper given at the University of Birmingham, April 19-23, 2004.
[19] *Ibid.*
[20] *Ibid.*
[21] Samuel P. Huntington, "*The Clash of Civilizations? The Debate*," *Foreign Affairs* (1996), pp. 10-11
[22] *Ibid.*
[23] *Ibid.*
[24] Muhammed Haron, , *op. cit.*
[25] *Ibid.*
[26] *Ibid.*
[27] *Ibid.*
[28] *Ibid.*
[29] Wikipedia, "Islam in South Africa,"
http://en.wikipedia.org/wiki/Islam_in_South_Africa (accessed April 20, 2009).
[30] Paul Sperry, *Infiltration: How Muslim Spies and Subversives Have Penetrated Washington* (Nashville, Tennessee), p. 19
[31] Rita M. Byrnes, *South Africa: A Country Study*, Washington: GPO for the Library of Congress, 1996.
[32] Jane Hunter, "The Israeli-South African-U.S. Alliance," *The Link*, Volume 19, Issue 1, March- April 1986
[33] *Ibid.*
[34] Roger Scruton, *The West and the Rest: Globalization and the Terrorist Threat* (Wilmington, Delaware, 2003).

[35] Keith Gottschalk, "Vigilantism v. the State: A case study of the rise and fall of Pagad, 1996-2000," *Institute for Security Studies,* February 2005.
[36] Serge Trifkovic, *The Sword of the Prophet: Islam: history, theology, impact on the world* (Boston, 2002), p. 218.
[37] *Ibid.*, p. 219.
[38] *Ibid.*, p. 227
[39] Paul Sperry, *op. cit.*, p. 87.
[40] Jeremiah W. (Jay) Nixon, John M. Britt, James F. Keathley, Van Godsay, "The Modern Militia Movement," *MIAC Strategic Report,* February 20, 2009.
[41] Anneli Botha, "PAGAD: A Case Study of Radical Islam in South Africa," *The Jamestown Foundation*, September 14, 2005.
[42] Gottschalk, *op. cit.*
[43] *Ibid.*
[44] James Kirchick, "South Africa's Betrayal," *The Wall Street Journal Opinion Journal*, August 8, 2007.
[45] *Ibid.*
[46] Keith Gottschalk, *op. cit.*
[47] *Ibid.*
[48] *Ibid.*
[49] "Intruders are targeting secret facility," *The Sowetan*, November 13, 2007.
[50] Sperry, *op. cit.,* p. 90.
[51] Steven Tau, "Terror claim angers Muslims," *The Citizen* (Johannesburg), August, 21, 2008.
[52] Alex Perry, "The Rise of Extremism in Somalia," *TIME*, March 1, 2010
[53] *Ibid.*
[54] *Ibid.*
[55] Michael Schmidt, "Islamic terror is not a problem for SA," *Saturday Star* (Johannesburg), November 20, 2004.
[56] *Ibid.*
[57] *Ibid.*
[58] Cnaan Liphshiz, "South Africa Jews slam deputy PM's anti-Semitic comments," *Haaretz,* January 28, 2009.
[59] An Alan Dershowitz coinage, from *The Case for Israel* (Hoboken, New

Jersey, 2003).
[60] COSATU Week, April 13, 2007.
[61] Heinz de Boer, "Cosatu targets Israel," *IOL,* February 4, 2009.
[62] Lionel Slier, "Jews gather at Beyachad to show Israel solidarity," *SA Jewish Report,* February 13-20, 2009.
[63] *Ibid.*
[64] Sam Kretzmer, "Taking A Dim View Of CSO Presence At PSC Rally," Letter to the Editor, *SA Jewish Report,* February 13-20, 2009
[65] Shelley Elk, "Emotions run high at Cosatu/PSC rally," *SA Jewish Report,* 13-20 February, 2009.
[66] James Kirchick, *op. cit.*
[67] "Riz Khan Interviews Amos Oz," *Al Jazeera Net,* February 18, 2009.
[68] Canadian Coalition for Democracies, "Canada Joins Running of the Jew at the U.N," November 30, 2006
[69] Ilana Mercer, "Thugs Unite At The UN Again," *WorldNetDaily.com*, February 1, 2008
[70] Naresh Raghubeer and David Harris, "Harper Government Withdraws From U.N.," *Global Politician* (New York), January 30, 2008.
[71] *Ibid.*
[72] Rabbi Ben Isaacson, "Do Not Attend Racist Conference In Durban," *The Jewish Report*, August 17, 2001.
[73] *Ibid.*
[74] *Ibid.*
[75] *Ibid.*
[76] *Ibid.*
[77] *Ibid.*
[78] Hermann Giliomee, *op. cit.,* p. 586.
[79] *Ibid.*, p. 646.
[80] W. A. De Klerk, *op. cit.,* pp. 285-287.
[81] *Ibid.*
[82] *Ibid.*
[83] *Ibid.*, p. 310.
[84] Samuel P. Huntington, *The Clash of Civilizations,* p. 318.
[85] *Ibid.*
[86] Paul Edward Gottfried, *After Liberalism: Mass Democracy in the Managerial State* (Princeton, New Jersey, 1999), pp. vii-xiv.

[87] Robert D. Putnam, "E Pluribus Unum: Diversity and Community in the Twenty-first Century," The 2006 Johan Skytte Prize Lecture, 2007
[88] Paul Edward Gottfried, *Multiculturalism and the Politics of Guilt* (Columbia [Missouri] and London, 2002), p. 16.
[89] Hermann Giliomee, *op. cit.*, p. 646.
[90] Matthew Parris, *op. cit.*
[91] *Ibid.*
[92] *Ibid.*
[93] Nicole Itano, "In South Africa, many blacks convert to Islam," *The Christian Science Monitor*, January 10, 2002.
[94] Samuel P. Huntington, *The Clash of Civilizations*, p. 256
[95] Jon Meacham, "The End of Christian America," *Newsweek*, April 13, 2009.
[96] *Ibid.*
[97] Samuel P. Huntington, *Who are We*, p. 83.
[98] Matthew Parris, *op. cit.*

CHAPTER 7: THE ANGLO-AMERICAN-AUSTRALIAN AXIS OF EVIL

[1] Samuel P. Huntington, *The Clash of Civilizations*, p. 269.
[2] Patrick J. Buchanan, "Nation or Notion?", *The American Cause,* October 4, 2006.
[3] Russell Kirk, *The Essential Russell Kirk: Selected Essays* (Wilmington, Delaware, 2007), p. 380.
[4] Buchanan, *op. cit.*
[5] Paul E. Gottfried, *Encounters: My Life with Nixon, Marcuse, and Other Friends and Teachers* (Wilmington, Delaware, 2009), pp. 39-40.
[6] Ilana Mercer, "The Gore Gospel: Act Globally, Trash Locally" *WorldNetDaily.com*, November 2, 2007.
[7] *Ibid.*
[8] Samuel P. Huntington, *The Clash of Civilizations? The Debate (* New York, 1996), p. 56.
[9] *Ibid.*
[10] Rita M. Byrnes, *op. cit.*
[11]*Ibid.*

[12] James Burnham, *op. cit.,* p. 270.
[13] *Ibid.*, pp. 270-273.
[14] Dennis O'Keeffe, *op cit.,* p. 17.
[15] *Ibid.*, p. 40
[16] Rita M. Byrnes, ed., *op cit.*
[17] *Ibid.*
[18] Wikipedia, "Constructive Engagement" http://en.wikipedia.org/wiki/Constructive_engagement (accessed Feb. 2009).
[19] Christopher Hitchens, "The Stupidity of Ronald Reagan," *Slate,* June 7, 2004.
[20] Edwin J. Feulner, Ph.D., "The Roots of Modern Conservative Thought from Burke to Kirk," *The Heritage Foundation*, July 9, 2008.
[21] *Ibid.*
[22] Russell Kirk, *op cit.*, p. 508.
[23] *Ibid.*, p. 380.
[24] Ilana Mercer, "Nation, State & Mass Immigration," *WorldNetDaily.com*, April 7, 2006.
[25] Hermann Giliomee, *op. cit.*, p. 625.
[26] *Ibid.*
[27] *Ibid.*, pp. 604-605.
[28] *Ibid.*, p. 611.
[29] Donald L. Horowitz, *A Democratic South Africa?: Constitutional Engineering in a Divided Society* (Berkeley: California, 1991), p. 7.
[30] Ben Temkin, *Buthelezi: A Biography* (London, 2002), p. 267.
[31] Hermann Giliomee, *op cit.*, p. 611
[32] Fredrik van Zyl Slabbert , *op cit.*, p. 73
[33] Martin Meredith, *The State of Africa* (The Free Press, Great Britain, 2006), p. 626.
[34] Donald L. Horowitz, *op cit.*, p. 103.
[35] *Ibid.*
[36] Hermann Giliomee, *op cit.*, p. 608.
[37] BBC Summary of World Broadcasts, "KwaZulu Assembly Approves Draft Federalist Constitution," December 3, 1992.
[38] Hermann Giliomee, *op cit.*, p. 608
[39] *Ibid.*
[40] *Ibid.*

[41] Donald L. Horowitz, *op cit.*, p. 102
[42] Hermann Giliomee, *op cit.*, p. 629
[43] *Ibid.*, p. 639.
[44] Hermann Giliomee, "Liberal and Populist Democracy in South Africa: Challenges, New Threats to Liberalism," February 15, 1996, p. 18 (address delivered in Johannesburg).
[45] *Ibid.* p. 18.
[46] *Ibid.* p. 19.
[47] Samuel P. Huntington, *Political Order in Changing Societies* (New Haven, Connecticut & London, 1968), pp. 7-8.
[48] Azar Gat, *op. cit.*
[49] *Ibid.*
[50] *Ibid.*
[51] Donald Horowitz, *op cit.*, p. xv
[52] *Ibid.*, pp. 242-244.
[53] *Ibid.*, p. 283.
[54] Hermann Giliomee, *The Afrikaners.*, p. 617
[55] Elie Kedourie, "One-Man-One-Vote," *South Africa International*, July 1987, p. 3
[56] Hermann Giliomee, "Liberal and Populist Democracy," p. 17.
[57] *Ibid.*, p. 18.
[58] *Ibid.*, p. 22.
[59] Lawrence Auster, "Global democratization: the unasked questions," *American Thinker*, August 17, 2005
[60] Hans-Hermann Hoppe, *Democracy The God That Failed: The Economics and Politics of Monarchy, Democracy, and Natural Order* (New Brunswick, London, 2001), p. 39
[61] *Ibid.*, p. 27
[62] *Ibid.*
[63] Ilana Mercer, "Classical Liberalism And State Schemes," *Free-Market News Network*, September 2, 2005,
[64] John C. Calhoun, *A Disquisition on Government* (Charleston, South Carolina, 1851)
[65] *Ibid.*
[66] *Ibid.*
[67] Philip du Toit, *op. cit.*, p. 268
[68] Donald R. Morris, *op. cit,* p. 228

[69] Ilana Mercer, "The Hillary, Hussein, McCain Axis of Evil," *WorldNetDaily.com*, February 15, 2008
[70] Hermann Giliomee, *The Afrikaners*, p. 537.
[71] Lawrence E. Harrison and Samuel P. Huntington, *op. cit.*, p. 168
[72] Randy E. Barnett, *Restoring the Lost Constitution: The Presumption of Liberty* (New Jersey, 2004), p. 16-17
[73] Samuel P. Huntington, *Political Order*, pp. 7-8.
[74] Rudi Prinsloo, "Praag Celebrates New ANC-Afrikaner *Entente,*" *Praag.co.uk,* April 4, 2009 http://www.praag.co.uk/news/southern-africa/340-praag-celebrates-new-anc-afrikaner-entente.html (accessed August 3, 2009)
[75] Hermann Giliomee, *op. cit.,* p. 639.
[76] Herman J. Cohen, *South Africa: the current situation*, US Department of State Dispatch, July 27, 1992.
[77] Giliomee, *op. cit.*, p 608.
[78] Paul Kelly, "New book reveals freed Mandela told Hawke: I owe it to you," *The Australian,* July 9, 2010.
[79] Anthony McAdam, "Malcolm's African ghosts," *Spectator Australia*, June 17, 2010.
[80] Hermann Giliomee, "Liberal and Populist Democracy," pp. 19-20.
[81] Leslie Dach, "Kennedy in the Land of Apartheid," *The Daily Beast,* August 30, 2009 http://www.thedailybeast.com/blogs-and-stories/2009-08-28/kennedy-in-the-land-of-apartheid/ (accessed August 31, 2009)
[82] Moeletsi Mbeki, "South Africa: United States Relations—The Political Dimension," *Woodrow Wilson Center*, June 10, 2009.
[83] David T. Jervis, "Book Review: Partner to History: The US Role in South Africa's Transition to Democracy", *International Third World Studies Journal And Review*, Volume XIV, 2003.
[84] Princeton Nathan Lyman, *Partner to History: The US Role in South Africa's Transition to Democracy* (Washington, D.C, 2002), p. 144.
[85] *Ibid.*, p. 133.
[86] *Ibid.*, p. 135.
[87] *Ibid.*, p. 145.
[88] Editorial, "South Africa's Wreckers," *The New York Times*, February 15, 1994.
[89] Princeton Nathan Lyman, *op cit.*, p. 128.

[90] Ben Temkin, *op cit.*, p. 268.
[91] Hermann Giliomee, *The Afrikaners*, p. 640.
[92] *Ibid.*, p. 640.
[93] Polity.org.za, "State is responsible for 'civil discord'—Buthelezi," July 28, 2009
[94] Elie Kedourie, *op cit.*, p. 4.
[95] Ilana Mercer, "Democratic Despotism," *Ludwig von Mises Institute*, September 16, 2004.
[96] Samuel P. Huntington, *Political Order*, p. 7
[97] Dan Roodt, "US, Britain wanted ANC in power," *Praag.co.uk*, July 14, 2009 http://www.praag.co.uk/columns/dan-roodt/441-us-britain-wanted-anc-in-power.html (accessed August 15, 2009)
[98] *Ibid.*
[99] Donald L. Horowitz, *op cit.*, p. 95.

CONCLUSION: SAVING SOUTH AFRICANS S.O.S.

[1] "O Tempora, O Mores!", *American Renaissance,* June 2004.
[2] Donna Casey, "White South African granted refugee status," *Ottawa Sun,* August 28, 2009.
[3] Adriana Stuijt, "Two more S. African farmers killed: death toll now at 3,037," *WorldHum.com,* Feb 17, 2009, http://www.digitaljournal.com/article/267463 (accessed June 14, 2009).
[4] *Ibid.*
[5] *Ibid.*
[6] David Brooks, "The Next Culture War," *The New York Times,* September 28, 2009.
[7] Peter D. Schiff, *The Little Book of Bull Moves in Bear Markets* (Hoboken, New Jersey, 2008), p. 196
[8] *Ibid.*, p. 197-198
[9] Vox Day, *The Return Of The Great Depression* (Los Angeles, 2009), p. 211
[10] Jon Hilsenrath, "Bernanke Calls for Action on Trade Gap," *The Wall Street Journal*, October 20, 2009
[11] Philip du Toit, *op cit*, p. iii.

[12] *Ibid.*, p. 259.
[13] Ilana Mercer, "Bush Answers Kennedy's Calling," *WorldNetDaily.com,* May 19, 2006.
[14] Dr. Stephen M. Steinlight, "High Noon to Midnight Why Current Immigration Policy Dooms American Jewry," *Center for Immigration Studies*, April 2004
[15] "Three Decades of Mass Immigration: The Legacy of the 1965 Immigration Act," *Center for Immigration Studies*, September 1995.
[16] Peter Brimelow, "Time to Rethink Immigration?," *VDARE.COM*, June 22, 1992
[17] *Ibid.*
[18] Ann Coulter, "I feel your pain. Not theirs. Yours.," *www.anncoulter.com,* May 27, 2009.
[19] Donald R. Morris, *op cit*, p. 128
[20] David Gordon (ed.), *Secession, State & Liberty* (New Brunswick, London, 1998), p. xiii.
[21] *Ibid.*, p. 212.
[22] *Ibid.*, p. 92.
[23] *Ibid.*, p. 94.
[24] Ilana Mercer, "Statists Struggle With States' Rights," *WorldNetDaily.com*, May 22, 2009.
[25] David Gordon, *op cit.*, p. 92.
[26] *Ibid.*
[27] David Gordon, *op cit.*, p. 97.
[28] Hermann Giliomee, "Liberal and Populist Democracy," p. 32,
[29] David Gordon, *op cit.*, p. 182.
[30] *Ibid.*, p. 218.
[31] *Ibid.*, p. 212.
[32] *Ibid.*, p. 218.
[33] *Ibid.*, p. 184.
[34] *Ibid.*, p. 184.
[35] *Ibid.*, p. 182
[36] Hermann Giliomee, *op cit.*, p. 28.
[37] *Ibid.*, p. 27.
[38] Andrew Simpson, *Language and national identity in Africa* (Oxford, 2008), p. 334
[39] *Ibid.*, p. 28.

INDEX

N

O

Q

R

S

T

U

V

W

BIOGRAPHICAL NOTE

ILANA MERCER HAS been lauded by iconic author and psychiatrist Thomas Szasz as "dangerous … intelligent, informed, independent, courageous." Historian, and *New York Times* bestseller-list author, Thomas Woods has called her "one of the few writers on earth whose talents I truly envy, adding that, in his opinion, "She should be a household name." Joseph Farah (CEO of WND.com) has described her as "standing out like a beacon in a vast sea of punditry. She's always hard to pigeonhole. She's always witty and incisive." Paul Gottfried (historian and author of such books as *Conservatism in America*) wrote: "Ilana takes on indelicate cultural, social, and political issues and challenges her opponents to rethink their positions." The outspoken libertarian broadcaster Ron Smith of Maryland's WBAL Radio has called her "a refreshingly original writer on the issues of our time."

As the only writer to have defended NFL quarterback Michael Vick on the basis of libertarian (propertarian) principles—or so said Fox News TV commentator Sean Hannity—she was invited, in 2007, to debate the matter with Mr. Hannity, after which he commented:

> Having read your columns throughout the years, I think I know you a little bit—I know you come from a very intellectual point of view, an intellectually honest point of view—you have given the most articulate argument I've heard on the other side of this [animal rights issue], one that is consistent with many of the views you have.

Ms. Mercer was born in South Africa—her father, Rabbi Abraham Benzion Isaacson, was a leading anti-apartheid activist eventually forced to leave the country—and spent her formative years in Israel. In the 1980s she returned to South Africa, where she married, had a daughter, and after completing her degrees, including a double major in psychology and Hebrew, worked as an AIDS counselor. In 1995, she and her family immigrated to British Columbia, Canada, before moving with her husband to America's Pacific Northwest, which she calls home. Ms. Mercer left South Africa with the proceeds from the sale of her apartment stashed in the soles of her shoes. Had she been apprehended smuggling her property out of that country, she'd have been jailed together with her husband; they both stood taller on that trip. Ms. Mercer, who happens to know what living without freedom is like, has seen first hand the same oppression sneak-up on unsuspecting Americans. (For instance, the South-African model of detention-without-trial is slowly becoming a fixture of the American legal landscape.)

Her book *Broad Sides: One Woman's Clash with a Corrupt Culture* (2003) was hailed by the late Aaron Russo (former libertarian presidential candidate) as the work of "a true warrior—a modern-day Joan of Arc—in the fight for freedom." A Fellow at the Jerusalem Institute for Market Studies, and the Jeffersonian think-tank Free New York, Inc., she has appeared as a guest on scores of broadcast talk programs: including those of Sirius Satellite Radio's Mike Church; of the late, legendary talk-show host George Putnam; and of the Australian Broadcasting Corporation. In addition to appearing on RT, the global Russian television news network, she was among the participants in the 2003 Public Network television series *America At War,* debating the media's dereliction of duty during the invasion of Iraq.

Ms. Mercer is—and has been for the last decade—a featured columnist for WND.com (which, according to Web monitoring site Quantcast, had one million daily visitors as of September 2009). Other publications where her articles, essays, columns, editorials, book and film reviews have appeared are *The American*

Spectator, The American Conservative, The Orange County Register, Insight On the News (an affiliate of *The Washington Times*), London's *Jewish Chronicle* and *Quarterly Review*, *The Ottawa Citizen, The Calgary Herald* (for which she penned a regular weekly column), the two Canadian national newspapers, the *Financial Post* and the *Globe and Mail, The Journal of Social, Political and Economic Studies, Free Life: a Journal of Classical Liberal and Libertarian Thought,* and the Foundation for Economic Education's *Ideas on Liberty*.

Ms. Mercer's work has been cited by *The New York Times*, the *Boston Globe*, and *Time*'s European edition, among other prominent publications. She maintains a popular blog, where she comments on the issues of the day. In her role as proprietor of the libertarian *Barely A Blog* (BAB), she has attracted such contributors as Tibor Machan (Cato Institute adjunct scholar), George Reisman (emeritus economics professor at California's Pepperdine University), and the aforementioned Thomas Szasz.

CPSIA information can be obtained at www.ICGtesting.com
Printed in the USA
LVOW061728210212
269754LV00011B/1/P